APARTHEID
A History

By the same author

The Labour Government 1964–1970
End of Empire

(as Editor)
More Power to the People
The Bounds of Freedom

BRIAN LAPPING

APARTHEID
A History

George Braziller

NEW YORK

Published in the United States in 1987 by
George Braziller, Inc.

First published in England by Grafton Books, a Division of the
Collins Publishing Group, 8 Grafton Street, London W1X 3LA.

George Braziller, Inc.
60 Madison Avenue
New York, New York 10010

[Library of Congress information to come]

Printed in the United States
First printing, February 1987

In memory of
JOE HUNT,
teacher and friend

CONTENTS

MAPS

LIST OF ILLUSTRATIONS

Troops at arms during the 1922 miners' strike – IDAF
Black and coloured troops in World War 2 – IDAF
John L. Dube – IDAF
Smuts photographing the royal family – Popperfoto
Dr Malan and his wife – Camera Press
Jan Hofmeyr – Popperfoto
The first all-Afrikaner cabinet – Popperfoto
The Voortrekker Monument – Topham Picture Library
Passive resistance campaign in Durban – Topham Picture Library
Congresses' Defiance Campaign – Jurgen Schadeburg/IDAF

SECTION IV
Chief Albert Luthuli – Topham Picture Library
Nelson Mandela with Jusuf Dadoo – Eli Weinberg/IDAF
Sisulu arrested – Topham Picture Library
Treason trial – Eli Weinberg/IDAF
Sharpeville before the shooting – Camera Press
Sharpeville after the shooting – Popperfoto
Sharpeville, the crowds return – Camera Press
J. G. Strijdom – Topham Picture Library
B. J. Vorster – Camera Press
Dr Hendrik Verwoerd – Camera Press
Steve Biko speaking in 1971 – John Reader
Chief Kaiser Matanzima – Camera Press
B. J. Vorster with leaders of black homelands – Camera Press
A removal – IDAF
Pass-book inspection – Eli Weinberg/IDAF
'Bachelors' single-sex dwellings' – Camera Press
Winnie Mandela at a funeral – Eli Weinberg/IDAF
P. W. Botha – Dale Yudelman (*The Star*, Johannesburg)
Oliver Tambo – Topham Picture Library
Rev. Allan Boesak – Popperfoto
Bishop Desmond Tutu – Dale Yudelman (*The Star*, Johannesburg)

ACKNOWLEDGEMENTS

Granada Television's decision to follow 'End of Empire' by making programmes on the history of apartheid was the starting-point for this book. I am grateful to the company for enabling me to undertake both the programmes and the book.

Some of my colleagues on the programmes, Mark Anderson, Norma Percy and Allan Segal, have kindly commented on some chapters. In thanking them, I do not wish to imply that my other colleagues have been unhelpful. John Blake, Max Graesser, Gary Mead and Alison Rooper have all helped with documents and advice which, given the difficulties we have faced in working in South Africa, have in every case gone well beyond the call of duty.

Three specialists in South African history, Shula Marks, Merle Lipton and Saul Dubow, have saved me from many errors. Elsie Donald, Anna Grimshaw, Tony King and Andrew Robinson have made valuable critical comments. My wife, Anne, and my elder daughters, Harriet and Claudia, helped remove some infelicities. My youngest daughter, Melissa, has kindly encouraged me to return to the word-processor when most people of her age would have caused trouble.

The standard clause about final responsibility being mine alone is in this case important. I have received a lot of advice. I have accepted much of it, but not all.

INTRODUCTION

South Africa is on the verge of civil war or revolution. Thousands have already been killed. The conflict seems set to become worse and to last for many years. The cause is generally agreed to be the government's policy of apartheid. This book casts light on two questions: how did the peoples of one of the most richly endowed countries in the world come to adopt so inefficient a social arrangement, and why did they persist with it when all the world could see it was not working? The book is not a history of South Africa. Rather it is the history of a strange disease that afflicted the South African body politic.

What is 'apartheid'? Pronounced apart-hate, the word is Afrikaans – the South African language derived from Dutch – for apartness or separation. The man who brought the word to the world's attention in its political sense was Dr Daniel François Malan, leader of the National Party in the South African general election of 1948. His party's victory, and its retention of power ever since, brought about the introduction of apartheid, not just as the government's overriding policy but as the means – they repeatedly said – of saving western civilization from destruction by black hordes.

However, racial segregation had already been practised in South Africa for almost three hundred years. So is apartheid merely the term used to describe its continuation since 1948?

No. It is more than that. South Africa's earlier racial segregation was not different in kind from that of many other countries, particularly the colonies of European states. Some people found it distasteful, but most accepted it as the way ruling groups behaved towards the conquered, especially those of a different skin colour.

In the decades after 1948, however, while the European empires were collapsing and the imperial relationship was everywhere being rejected, South Africa's white population clamped the race relations of the past on to their society. But where, in imperial times, most social rules were informal and capable of some flexibility, since 1948 in South Africa they have been made rigid and enforced by law. For thirty years the white majority persisted with this policy, even though it turned the country into the world's pariah. This obsessional, anachronistic law-making and its harsh policing are what constitute apartheid.

At the time of the 1948 election, National Party candidates told voters that apartheid meant 'total segregation' – sending all blacks to 'homelands' and running a white-only economy. This idea appealed to white industrial workers who feared growing black competition for jobs, and to some white intellectuals, embarrassed at having blacks in the towns as second-class citizens: sent to 'homelands', they could rule themselves, enjoy full civil rights and be off the white man's conscience.

Such a policy could not work. By 1948, the English-speaking whites in South Africa had developed manufacturing industries which were dependent on a stable African workforce. Expel the blacks from the towns and before long the fastest-growing sector of the economy would collapse. The mine-owners and the farmers – the extractive and primary producers typical of the colonial economy – had few complaints about apartheid. Indeed, the mine-owners had long employed migrant black workers and forced them to live in single-sex barracks because this had proved an efficient way to keep wages down. But the future lay with more sophisticated industries that needed an educated, skilled workforce and could not survive if restricted to temporary sojourners from African reserves. So apartheid was from the beginning a cheat. The National Party's leaders knew that it was economic nonsense.

Most sensible white South Africans also shared a debilitating characteristic with the whites of Mississippi and Louisiana: slave-owning had taken from them the love of hard work. That they knew it is revealed in an Afrikaner joke: 'Van der Merwe (the typical Afrikaner) was in London watching two white Englishmen digging a hole. He said to his wife, "Man, these guys are slow. Give me twelve blacks and I do it on my own".'

Accustomed to having black servants, the whites had no intention of fending for themselves. Consequently, throughout the years when National Party governments enacted and applied volumes of apartheid laws, the number of blacks, coloureds and Indians working in the towns and contributing to the white-controlled economy steadily increased.

(The laws and their enforcement are what make apartheid unique.) 'Bantu education' is one example. At a time when manufacturing industry was expanding fast and needed well-trained African employees, when many schools, notably those run by Christian missions, were offering education to a high standard, the South African government banned academic teaching for Africans and closed schools which tried to continue it. Population registration is another example. For every South African, the 'racial group' in which he was registered became the decisive indicator of where he could live and what he was allowed to do. 'Relocation' is a third. Skilled

African workers, eager to stay in towns where their employers valued them, were arrested in their tens of thousands and evicted to live in semi-deserts.

Joseph Lelyveld, in his brilliant book *Move Your Shadow*, described one consequence of the eviction policy. In order to limit the number of Africans staying overnight in 'white' towns, the government developed subsidised 'busing'. Blacks who had lived in towns were resettled in 'native reserves' or 'homelands' and buses were provided to take them to the towns each morning.

At 2.40 a.m. No. 4174 left the depot [Lelyveld reported]. The first man on board said he worked six days a week on a construction site. Even at the concession rates arranged by the authorities . . . bus fares gobbled up 25 per cent of his wages. When he did not have to work overtime, he could get home by 8.30 p.m. Only on Sundays did he see his family in the light of day . . . With four hours sleep at home and a couple of hours on the bus, he managed to stay awake at work . . . [A second passenger] was on her way to a part-time job as a cleaning-woman . . . She was expected at work by 7 a.m. to prepare breakfast . . . Another 'commuter', a construction worker, had received several reprimands for falling asleep on the job.

[The first] reached into a bag he was carrying and extracted a little rectangle of foam rubber about the size of a paperback book . . . pulled his cap over his eyes, pressed the foam rubber to the back of the seat in front of him, rested his forehead against it and . . . was out like a light . . . [The second] unfolded the collar of her turtleneck sweater so it covered her face, and slumped . . . [The third, who had no seat] spread a piece of folded newspaper neatly on the floor between his feet and, with the suppleness of a yogi, collapsed himself into a seated position on the paper with his knees drawn up to his chin and dropped his head . . . [In just over an hour] the bus had reached the highway and the ride was smoother . . . More than ninety people aboard had dozed off. The centre aisle was packed with bodies, wound round themselves like anchovies in a can. No. 4174 ended its ride at 5.40 a.m. three hours after it had begun.

In some parts of the world, wealthy people choose to commute because they have found a house and garden they like some way from their work. For none of the 'homelands' commuters is this so. They have been forced to live, in Lelyveld's words, in 'vast rural slums with urban population densities but no urban amenities'. The reason is the guiding belief behind apartheid: that in everything that matters whites must be on top and meticulously separated from blacks.

One device, invented in the days when South Africa's race policy was merely segregation, became the key to enforcing apartheid. It was the pass. All blacks had to carry passes. To be without one was a punishable offence. The pass had to contain an employer's stamp. Without it a black was liable to be ordered to leave town. As an administrative device this was brilliantly simple. It gave the authorities legal power to send almost any black they thought undesirable to a 'native reserve' and it gave employers enormous power over workers. As human relations it was wounding and cruel. The Pass Laws provoked more campaigns and protests than any other law of the apartheid state.

———

The South African whites did not go wrong suddenly in 1948 – or any other year. They did not go wrong because they are a uniquely evil or racist or authoritarian people. They went wrong because the experience of the previous three hundred years had brought them to a state of frustrated and enraged nationalist fervour that desperately needed a target. That is why the only way to make sense of apartheid is by looking at its roots in history.

A person who has been humiliated at work and comes home to thrash the children is acting as the Afrikaners did when they invented apartheid. The majority of Afrikaners – white South Africans who speak Afrikaans – developed a gnawing resentment against the British Empire, which had arrived uninvited at the start of the nineteenth century to rule what they considered their country. Until the 1930s the terms 'racial conflict' or 'the two races' when used in South Africa did not mean black *v* white. They meant Afrikaner *v* British.

The British dominated the vast gold- and diamond-mining companies, the civil service, the professions, the army; they were the superior class. The Afrikaners were mostly farmers and, increasingly in the first half of the twentieth century, a white, urban proletariat; they formed an under-class. The Afrikaners claimed with some cause that they had been dispossessed, deceived and brutally defeated by the British. (The fact that blacks could make a similar complaint with even more justification did nothing to alleviate the morose feelings of the Afrikaners.) They worked up a national resentment titanic in its bitterness and determined that, in order to take control of their country, they would remove from all top positions the arrogant, cliquey, exploiting minority whose first loyalty was not to South Africa but to Britain.

The Afrikaners were the first people in Africa to attempt to throw off imperial power. Their great war against the British Empire, the Boer War of 1899–1902, was an inspiration to subsequent anti-imperialists – except that the British won. The Afrikaners saw themselves as a nation. They demanded their own flag, official language, national anthem, head of state and a fair share of the revenue from their country's vast mineral reserves. Like the African nationalists who throughout the continent were to follow in their footsteps, the Afrikaners demanded absolute power in their own state.

From 1910, when Britain unexpectedly gave South Africa independence, every Prime Minister of South Africa was an Afrikaner, as were the majority of those allowed to vote. But, until Malan came to power, each Prime Minister in turn – Louis Botha, Jan Smuts, J. B. M. Hertzog – became convinced that independent South Africa must retain constitutional links with Britain, which was still a world power and brought big commercial advantages. To the average Afrikaner voter, the perfidious British Empire remained the conspirator behind the scenes, with the English-speaking South Africans as its local agents.

Afrikaner resentment against the blacks was not of comparable intensity. The Africans, after all, were subject peoples. They were cowed after a succession of nineteenth-century defeats, nearly all, despite Afrikaner claims to the contrary, at the hands of imperial armies sent from Britain. In 1948, the blacks of South Africa had not yet built an effective united nationalist movement that offered any real challenge to the whites. But Afrikaner nationalism was on the march, ready to cut down any opponent. And, since the English-speaking whites remained difficult to displace, particularly from the heights of economic power, the full force of the resentment the Afrikaners had been burnishing for generations was turned against the blacks. Many Afrikaners truthfully said: 'We have no quarrel with the blacks, only with the British.' But it was the blacks who felt the lash.

This does not mean that segregation resulted from Afrikaners' anger against the British. Segregation was a policy in which Afrikaans- and English-speaking whites were at one. What needs explaining – and is explained by the excesses of frustrated nationalism – is the more intense form of segregation called apartheid.

———

On 28 March 1979 a distinguished Afrikaner historian, Professor Floors van Jaarsveld, was addressing a theological symposium in Pretoria, the administrative capital of South Africa. He was seven minutes into a scholarly analysis of an event that had occurred 140 years earlier, when he was interrupted. A posse of well-built young men broke into the hall, pushed aside the religious sister at the door, encircled van Jaarsveld, lifted him up and poured a tinful of tar over his head and clothes, followed by a shower of feathers.

The group then left the hall. The shaken professor tried to go on, but his spectacles, which had shielded his eyes, were covered in tar. The bully-boys left behind a press release explaining that they were tired of the way the spiritual values of Afrikanerdom were being destroyed by 'worn-out academics'.

Van Jaarsveld's carefully researched paper was about the 'Covenant' said to have been made with God in 1838 on the day before a battle against Zulu armies: if God gave them victory, the Afrikaners promised to celebrate the day each year and keep it holy. Van Jaarsveld had examined the reports of the Afrikaner commander and his clerk and found that neither described such a promise. The religious ceremonies with which Afrikaners each year solemnized the Day of the Covenant were therefore not historically justified. Van Jaarsveld went on to show that the 'Covenant' in the form it was celebrated was largely the invention of a man on his death-bed thirty-three years after the event, as perpetuated by a professor a further forty-eight years after that.

The tarring and feathering of van Jaarsveld conveys a sense of Afrikaners' feelings about their history. They have been inclined to depict themselves as a modern version of the Children of Israel, God's chosen people, fighting His battles against the infidel, driven by a Calvinist ethic to serve God and protect Christian civilization. The most recent historical research suggests that such stories about their early religious devotion are, like the story of the 'Covenant', largely a modern invention. The decisive role of the Dutch church, heavily emphasized in some histories of South Africa, is therefore excluded from this book.

A visit to South Africa offers many surprises. In May 1986 I flew into Cape Town, having read that the road from the airport was dangerous – it runs near some African townships from which young blacks emerged to throw bricks at passing cars. I feared I might be entering a town under siege.

Nothing seemed further from the truth. Cape Town, one of the world's most beautiful cities, is backed by a group of mountains. Look up from most streets or windows and you see them. Turn round and you see the blue south Atlantic through the flowering trees and shrubs that everywhere adorn the coastline. Cars dawdle by, their drivers, nearly all whites, relaxing in the summer clothes which are here adequate throughout the year. On the road from the airport and later the road to the nearby Cape of Good Hope, separated from the South Pole by nothing but open sea, no sense of danger seems to trouble anybody. White people walk to the sandy beaches or over the hillsides, white girls bicycle happily. It might be the South of France or California. The few black people one meets are smiling and courteous.

To find the troubled black 'locations' requires some map-reading. The area within Cape Town where coloureds and Indians once lived has been totally demolished and every inhabitant removed. Out of sight, several miles from the white city, inadequately signposted, are the 'townships'. This one is Mitchell's Plain, for 'coloureds' (people of mixed race). This one is Khayelitsha, recently constructed for blacks. We drive through nervously with the windows closed. Will some young African throw a brick? It does not seem likely. The government has built the main roads through the townships wide enough for a tank to turn round. With so many lanes to choose from, our car is alone. The small, breeze-block, identical houses behind their walls show few signs of life. At the edges of the township, separating it from the perimeter road, is a broad space, wider than the range of a .303 rifle, a free-fire zone, so that, in an emergency, a small number of troops can contain a large rising. The South African planners have learned all the lessons of Haussman's Paris, except the elegance.

Next we drive to Crossroads. This is a squatter area, its corrugated iron shacks tightly crammed together like any third-world shanty-town, children and chickens running in the dusty alleys, sellers of vegetables and fruit perched at corners; bustle everywhere. In April 1986, this was a no-go area for the South African police. Black collaborators with the government had been killed here, whites' cars stoned. The government came no nearer than the free-fire zone, a wide strip of scrubland, where those huge, high, uncomfortable-looking military vehicles the South African army uses, each one manned by half a dozen young white soldiers with guns, provided the appearance of some state control.

Many of those young soldiers were conscripts who had never seen townships or shanty-towns before. Like most white South Africans they could honestly say that they had no idea blacks lived in such conditions. Some of them were shocked by what they saw. A group of students, returning to Stellenbosch from a black resettlement area, wrote in Afrikaans in the university magazine: 'When a person is led into a first-hand "black experience" he discovers a South Africa radically different from the one in which he lives. This was perhaps the biggest shock of all. We live in one land and we don't know each other, we children of apartheid.'

In my hotel in Cape Town the service was impeccable. The black waiters in the restaurant were deferential, quick with the wine. Did some of them live in Crossroads? What did they think of me, eating a four-course meal that cost more than a week of their wages? Steve Biko, the Black Consciousness leader of the 1970s, wrote that many black workers, after a day of smiling subordination, returned to township or shanty-town and there, in the privacy of their lavatories, howled their rage.

Many returned also to pay their dues to protection gangs. People who feel that the ruling institutions of the state are illegitimate and incapable of offering reliable protection do not rush to the police to report crime. And many of the criminal gangs that flourished in black townships and shanty-towns preyed – or claimed that they preyed – on whites. Thus apartheid helped to spread criminality and give it a tinge of heroism.

———

By 1986, apartheid had obviously failed. A few fanatical Afrikaners in the northern Transvaal, angry Canutes, broke up the meetings of National Party ministers and threatened that, if the government backed away from apartheid, they would launch a civil war. But the government had no choice. Apartheid was already crumbling. In two of the principle purposes for which it had been introduced its failure was manifest. It was intended to strengthen the Afrikaners' grip on power. But that grip was becoming steadily harder to maintain. And it was intended to secure the permanent exclusion from power of blacks, but the longer it was enforced the more it provoked the mobilization and radicalization of the black majority. So South Africa's State President, P. W. Botha, who in 1948 had been one of the strident new MPs demanding apartheid's immediate and full introduction, in the 1980s cautiously led his party in the opposite direction. Not only the government but the majority of whites realized they had reached a dead end.

The English-speaking whites had by and large held aloof from apartheid. Most of them did their best to depict it as a wicked or ludicrous obsession of the Afrikaners, while benefiting from it in any way they could. Politically, once the National Party had established itself in power, the English-speaking whites vanished. They cultivated their gardens, made money in their businesses and laughed at the Afrikaners for concentrating so disproportionate an amount of their political fire-power on the blacks. By the 1980s the party with most support from English-speakers, the Progressive Federal Party, was demanding that apartheid be dismantled.

P. W. Botha was not far behind them. If he seemed to be dragging his feet it was because no group that enjoys power gives it up readily and a vast bureaucracy of Afrikaners was employed enforcing apartheid: remove the policy and a significant part of the electorate would be out of work. In 1986, Botha announced publicly that no major constitutional changes could be made without the consultation and consent of all the racial communities; that one-man one-vote was not to be ruled out; that there was no alternative to power-sharing. He had laws and regulations that embodied apartheid repealed as fast as the civil service could work out the consequences – sometimes faster.

Every concession was too little too late. The Africans would, in previous decades, almost certainly have accepted power-sharing and a phased transition to majority rule. By 1986, the impression that white rule was on the slide made it difficult for black leaders to agree to such compromises.

The white areas remained as safely white-dominated as ever. Although occasional bomb-blasts killed by-standers and left the message that the black nationalist movement too was a force to be reckoned with, the army was still able to handle any military assault the blacks could launch. But the experiment was drawing to a close. The time of apartheid, and therefore of white rule, was near its end.

In writing about history in South Africa, some words cause peculiar difficulty. A white who calls himself 'a native of California' may wonder why South African blacks find the word 'native' offensive. Those who have suffered a lifetime of 'native' policy, however, find it insulting. When the government replaced 'native' by 'Bantu' in official designations, they made that word too an insult.

I have found no resolution to this problem. 'Non-white', 'homeland', 'native', 'Bantu' pepper the pages that follow. At every point I have used the word I think most clear. If my usage, and my failure sometimes to use inverted commas, cause offence, I should like to apologise. Likewise I have used the word 'Afrikaners' throughout the book for people who in the earlier period were usually called Cape Dutch or Boers. Again, my purpose was clarity and consistency and no offence was intended, to the Cape Dutch or to anybody else.

TABLES: THE POPULATION OF SOUTH AFRICA

1 Since the creation of the Union

Year	Africans m	Asians m	Coloureds m	Whites m	Totals m
1911	4.02 (67.3%)	0.15 (2.5%)	0.53 (8.8%)	1.28 (21.4%)	5.98
1960	10.93 (68.3%)	0.48 (3.0%)	1.51 (9.4%)	3.09 (19.3%)	16.01
1980	19.95 (71.9%)	0.79 (2.8%)	2.55 (9.2%)	4.45 (16.1%)	27.74

Note: These figures include the populations of all the 'homelands', including those that are officially independent.

2 The Apartheid categories, 1986

Africans	Millions	Total millions
Zulu	5.5	
Xhosa	5.2	
Sotho	4.3	
Tswana	2.1	
Shangaan	0.9	
Swazi	0.7	
Venda	0.5	
Ndebele	0.7	20.0
Indian		0.9
Coloured		2.8
White		
Afrikaners	2.9	
English-speakers	1.9	4.8
SOUTH AFRICA		28.5

Note: A table showing the land allocated for 'native reserves' under the 1913 Land Act is on page 53.

APARTHEID
A History

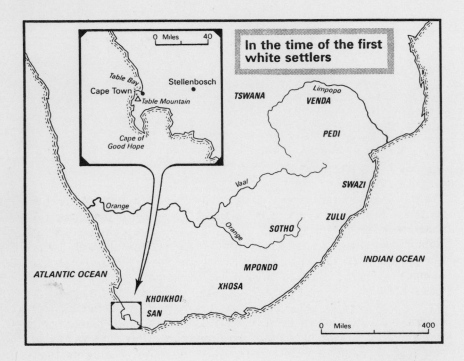

In the time of the first white settlers

O Miles 40

Table Bay
Cape Town
Table Mountain
Stellenbosch
Cape of
Good Hope

TSWANA

Limpopo
VENDA

PEDI

Vaal

SWAZI

Orange

Orange

ZULU

SOTHO

ATLANTIC OCEAN

MPONDO

XHOSA

KHOIKHOI
SAN

INDIAN OCEAN

O Miles 400

CHAPTER ONE

White Men Arrive, 1652–1795

The racial conflict that arouses worldwide interest in South Africa has its roots in a series of decisions pressed upon a reluctant group of Dutch merchant princes by one man, Jan van Riebeeck. He was an ambitious young burgher living in the Netherlands in the 1630s, when the quick way to a fortune lay in joining the Verenigde Oostindische Compagnie (VOC), the Dutch East India Company. He applied, and was sent out to the company's Far Eastern trading posts, centred on Java. He worked in China and Japan and his reliable reports to his superiors, diligent obedience to instructions, meticulous handwriting and commercial acumen led to rapid promotion. Then he was caught out. Most company servants in the East did some trading on their own account. It was against the rules but hard to prevent. From time to time the company clamped down. Van Riebeeck was accused of such trading, found guilty and ordered home to be dismissed from the service.

On his way back to the Netherlands in 1648 his ship called at the Cape of Good Hope, a watering place increasingly used by the VOC's trader-privateers, also by some British and French ships. In the 1490s the first white men to sail past, the Portuguese, had called it the Cape of Storms, and when van Riebeeck arrived there he saw a Dutch ship that a storm had recently beached. Its crew had stayed camped on the shore for more than a year to protect their cargo, some of which van Riebeeck helped transfer to his own ship. During his three weeks' stay, he visited the small garden that the stranded crew had planted with lettuce and cress.

The next year two crew members of the beached vessel returned to the Netherlands and suggested that the VOC set up a permanent staging post at the Cape. The company referred their proposal to the dismissed merchant who had recently been there. Van Riebeeck seized the opportunity to reinstate himself, volunteering to head a team of seventy to eighty colonisers.

The Cape – a small bay and a few miles of hinterland – was then inhabited by two closely related stone-age peoples, yellowish-brown in skin and small in stature. The San, whom the whites called Bushmen, probably numbered fewer than 20,000. They kept no animals except dogs and constantly traversed vast areas in search of game, which they stalked with such skill, communicating by means of verbal clicks, that, when most communities of hunter-gatherers had become extinct, they survived. Their contacts with white men were limited.

The Khoikhoi were more numerous than the San – perhaps 100,000 in all. The Dutch thought their speech a mere series of stutters and so called them Hottentots. They kept herds of cattle and sheep in regular, seasonal pastures. They planted no crops but possessed something the white men wanted – meat. Their contact was therefore bound to be more eventful.

The Cape lay at the mid-point of the voyage from Europe to the East Indies. After three months eating salty or rancid pork, nearly all sailors were hit by scurvy, which causes swollen joints and internal bleeding, visible at the gums. Sometimes as many as half the crew died of it on a single voyage. To overcome the disease and launch them on the next three months of their journey, they needed fresh fruit and vegetables.

No better stopover was ever found than the bay where a delectable brook of pure water flows all year round from Table Mountain. The climate is Mediterranean. Herbs grow everywhere. In spring a ship's crew would take wicker baskets and indulge in an orgy of sorrel salad, sorrel soup and sorrel posset. According to van Riebeeck's journal, asparagus with as good a flavour as the best to be had in the Netherlands grew wild and in abundance. The bay swarmed with fish, easily dried or salted. And the Khoikhoi, in return for tobacco, copper and iron, were willing to sell old sheep and cattle.

From the 1590s, knowledge of the virtues of Table Bay had spread among ships' masters, testing to the limit the Khoikhoi's willingness to supply meat. Like many African peoples they regarded cattle as their principal form of wealth, an asset that could increase as well as provide food and clothing. Rather than sell young animals for slaughter, they sharply raised the price and withdrew their herds from the coast. Sailors who had for weeks been dreaming of fresh meat took guns inland and stole cattle.

The VOC was making huge profits on its spice trade with the East. Its ships were the heaviest users of Table Bay, and in 1652 it instructed van Riebeeck to set up a permanent post there. He was neither to conquer nor to enslave the Khoikhoi: they were a free people who must be treated with respect and consideration, to encourage them to supply meat. Thus the company hoped to establish a comfort station but not a settled colony.

Van Riebeeck was not happy with these instructions. He wrote to the directors begging to be allowed to enslave the Khoikhoi and seize their cattle. But when the mild and economical policy of the company was reasserted, he obeyed. He entertained Khoikhoi delegates at his fort, offering them gifts and services. He duly restrained his subordinates and ships' captains who wanted to plunder.

This policy, however, did not work. The Khoikhoi could not be induced to increase the supply of beef without unacceptable rises in price. And the kitchen gardens that van Riebeeck had company servants plant, although they were soon delivering two weeks' supply of carrots, beet, parsnips, turnips and cabbages to every departing ship, were proving too expensive. The gardeners received company wages even if they were careless about weeding and let the vegetables run to seed. So in 1657, just five years after his party had landed, van Riebeeck persuaded the company to let him introduce a change. Nine company servants were invited to set themselves up as farmers. Van Riebeeck allotted them plots of land near Table Bay, so that they could supply not only vegetables, citrus fruit and grain but also meat at prices fixed by the company. Van Riebeeck's plan was that these 'freeburghers' would be motivated to farm intensively, like their cousins in the Netherlands, rotating crops, gathering manure as fertilizer, enabling them to supply the garrison and passing ships cheaply, without encroaching too far on to the grazing areas of the Khoikhoi.

This policy worked better, though not altogether as planned. Sheep shipped out from the Netherlands and kept in the freeburghers' restricted plots grew thin and died. The local species did best, bought or stolen from the Khoikhoi and allowed, as they were accustomed, to wander freely in the open veld. So van Riebeeck persuaded the company to let him grant larger farms to freeburghers, taking over land the Khoikhoi regarded as their commons.

Conflict was inevitable. In 1659, seven years after the settlement began, a Khoikhoi named Doman, who had worked for the VOC as an interpreter and had sailed in a company ship to the Dutch possessions in Java, led his people in an attack on the spreading Cape colony, destroying most of the freeburghers' farms and stealing their sheep and cattle. The battle was touch and go. Doman told the Khoikhoi that the Dutch muskets did not fire in the rain and was therefore able, by timing his attacks, to lay waste at will. His purpose was not to kill the Dutch, only to make them buy Khoikhoi cattle.

Gradually Dutch firearms proved their superiority over the spears of the tiny, stone-age Khoikhoi. Within twenty years van Riebeeck's successors had begun endorsing the appointment of each new chief by ceremonially presenting him with a cane of office, its handle engraved in copper. The canes signified that the Khoikhoi had become clients of the great company. Some began to work in the colony as cattleless labourers, in the kitchens, on building sites and as dispatch runners. Several became interpreters to the expeditions the company sent into the interior to buy additional cattle and sheep from more distant Khoikhoi. Some set up as traders, buying cattle inland and delivering them to Table Bay. Their traditional herd-based way of life gradually disappeared.

From the beginning, van Riebeeck found Khoikhoi labour inadequate. To build his fort, store-rooms and dwellings, to cut and haul timber and firewood for the ships, to make bricks, till the soil and catch fish he needed workers. Most Khoikhoi lacked the skill or inclination for such tasks and his garrison, rising to 200 men, was equally unenthusiastic and in any case too small. He wrote to the company asking to be sent slaves.

By the 1650s, the Dutch were benefiting from slavery in the East Indies and had become active in supplying slaves from West Africa to the Americas. Elsewhere in Africa, slavery and the slave trade were practised before the white man arrived, but in the Cape they were unknown until brought by van Riebeeck. Others argued for free white men to be imported as labourers, but van Riebeeck won his way by showing that they would cost more.

Thus he persuaded the company to take the four decisions that shaped South Africa: to found the colony, to settle freeburghers, to establish superiority over the local tribes and to import slaves. Afrikaners remember him as the founder of their nation and way of life. But he was a company man aspiring to higher things. In 1662, after ten years at the Cape, he was rewarded with a position in the Indies, where the real money was to be made. There he rose to be President of Malacca and (in the words on his gravestone) 'Secretary to the exalted government of India'. He died and was buried at the capital of the Dutch eastern empire, Batavia, in 1677.

The main labour needs of the tiny colony he founded were met by a few shiploads of slaves. They arrived from Madagascar, Angola and Dahomey and later from Mozambique and Zanzibar. They provided the strength to work the farms. From the East Indies and India came the more highly valued domestic slaves, trained in household skills or craftsmanship. They were generally bought from owners they accompanied on the homeward voyage. Taking slaves to the Netherlands or England made them liable, on landing, to be declared free. Selling them at the Cape maximized for the returning company man both convenience and profit.

Male slaves always fetched a higher price, but the women too were valued. The company maintained a slave lodge at the Cape which soon became the leading brothel. Each evening VOC officials, before locking the gates and counting the slaves, asked the European visitors, mostly soldiers and sailors, to leave. In 1671 the VOC's commissioner of the Cape, Isbrand Goske, reported that three-quarters of the children born to company slave-women had European fathers. Many of the early white settlers married slaves, particularly women from the Indian state of Bengal. Later, such mixed marriages as occurred were more often with local women of mixed race. Thus was founded the significant population group known as the Cape Coloured – varied in racial origin, but Dutch-speaking, Christian and, after a generation or two, predominantly European in culture.

The vast majority of the slaves were sold to freeburghers. One visitor wrote that in the eighteenth century the teenage sons of respectable Cape families commonly became 'entangled with a handsome slave-girl belonging to the household' and got her pregnant. The girl would be 'sternly rebuked for her wantonness' but for the boy 'his escapade is a source of amusement and he is dubbed a young fellow who has shown the stuff he is made of'.

Van Riebeeck's original crew of seventy were mostly poor Dutchmen, though, in accordance with the VOC's normal practice, some of the less attractive posts were filled by Germans. Their language was not van Riebeeck's elegant Dutch but the seamen's dialect of Amsterdam, larded with Portuguese and Malay words picked up from the eastern trade and the domestic slaves. Over the next two hundred years the mixture was to evolve, first into a patois of Dutch known as the *Taal* (Dutch for 'the language') and, by the beginning of the twentieth century, into a distinct language, Afrikaans.

Since the VOC's purpose at the Cape was merely to maintain a refreshment station, no further shiploads of Dutch were sent to colonize, just the occasional orphan girl and, after an outbreak in 1688 of religious persecution in France, some two hundred French Huguenots. These were carefully dispersed among the Dutch farmers, whose numbers grew through natural increase in this unusually healthy colony. The Huguenot immigration was soon stopped because the Cape was too poor to sustain a large population. Farmers had nowhere to sell their surplus grain, wine, fruit and vegetables. The produce was neither valuable nor durable enough to merit shipment to Europe. During the 150 years that the VOC rule was to last, Cape Colony remained what the company had intended: a facility for passing ships, no more.

In a slave-owning society, freedom is defined by slavery. Everyone wanted to own slaves and thus avoid manual work. Within two generations the widespread intermarriage of the early years had ceased. White farmers married only white women. Families became established, and many soon came to be related. According to their generations, one white would address another as 'grandfather', 'uncle', 'aunt', or 'nephew'. Like any slave-owning caste, they behaved in ways that reinforced their unity and sense of superiority.

For the VOC the Cape was an administrative anomaly. Once its original plan – to have its staff grow vegetables and rely on the Khoikhoi to supply meat – had gone wrong, the company found it had created a new and potentially troublesome group: independent settlers. They were less amenable than company servants to the narrow regulation that the lordly council in Amsterdam was accustomed to impose. Company men in Cape Town could be disciplined and, if necessary, ordered home. A settler facing the prospect of an unfavourable judgement from the VOC court could move into the interior.

To seek to control them was uneconomic. From many it was difficult even to collect taxes. As generations passed, they felt that the land and the slaves were theirs by right of immemorial possession. Increasingly they resisted attempts by company men, on short-term assignment, to regulate them. In theory the company, like a sovereign state, protected the farmers. It fortified Cape Town to resist invasion by European powers from the sea. On the inland frontiers, however, if the farmers came into conflict with indigenous peoples, the local magistrate, the field-cornet, had to gather such volunteers as he could and engage in action when they would spare him the time.

In 1702 such a group, consisting of forty-five young Afrikaners with Khoikhoi servants, rode east from the grain- and fruit-growing area of Stellenbosch – a mere twenty-five miles from Cape Town – and launched the first recorded battle between the white man and the Xhosa, the predominant black population inland from the Cape. The fight was indecisive, but was the basis of the common claim of twentieth-century Afrikaners that 'we were here before the black man'.

The evidence is against this myth. Even though the only dwellers close to Cape Town were the yellow Khoikhoi and San, black clans or states had been established in the rest of southern Africa for centuries before van Riebeeck arrived. The Xhosa belonged to a group of states, along with the Zulu and the Swazi, who spoke mutually understood languages together known as Nguni. As early as 1552, Portuguese shipwrecked on the south-east coast had reported that a yearly ship visited the Xhosa people to buy ivory. In 1554 another Portuguese shipwreck produced reports of men 'very black with woolly hair'. In 1593 some shipwrecked Portuguese were rescued, but had to leave behind a boy who was too ill to travel. He was looked after by a Xhosa chief and in 1635, when another shipwrecked group met him, he 'was now very rich and had three wives and many children' and helped arrange for them to buy 219 cattle. The 1593 party were told on the coast that if they travelled inland they would 'always find villages with provisions'. Their journal described the village huts as 'round and low, made of reed mats which do not keep out the rain'. Finally, in 1686 a Dutch ship, the *Stavenisse*, was wrecked on the south-east coast and the Governor of Cape Town, Simon van der Stel, summarized the survivors' reports for the VOC directors. The Xhosa, he wrote, were 'civil, polite and talkative', kept 'cows, calves, oxen, steers and goats', grew 'three sorts of corn' and 'would not sell their children as slaves'.

The Xhosa and their linguistic relatives were not the only inhabitants of the interior. Unknown to the Dutch at the Cape, black peoples speaking another group of languages, Sotho, had for centuries been constructing stone buildings, smelting iron, working copper into fine wire, selling ivory and ostrich feathers for overseas trade and, in one case, mining and working gold. This group included the people of modern Lesotho, Botswana and Bophuthatswana as well as the Pedi and the Venda. The nineteenth-century Scottish missionary, David Livingstone, wrote: 'The manufactory of iron seems to have been carried on here from a very remote period . . . [the people] smelt iron, copper and tin, and in the manufacture of ornaments know how to mix the tin and copper so as to form an amalgam. Their country abounds in ores.' A large group of the Tswana bear the surname Baralong (smith), which has been traced back to the fourteenth century. Archaeological evidence of smelting has been carbon-dated in Sotho-speaking areas as early as the eighth century. Some fragments of Sung porcelain dug up in ancient sites suggest that Sotho-speakers were linked in trade with China between the twelfth and fourteenth centuries.

The *Boers* – Dutch for farmers – would have dismissed all this evidence as fanciful. They led an isolated, simple life and were not well informed. No journals or newspapers were published in the colony, no plays were performed. Though parish clerks of the Dutch church ran elementary schools, demand for higher education was negligible. It was enough for children to be taught to read and to be confirmed as Christians. The ferment of eighteenth-century Europe – the Enlightenment, rationalism, the growing potential of science and industry – excited some American slave-owners on the huge plantations of Virginia and Maryland, but here everything was on a smaller scale, the slave-owners were merely a more prosperous class of peasant, and new ideas were scarcely noticed.

By the end of the eighteenth century, van Riebeeck's seventy had multiplied to some 20,000 Afrikaners, employing 26,000 slaves and some 13,000 Khoikhoi (their earlier numbers reduced by smallpox). To prevent slaves or Khoikhoi from fleeing or rising against their masters, punishments of unimaginable cruelty were imposed. This was an age when a sailor found guilty of malpractice on a company ship, a free, white man, could receive 200 lashes or be keelhauled – thrown overboard and dragged by rope beneath the keel and up the other side, alive if he was lucky. Criminal justice in Europe was still barbaric. The almost God-like – or diabolical – authority of a master over his slaves was merely the most extreme way society kept order. It made the Cape farmers, even more than the gentlemen of the Carolinas and Georgia, immune to the libertarian ideas of the time. Anybody coming from Europe to tell the Afrikaners how slaves or Hottentots should be treated was asking for trouble.

CHAPTER TWO

The Great Trek, 1795–1854

In the burst of aggression that followed the French Revolution, the armies of France swept over the Netherlands. The Dutch could no longer protect their colonies. To prevent these too from falling into French hands, the British, with Dutch consent, occupied the Cape and the Dutch East Indies. At the end of the wars, in 1815, Britain paid the Dutch £6 million and kept the Cape.

The British tried to be amiable to their new Dutch-Afrikaner subjects. Lady Anne Barnard, wife of Britain's first Colonial Secretary at the Cape, held banquets in the governor's residence. The Cape Town women who came reminded her of those one might find at an assize ball in an English country town, but she did her best (as she wrote) to 'reconcile them by the attraction of fiddles and French horns'.

In 1809 the British introduced a law to help Afrikaner farmers, which later became one of the most bitter causes of complaint. It was called the Hottentot Code and decreed that every Hottentot (or Khoikhoi) was to have a fixed 'place of abode' and that if he wished to move he had to obtain a pass from his master or from a local official. Any landholder could demand this pass and any Khoikhoi found abroad without one was to be taken to the *landrost* or field-cornet who would act 'as they shall feel incumbent to do'.

This was the first of the Pass Laws. It compelled the Khoikhoi to work for the Afrikaners, as without a pass a Khoikhoi had no right to be outside his master's property, and the masters controlled the issue of passes. Although introduced by a British governor, the measure was largely a codification of the long-standing practice of the settlement. It was not like the obligation to carry identity cards, common to citizens of many societies, but more akin to a badge of slavery: caught without his pass, a Khoikhoi was liable to be thrown into prison, punished and sent back into service.

Afrikaner farmers welcomed the measure. Compared to the pettifogging bureaucracy of the Dutch East India Company, in the early years of British rule they found much to commend. British officials were better paid than those of the Dutch company and were praised for being, as a whole, less corrupt. They were shocked by the general illiteracy at the Cape and set about improving the schools. In 1800 they founded the first newspaper in southern Africa, the *Cape Gazette*. For thirty years the Afrikaner settlers in the eastern Cape and the inland peoples there, the Xhosa, had engaged in intermittent killing and cattle-stealing, neither able to drive out the other. British troops quickly expelled the Xhosa and set up military posts to prevent their return. The duty on Cape wines entering Britain was reduced, stimulating an enormous increase in production and exports. Under Dutch rule farmers had distilled excess wine to make brandy for their own consumption. By the 1820s the Cape supplied more than 10 per cent of the wine drunk in Britain.

But British merchants spoke the right language and had the connections to seize most of the new opportunities in trade. And the Afrikaners soon began to find that the improvements in administration and law-enforcement were, likewise, not primarily for their benefit.

For the first time judges were sent on circuit round the country. In 1815 one of them faced a dilemma. A Khoikhoi herdsman had charged his boss, Freek Bezuidenhout, with maltreating him. The court had summoned Bezuidenhout three times. Three times he had ignored the summons. The Dutch company's courts had generally not pursued such charges by a black servant against his white master. The British-appointed judge (actually an Afrikaner) took the British view of the dignity of the law. He sentenced Bezuidenhout to one month's imprisonment for contempt of court and sent a party of soldiers to fetch him. Bezuidenhout took a gun into a cave to resist arrest and was shot dead.

His family and local sympathisers responded by taking the law into their own hands. Not only were the British sending a judge to remote areas where they had no business, to hear cases brought by black servants against white masters – a certain way to encourage trouble – but they had sent a troop of twelve Khoikhoi soldiers, under two white officers, to arrest a white man. Some sixty Afrikaner farmers rose in an armed rebellion, but were quickly defeated. Five of them were found guilty of treason and hanged. Many years later, when the Afrikaners' resentment against British oppression had intensified, the five hanged for avenging Bezuidenhout became 'the heroes of

Slachter's Nek' – Afrikanerdom's first martyrs. The fact that during the hanging the ropes broke, dumping four of them on the ground, which they pleaded entitled them to mercy, only strengthened the martyrdoms' message. The four were picked up and rehanged.

In 1820 the government in London, faced with severe unemployment and mounting disorder following the war against France, tried to encourage settlement in its colonies. It paid for 4,000 Britons to travel to the Cape, where its local administration allotted each family 100 acres of frontier land. In 1822 Lord Charles Somerset, the Governor, proclaimed that within five years English would be the only language used in the courts. Afrikaner resentment grew when members of their community were forced to answer questions put to them by court interpreters, who were usually coloured, and when Lord Charles recruited British teachers and gave subsidies to schools that taught in English.

More trouble between the British and the Afrikaners arose from the arrival of missionaries. The Dutch church in the seventeenth and eighteenth centuries had not sought converts among the Khoikhoi, San or Xhosa. The few pastors had had their salaries paid by the Dutch East India Company to serve the Dutch community and had prudently avoided pleading for the equality of man or delivering sermons that might justify slaves or Khoikhoi rising in revolt. The new wave of missionaries – English, Scottish, German, American, and of many denominations – were different. They came to the Cape to save souls, particularly black, heathen souls. They hoped to create an African clergy with whose help they would transform African society, introducing Christianity, civilization and the idea of the dignity of labour. Financed independently of government, they bought land or negotiated its cession from African chiefs in return for diplomatic, technical or administrative help. They then created self-supporting agricultural-religious settlements, providing medical, social and religious services. To these Christian radicals the illiteracy and poor living conditions of the slaves on Cape farms were a moral outrage.

In England allies of the missionaries had by 1807 forced Parliament to outlaw the trade in slaves throughout the empire. This meant that Afrikaner farmers were allowed to keep the slaves they had, but not to buy any more. The Royal Navy and the Cape administration gradually overcame the smuggling and the sales of 'prize negroes' that immediately followed the ban. The anti-slavery movement went on from this first success to demand that all slaves throughout the Empire must be freed. In such an atmosphere, Lord Charles Somerset felt obliged to keep up the pressure on the Cape slave-owners. He made them complete a register of slaves and declared that any not registered would be regarded as free. He appointed a protector of slaves in each district. He supported the setting up of fifteen schools for slaves and issued an order allowing slaves to give evidence before a magistrate against their masters. To the Afrikaner slave-owner it was all madness, the ignorant action of malevolent foreigners.

Naturally the 4,000 English settlers of 1820 were not allowed to buy slaves. This created a problem. No wage-labourers seeking work were available to help them turn their land into farms. The local Khoikhoi (or Hottentots) were nearly all by now paid servants of the Afrikaners, treated not as free but as semi-slaves, forbidden to move about the country. The evidence of missionaries reinforced the pleas of the 4,000 English settlers. Black labour had to be eased out of Afrikaner control and made available in a free market. This coincidence of economic and humanitarian interest led the British in 1828 to issue a famous ordinance:

> As it has been the custom of this colony for Hottentots and other free persons of colour to be subject to certain hindrances as to their place of living, way of life and employment, and to certain forced services which do not apply to other subjects of His Majesty, be it therefore made law that no Hottentot or other free person of colour shall be subject to any forced service which does not apply to others of His Majesty's subjects, nor to any hindrance, interference, fine or punishment of any kind whatever under the pretence that such person has been guilty of vagrancy or any other offence unless after trial in the due course of law.

The Pass Law which the helpful British had introduced in 1809 was thus inconsiderately repealed. It was stipulated, moreover, that the ordinance could not be altered without authority from London. The measure was essential, in the eyes of the free-market British, to create a mobile supply of labour. In the eyes of the Afrikaners, the servants on whom their prosperity depended were being taken from them and turned into a plague of thieving vagrants.

In 1833 the law abolishing slavery throughout the empire was passed. The reformers in Westminster were primarily concerned – for reasons economic and political as well as humanitarian – to stop the plantation slavery of the West Indies, where the owners were rich and conveniently able to travel to London for their compensation – about a third of the assessed value of the slaves. The slave-owning farmers of the Cape were not so rich. Most could not get to London and, having fewer slaves (some 36,000 valued at £3 million), had less compensation to collect. They had to employ London agents, who charged a high commission. The four to six years' 'apprenticeship' before the slaves were free to leave did little to cushion their owners' resentment.

Meanwhile the missionaries were marching out to the frontiers of the white settlement, and then beyond into the land of the Xhosa, the Sotho, the Zulu, the Tswana, the Pedi and the Venda. One group of British missionaries began making complaints to London against the farmers on the eastern frontier for grabbing the black people's land. After investigations, the Secretary for the Colonies ordered the return of substantial areas that the governor himself had, with enthusiastic Afrikaner support, recently conquered. The House of Commons appointed a Select Committee on the treatment of aborigines. Some missionaries were even reported to have supplied guns to the black peoples, as a quick way to win converts.

To Afrikaners the most hated figure of all, worse than Lord Charles Somerset, was the Superintendent of the London Missionary Society (LMS) at the Cape from 1818 to 1851, Dr John Philip. The LMS had more than thirty missions in the Cape and nearby African areas, and Philip as their chief administrator made twelve treks inland, each lasting some six months, during which he wrote detailed journals. The knowledge he thus acquired was complemented by the steady flow of reports he received from the missions and by missionaries visiting his Cape Town home on their way out of the colony. Thus Philip was able to present a more complete view of the condition of Africans than either the government or his critics. He campaigned ceaselessly on behalf of the Africans and against the Afrikaners.

In the face of all these provocations some 6,000 Afrikaners set out in 1837 on what became the most important of all events in their popular mythology, the Great Trek. By 1854, when it was completed, almost a quarter of the European population, more than ten thousand men, women and children, had left Cape Colony for ever, taking as many servants with them. Some sold their homes at a loss. Others abandoned them. A hundred years later Afrikaners came to revere the Great Trek, as though it were the flight of the Children of Israel from Egypt to the Promised Land.

Little treks had been going on for more than a century. As the original settlement spread from Cape Town eastwards, the early generations filled up all the land suitable for vegetables, fruit, grain and vine. In the eighteenth century many Afrikaner farmers' sons found work in Cape Town. But after 1815, the best commercial opportunities in Cape Town came to require fluency in English. So the sons of *boers* became *trekboers* (frontier farmers). They drove off in their wagons to remote areas without roads – and in the whole of South Africa none of the rivers is navigable – and concentrated on breeding the produce that could get to market on its own legs: cattle and sheep. The life of *trekboers* came increasingly to resemble that of the African peoples whose pastures they took over.

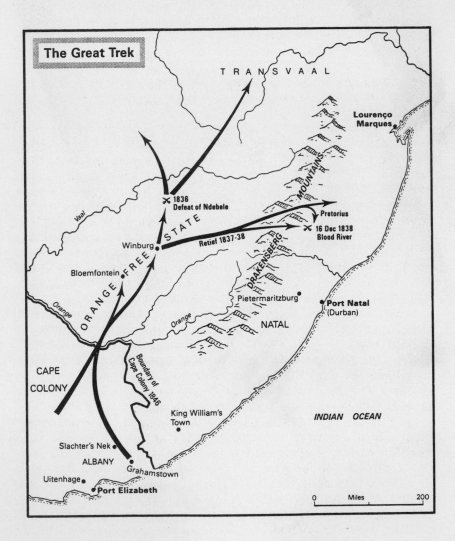

The Great Trek

TRANSVAAL

Lourenço Marques

1836
Defeat of Ndebele

MOUNTAINS

Vaal

Pretorius

16 Dec 1838
Blood River

Winburg

Retief 1837-38

ORANGE FREE STATE

Bloemfontein

DRAKENSBERG

Orange

Pietermaritzburg

Port Natal
(Durban)

Orange

NATAL

CAPE
COLONY

Boundary of
Cape Colony 1846

King William's
Town

INDIAN OCEAN

Slachter's Nek

ALBANY

Uitenhage

Grahamstown

Port Elizabeth

0   Miles   200

Repeatedly the *trekboers* had come into conflict with African tribes. The San (Bushmen), the primitive hunter-gatherers, had proved particularly troublesome. Having no herds of their own, they had greeted the roaming animals of the *trekboers* as fair game. The *trekboers* tried to inculcate a sense of their property rights by launching punitive expeditions, but these failed in their educational purpose and soon frontier farmers were shooting San on sight. Some went out with guns to hunt them and enslaved San women and children. By the nineteenth century the San were exterminated, except for those living hundreds of miles to the north in the Kalahari desert, where neither white nor black pastoralists claimed wandering animals as their property.

With the Xhosa peoples the *trekboers* had generally maintained a better understanding. Both measured their wealth in the ownership of cattle. Both were possessive and combative over animals but ready to move their homes and abandon land as soon as the grasses were exhausted. Their long years of neighbourly rivalry punctuated by raids had ended temporarily in 1811–12 when the British defined the frontier and expelled the Xhosa from the area within it. By the 1830s, however, when Afrikaner resentment at British rule was becoming uncontainable, the pressure at the frontier was reaching explosion point. The *trekboers*, increasing in numbers, were pressing eastward into pasture long used by the Xhosa, who were pressing westward against the land, albeit unregistered, of the *trekboers*.

Some *trekboers* rode far into Xhosa country. They were armed and went unmolested. Away to the east and the north, beyond the Xhosas' seasonal pastures, they found areas of unoccupied land. Better still, some of it was near a small harbour the British were developing at Port Natal (later renamed Durban) offering the promise of a market. The early scouts were followed by a few intrepid families. Reports back were favourable.

On 2 February 1937 the *Grahamstown Journal*, in the frontier district of Albany where the British settlers of 1820 had been allotted land, announced: 'A document has been handed to us purporting to be the cause of the emigration.' The author was Piet Retief, a fifty-seven-year-old Afrikaner of Huguenot origin. He had quit his family's fruit farm near Cape Town, moved to the frontier and earned his living as cattle auctioneer, supplier of food to the new, British settlers, horse breeder and building contractor – in which role he failed to complete a government contract on time, sued for payment anyway and lost, at great personal cost. He was also the local *Veldkommandant* – commander of the militia force and magistrate. His document stated, in part:

1. We despair of saving the colony from the turbulent and

dishonest conduct of vagrants, who are allowed to infest every part;

2. We complain of the severe losses which we have been forced to sustain by the emancipation of our slaves;
3. We complain of the continual plunder which we have ever endured from the Caffres [i.e. the Xhosa] and other coloured classes;
4. We complain of the unjustifiable odium which has been cast upon us by interested and dishonest persons, under the cloak of religion, whose testimony is believed in England.

His reasons published, Piet Retief set off with his family to Winberg, the meeting point for the trek. There hundreds of ox-carts slowly assembled in dozens of encampments. Many of the trekkers were strong-willed people and disagreements had erupted. Some wanted to go far to the north, beyond the Vaal river, away from the British. The Dutch church – in South Africa a habitual supporter of the government – opposed the trek and would appoint no pastor, so the trekkers argued fiercely over who should be their senior priest. Retief was elected governor and chief commandant and spent months at Winberg, as the trekker encampment grew, trying to settle such arguments. But he was not successful. So he led any who would follow him towards a pass in the formidable Drakensberg mountains, down towards the east coast and the green, hot, fertile land of Natal.

Those opposed to him pointed out two main drawbacks in trekking to Natal. First, the Zulu already occupied much of the land there and had a terrifying military record, their conquests in recent decades far more extensive than those of the white man. The military organization of Shaka, the great Zulu king, had affected every settled tribe in the southern quarter of Africa. Most he had conquered. He then made their young men join his armies, learn his discipline and carry his weapons. And the more his armies grew, the more they had to move on and conquer. Second, the British who had opened Port Natal were incorrigible imperialists and would try to control their neighbours as they had at the Cape. Retief dismissed both arguments. More land was available in Natal than the Zulu could occupy and it was well known that Shaka had adopted many whites as 'his' and ordered that they must not be hurt. Retief would win the Zulu king's approval by honest diplomacy, a method he had repeatedly found successful in his role as frontier commander. As for the British, Retief was one of the few trekkers who spoke their language fluently: they were not yet well established in Natal and would be accommodating.

The trek was slow. The ox-drawn waggons were tough enough to be dragged over the mountains and be taken apart and repaired when they broke down. Their multi-layered canvas covers were impenetrable to spears. But they could advance only two or three miles a day, and every night each family's cattle and sheep had to be found pasture, often dispersed over vast areas. Where they found grass, shade, water and firewood they would stop for a day or two, sometimes even a week.

Retief used the months at Winberg and the slow rate of advance to send scouts over the Drakensberg range. They found passes which the ox-waggons could, with difficulty, negotiate. Retief set off ahead to clear the way with the British at Port Natal, who cheered his arrival, and with the King of the Zulu, Shaka's half-brother and successor, Dingaan. Retief offered to recover some stolen cattle for Dingaan, as a goodwill gesture, and to be a peaceful neighbour in a land that was big enough for both of them. In return Dingaan signed a document in English, which a Welsh missionary newly resident at his court translated, ceding a large part of Natal to Retief and his followers. The signing was followed by days of ceremonial, principally Zulu war-dances.

Retief had been warned that Dingaan was treacherous. At the centre of the king's capital, a military camp made up of thousands of beehive huts in huge concentric circles, Retief and his followers – seventy-one Afrikaners, thirty coloureds – were at the mercy of the Zulu army. Dingaan received news that the trekkers who had followed Retief over the passes had begun to establish themselves on the land before he had granted his royal assent. Retief boastfully told him of another group of trekkers, headed north towards Transvaal, who had overwhelmed the Zulus' kinsmen, the Ndebele, in battle. Such news was bound to make the Zulu king feel threatened.

Retief had concluded his business. Etiquette required him to sit through a final, ceremonial war-dance, at the climax of which Dingaan ordered that the visitors be dragged away. Zulu warriors took them to the tribe's place of execution and cracked open their skulls. Afterwards more warriors set off for the spreading encampments beside the streams that flowed from the Drakensberg and there wiped out almost five hundred of the settlers and their servants, mostly women and children.

The trekkers were more determined than Dingaan realized and quickly counter-attacked. They sent messengers to seek aid from their colleagues inland and from the British at Port Natal. Both sent forces against Dingaan, only to be defeated by the Zulu armies. By mid-1838 the trekkers in Natal seemed doomed. They were unwilling to climb back up the Drakensberg to return to the Cape, even though many thought it only a matter of time before the Zulu came to wipe them out.

In December 1838 the Zulu came. The trekkers had by then been

reinforced by fresh men and by cannon, and a well-armed group of
them advanced provocatively towards the Zulu. Each night they
retreated into their famous laager, a great circle of ox-waggons,
chained tightly together, with ladders and thorn-bushes blocking any
gaps. On the night of 15 December they placed the laager in the V
between two rivers, so that the Zulu could attack only from one
direction, towards which the trekkers pointed all their fire-power.
This was to be the moment of vengeance for the murder of Piet
Retief and his companions. It was also the occasion of the
subsequently hyped and later disputed Covenant with God (see page
xviii). The next morning the massed Zulu charged at the laager with
their spears, only to be mown down. Waves of them kept charging
with disciplined, suicidal bravery. Others tried to cross the rivers to
attack the laager from behind. Every tactic was met by bullets. At
the end of the day some 3,000 Zulu lay dead, while not a single
Afrikaner was lost. The rivers that protected the flanks of the laager
were red with blood and the day's events, which broke Dingaan's
authority over the Zulu armies and decisively shifted the balance of
power, have been remembered ever since by Afrikaners as the Battle
of Blood River.

Though important to Afrikaner folk memory, the battle did not
bring success to the trekkers. The British considered Port Natal of
strategic value rivalling Cape Town. They could not risk its falling to
an enemy. So the Independent Republic of Natalia which the few
thousand trekkers set up, eagerly seeking African 'orphan' children
to work as 'apprentices' (i.e. slaves) on their new farms, soon found
itself facing the military might of the British Empire. In 1842 the first
battle between Afrikaner settlers and British troops ended
indecisively, but the British Cabinet's determination was enough to
cause the trekkers in 1845 freely to dissolve the republic.

Most of them refused to be reabsorbed by the empire. Piet Retief's
first four reasons for setting out on the Great Trek amounted to an
objection to Britain's interfering with the white man's right to treat
blacks as slaves. The Afrikaner settlers left Natal mainly because
they thought the British about to do it again. The British government
did indeed assert that the laws of the Cape would apply in Natal and
courts would be set up in which the evidence of missionaries and
black men would be accepted against Afrikaners. The Dutch East
India Company too had had some inconvenient laws. What was
unacceptable about the British as rulers was that they seemed
determined to enforce laws, even in remote places, and made the
settlers pay taxes for the privilege of being browbeaten. The Natalia
trekkers wanted none of it. They reloaded their waggons and began,
only five years after triumphantly descending the Drakensberg,
slowly to climb back again to the high veld. There they resumed the

Great Trek northwards, to rejoin those who had rejected Piet Retief's leadership and, after defeating the Ndebele army, had moved into the interior.

The next trekker settlements after Natal were on the Orange river. They called them the Orange Free State. In 1848 the British Empire sent a force, under Sir Harry Smith, to conquer them. Hundreds of defeated Afrikaners were driven further north, across the Vaal river, where their final independent republic, the Transvaal – small, quarrelsome and disorganized – was promptly overwhelmed by the next forward step of Sir Harry. The heroic exodus which was to become the Afrikaners' inspiration appeared by 1848 to have produced, in the middle of nowhere, a mere mouse of a settlement – and under British rule.

The Afrikaners remained unwilling to have the British telling them what to do. Their republican ideals, derived from the Netherlands in the seventeenth century, were complemented by one overriding principle: the right of their white citizens to treat blacks as servants or slaves. When in 1839, after the Battle of Blood River, they had briefly set up the republic of Natalia, the central feature of its constitution was a *Raad van Representanten van het Volk*, a council of representatives of the people. Only white males could vote for the Raad, because, scattered and vulnerable as they were, their group survival depended on holding together against all outsiders. The Transvaal and Orange Free State had had the same basis to their constitutions: the determination of frontier escapees to run their own affairs and rule the natives. Britain found the trekkers cussed and unprofitable subjects and gave them back their independence, the Transvaal in 1852 and the Orange Free State in 1854. Neither flourished.

In Cape Colony and Natal, British control was only slightly more firm. When Britain had set up the first legislative council in Cape Colony in 1836, it enabled Africans to qualify for the vote for municipal boards in towns and villages. When representative government was granted in 1853, the local British demanded a high qualification for the vote, hoping to exclude both non-whites and poor Afrikaners. They were overruled by the Colonial Office, which set a low qualification. The Cape Attorney-General, William Porter, explained: 'I would rather meet the Hottentot at the hustings voting for his representative than in the wilds with his gun upon his shoulder.' From London the principle was spelled out: Her Majesty's subjects must have 'political rights enjoyed by all alike'.

This did not mean that there was any chance of power passing to the majority in the Cape, who were black. The British government had liberal principles, but did not expect them to be rigidly adhered to. Later in the century Cape white voters excluded tribal Africans from the electoral register; they feared that large numbers of 'blanket Kaffirs' were registering and passed a law providing that no person could vote 'by reason of his sharing in tribal or communal occupation of land'. The property qualification required individual freehold tenure to the value of £25. This allowed the non-white vote to grow modestly and a few blacks to sit in the Cape provincial and municipal councils. Thus in the Cape power was moving from London to a local élite, formed of English and Afrikaners, who laid down the qualifications under which *they* allowed Africans a few seats in the legislature.

In Natal matters were more straightforward. Here the few white settlers were nearly all British, intensely loyal to the empire, but free of the Cape liberal tradition. They would back London on any imperial issue, so long as London protected them and allowed them to dominate the local blacks by making the white government 'supreme chief of all natives'. Liberal-looking clauses were included in the Natal constitution, but just for show.

Thus, by the time the trekkers from Cape Colony had made good their escape, white rule in southern Africa was thoroughly disorderly. The Orange Free State and the Transvaal held clusters of land surrounded by Africans. Their future was far from secure. And the British at the Cape could not make up their minds what, if anything, to do about them.

CHAPTER THREE

Diamonds and Gold, 1854–96

In 1866 a boy called Erasmus Stephanus Jacobs picked up an unusual stone on a farm in the north of Cape Colony. The farmer showed it to a travelling trader who thought it might be a diamond. The nearest geologist, 200 miles away at Grahamstown, confirmed it and found the stone to weigh 21¼ carats. Sir Philip Wodehouse, the Governor, bought it for £500. Over the next four years more diamonds were found. One, the 'Star of Africa', was bought from an African shepherd for 500 sheep and ten oxen and soon afterwards fetched £30,000. Fortune-hunters rushed to the area, sorting the pebbles near the confluence of the Vaal and Orange rivers, and shuffling title deeds and forgotten documents. A harvest of stones reached Cape Town. Clerks, shopkeepers, farmers and young hopefuls streamed to the diggings.

It was unclear to whom the diamond zone belonged. The Afrikaner trekkers to whom the British had given back charge of their own independent republics, the Orange Free State to the east and the Transvaal to the north, both claimed the area. And to the west were the Griquas, a tatterdemalion group of half-castes who had come from the Cape, much like the trekkers. Britain had recently recognized their independence and they too claimed the area. Some 10,000 diggers, sifters, speculators and hangers-on were squabbling, drinking, stealing and selling in a no man's land between these three puny governments and the British in Cape Colony. Lawlessness spread. Some of the diggers announced they had set up a republic of their own.

The British government faced a dilemma. It claimed that all it wanted was to prevent disorder, more particularly to prevent the Afrikaners from oppressing the natives in a way that would make

expensive British intervention necessary. This had indeed become
the empire's policy towards the interior when it was thought to be
worthless scrubland. But diamonds made a difference. The British
continued to maintain that their motives were pure, but somehow
they secured the plums from the pudding. The Governor of Natal (a
British official) was accepted by all parties as arbitrator. He
pronounced in favour of the Griqua claim. Then, soon after, the
Griqua leader said it was all too much to handle and asked the British
to take over.

The diggers, flooding in from all parts of South Africa and the
world, soon concluded that they had come upon one of the extinct
volcanic pipes that are the source of diamonds. The truth was even
more impressive. The area contained not one diamond pipe, but four
– the richest deposits ever found. All were added to Cape Colony,
and thus became part of the British Empire, without a shot being
fired. To the British it was a triumph of diplomacy, to the Afrikaners,
particularly in the Transvaal and the Orange Free State, a crude
imperialist grab.

On average here one diamond was sifted from every fifty buckets of
earth. Never were jewels so common. Some were found in the
gizzards of hens, which liked to peck at them. Cooks sifted
ingredients with extra care. The British Colonial Secretary, Lord
Kimberley, complained that he could neither pronounce nor spell the
Dutch name of the farm where the biggest mine was found,
Vooruitzicht, so the place was renamed Kimberley.

Diamond-mining is an extraordinary business. A few diamonds
removed from the diggings can radically change a person's entire life.
Consequently, diamond mines come to resemble prisons. Nobody is
allowed to leave without being searched. Naturally this rule is
applied more actively to some than to others. Labourers go in and out
most frequently and tend to be most often and thoroughly searched.

The surest way to prevent labourers from smuggling out diamonds
is to stop them leaving the area, by housing them beside the mine in
enclosed compounds. Once a few companies had secured control of the
industry at Kimberley, such labour compounds were built. Diamond-
mining was the first industrial enterprise of any size in southern
Africa. By 1870 – just four years after Erasmus Stephanus Jacobs
picked up the unusual stone – Kimberley was reckoned to have 50,000
inhabitants, including more whites than had taken part in the entire
Great Trek. The way they organized their business, with the first
industrial disciplining of a large black labour force by compounds,
searches and Pass Laws, was to become a blueprint for South Africa's
future.

At first blacks came from native kingdoms far and near to make
their fortunes at the diggings, but the gun-carrying whites combined

to squeeze them out. In 1870 that was standard practice in southern Africa. The early arrivals were nearly all men. Who would want to bring his wife or children to such a violent, ugly place? But a change occurred. The whites who came were free to bring their wives; blacks could have a job in the mines only if they agreed to live in the compounds, which were for men only. And at the end of their contracts they had to submit to an extra indignity. To make sure they had no diamonds concealed on them, they were kept naked in a separate compound for several days and their bodies and excrement thoroughly searched.

For the bosses the compound labour system had many advantages. All the problems of wives, children and old people were kept at a distance – back in the native area. A labourer who fell ill or needed help could be sent home, to the all-purpose social services presumed to be provided by his tribe. And men housed in a compound could be paid less than those dwelling in the town with their families. Wives and families were assumed to have a field or a vegetable patch off which they fed; so the worker need not be paid enough to support them.

Until 1870 southern Africa had been a mixed bag of African kingdoms, Afrikaner republics and British colonies. They rubbed along together, the British mostly concerned with strategy and commerce, the Africans and Afrikaners with being left in peace to farm. When Britain had annexed the Afrikaner republics it had soon given them back. As for the African kingdoms, the British, like the Dutch before them, had considered conquest a foolish notion, a prescription for nothing but expense and trouble.

Diamonds changed everything. More specifically, British policy towards the African kingdoms changed because mining intensified the shortage of black labour. The influx of foreigners created a sudden demand for food. Africans seized the opportunity. Some sent their young men to the mines for a few years to earn the money to buy ploughs, seed and fertilizers. But the objective of nearly all was to avoid the horrors of mining and stay, if possible, on the family farm. So long as the Africans had access to land, the mines were to face a constant shortage of labour.

Blacks at Kimberley were soon in such short supply that they could refuse to live in the diggers' compounds or eat at the canteens. They insisted instead on high wages to enable them to use the mushrooming black eating houses, sleep where they wished, drink and take days off at will. Further, Kimberley became southern Africa's principal gun-market. Many Africans went to work there only because their chiefs sent them to earn the money to buy guns and gunpowder.

Tiny groups of white farmers scattered over a vast area were seized by panic, especially the British in Natal. They lived surrounded by Africans – Zulu to the north, Sotho to the west, Mpondo to the south. Why, they wanted to know, were thousands of Africans buying guns? Rumour spread that the Zulu were preparing to lead an African army 'to drive the whites into the sea'.

The first African nation to make effective use of guns bought at Kimberley were not the Zulu but the Pedi. Blacks who had worked on the land of Transvaal Afrikaners saw the chance the diamond mines had created to run their own farms for profit. Prevented by law from buying or renting land in the Transvaal, they walked to the Pedi kingdom, nearby to the east, and set up smallholdings. The Pedi king was determined to protect these new settlers on his land and insisted that the Transvaal whites could not seize them back. So in 1876 the Transvaal government mounted a military expedition against him. The war was indecisive, but a disaster for the Transvaal. The penniless little state was almost defeated and failed to secure the return of the black workers its farms needed. The next year, without resistance, the 8,000 burghers of the Transvaal allowed themselves to be re-annexed by Britain, and imperial troops soon afterwards defeated the Pedi. (Then, in 1881, after winning a spectacular victory over a British army at Majuba Hill, the Transvaal burghers again won back their independence.)

The need to keep order in the mining area, to maintain the supply of labour, to stop the spread of guns to Africans, to calm the panic in Natal, to prevent a widespread war between blacks and whites, all argued for a single policy: British imperial troops, the only power capable of disciplining a region shaken by its new wealth, must intervene. By coincidence Benjamin Disraeli was at this time the dominant force in policy-making in London and he pressed enthusiastically for this new imperialism. So the diamond finds triggered wars of conquest that were for the first time to bring the whole of southern Africa under white control.

In the Cape the Xhosa, after a hundred years of intermittent war, were finally defeated and their principal remaining homelands, the Transkei and Ciskei (the two sides of the Kei river), became British possessions. The Cape Parliament passed an Act aimed at confiscating African-owned guns. When attempts were made to enforce it in Basutoland, resistance there led to another war – which cost an unhappy Cape legislature £3 million. As with the Pedi, it was British imperial troops who settled the issue, making Basutoland a British 'protectorate'.

In the war against the Zulu, the British had an extra motive. Suspecting that the Zulu were behind all the black unrest throughout southern Africa, the British hoped that a victory over them would not only calm the whole area but also persuade the Afrikaner republics to join a British-dominated federation. Thus the security of the Cape route to India would be assured along with some control over the labour supply for the diamond-mines. It did not prove easy. The Zulu defeated the British at Isandhlwana and Rorke's Drift and it was eight years – 1879 to 1887 – before Zululand finally became a Crown colony.

The black states were fragmented and made no attempt to form an alliance. The Swazi waited discreetly on the side during the British-Zulu war, until they saw the British were winning and signed a protectorate treaty with them. The Tswana people were themselves divided, the northern Tswana waiting to see the fate of the southern, before deciding to sign their own protectorate agreement. By and large the wars did not lead to dispossession of the Africans. Their land had already been restricted by the expansion of the British colonies and the Afrikaner republics. What they lost now was their independence. Their lands became native reserves, with the British granted the right to approve the appointment of chiefs, to handle external relations and to recruit labour for the mines.

To make the Africans come and work, the governments of the colonies introduced poll-taxes or hut-taxes. To pay the tax, at least one member of most African families had to leave home and earn cash. In the 1890s the mining magnate and Prime Minister of the Cape, Cecil Rhodes, said of the policy: 'If you are really one who loves the natives, you must make them worthy of the country they live in . . . You will not make them worthy if you allow them to sit in idleness.'

No sooner had diamonds been discovered – and most of the African kingdoms been conquered – than a second and even bigger fortune was dug up. In the South African Republic, or the Transvaal, lay a small line of hills, the Witwatersrand or white water range, where a rumour circulating since the 1850s had it that some locals had found gold. Hopefuls who went to dig were disappointed, but the rumours intensified and men who had recently made fortunes at Kimberley came to inspect. Barney Barnato, the most flamboyant of the diamond speculators, refused to believe gold was present. Cecil Rhodes brought a geological expert who pronounced: 'If I were to ride over these reefs in America, I would not get off my horse to look at them.' In samples of Rand earth the traces of gold were so slight as to earn the contempt of experienced miners. But the traces were consistent and widespread. At Kimberley men had fought over plots thirty feet square. On the Rand the successful extraction of gold required them to buy huge farms and ranches. The proportion of gold to earth was lower than in any previously exploited mine and the

seams ran inconveniently deep. But throughout a vast area the
ore-bearing rock seemed endless. Never in the history of the world
had so much gold been found in one place.

Diamonds and gold transformed South Africa. This was no longer
the unwanted hinterland of a modest naval facility. It became for the
first time a country in which powerful foreigners – in Afrikaans
uitlanders – were to take an interest. It also became, thanks initially
to the requirements of diamond-mining, a region with a peculiar
employment pattern. In 1902 Gardner Williams, general manager
of de Beers diamond mines, described the largest compound in
Kimberley: 'Four acres are enclosed, giving ample space for the
housing of its three thousand inmates, with an open central ground
for exercise and sports. The fences are of corrugated iron, rising ten
feet above the ground . . . Iron cabins fringe the inner sides of the
enclosure, divided into rooms 25 feet by 30 feet, which are lighted by
electricity. In each room twenty to twenty-five natives are
lodged . . . The bed clothing the natives bring with them or buy at
the stores in the compound . . . In the centre of the enclosure is a
large concrete swimming bath.' This was fairly standard, based on
the labour compounds for convicts earlier used at Kimberley by Cecil
Rhodes. It was to remain standard for many decades.

Making black workers live in compounds was arguably necessary to
counter the theft of diamonds. Making them all carry passes – and
making those without passes liable to be thrown out of town – could
also be justified as a police measure to prevent thefts. On the
gold-mines, however, compounds and Pass Laws were not needed for
the reasons advanced at Kimberley. They were principally a means of
keeping down wages and controlling the workforce.

The big gold finds made from 1886 onwards on the Rand were in
the Transvaal, the poorest, most backward and least competently
administered of southern Africa's white-ruled territories. Twice – in
1848 and 1877 – Britain had annexed the Transvaal, and twice – in
1854 and 1881 – restored its shaky independence. Gold provided a
strong argument for a third British embrace. Ministers in London
remained concerned for the security of the sea-route to India, which
meant keeping rival powers and their potential helpers under control.
Their preferred methods were agreements or treaties. But the Cape
voters were increasingly powerful and the largely British mine-owners
began to use their influence, on both the South African and London
political scenes, to press for intervention.

In Cape Town the British – and many Afrikaners – looked jealously at
the new riches to the north. Accustomed to being at the centre of power
and commerce, a position reinforced by the annexation of the
diamond-mines to Cape Colony, they sought ways to obtain a share of the
curmudgeonly trekkers' amazing new wealth.

Paul Kruger, President of the Transvaal Republic from 1883 to 1902, was an Old Testament prophet. One British official (Roger Casement, later hanged as a traitor) called him an 'ignorant, dirty, cunning' old man. Disraeli called him an 'ugly customer'. In London his reputation was never high. At the age of nine he had been taken on the Great Trek. He spent most of his youth herding sheep and cattle, had no formal education, married and set up as a farmer when he was seventeen. As a commando he fought heroically against both Africans and British. He rarely read any books but the Bible. Where most Afrikaners were no more religious than the age they lived in, Kruger was a Dopper, a member of the smallest and most fundamentalist branch of the Dutch church. He was said to believe until the day he died that the earth was flat. He preached every Sunday. Most days he sat on the veranda of his iron-roofed house in Pretoria, available to chat to fellow-farmers. His wife kept cows at the back and sold milk. At state banquets, when others drank wine or champagne, Kruger insisted on milk.

Into his lightly administered state came gold-hunters of many nationalities but mostly British, soon to outnumber the Afrikaner inhabitants. Kruger considered Johannesburg, the town the *uitlanders* built high on the Rand, godless and debauched. It attracted hundreds of prostitutes, many of them black, and made him feel a foreigner in his own country. He once publicly contrasted Afrikaners – 'People of the Lord, you old people of the country' – with *uitlanders* – 'You newcomers, yea, even you thieves and murderers'.

Kruger was not all simple-minded piety. When the *uitlanders* arrived, his treasury was empty. He secured what he could from them to finance development projects. His import duties raised revenue for road-building and public services, but were unpopular with both *uitlanders* whose costs were raised and traders in the Cape whose anticipated profits were lowered. He refused to allow the railway from the Cape to be extended to Johannesburg until he had built the line to Lourenço Marques in Portuguese East Africa, which was both a shorter route to the sea and a way to free his republic of British and Cape domination. In this way he expanded trade with Germany. He sold monopolies – for the making of brandy, the sale and distribution of dynamite and water, the building of railways – with similarly sound intentions: both to raise money for investment and to bring some of his fellow Afrikaners into a share of the wealth beneath their soil. Again the *uitlanders* criticized him. They said they could supply brandy, dynamite and water more cheaply than Kruger's monopolists, who were merely his Afrikaner cronies. Kruger used his country's mineral wealth in a way that became, in the century after his death, a model for developing countries.

The mining companies caused damaging stories about him to be published in London newspapers. When his friend, Alois Nellmapius, a businessman, was found guilty of embezzlement, Kruger had him released from prison. What clearer evidence could be provided that Kruger was a corrupt dictator? Some of his Afrikaner officials were undoubtedly inefficient and bribable – with the state revenue rising from £196,000 in 1886 to £4 million ten years later, who can wonder? – and the details made good copy.

Kruger had seen the British secure the diamond fields from the Afrikaner republics and turn great areas of southern Africa into 'protectorates' by signing deals with black rulers – including Bechuanaland, which Kruger and his fellow Transvaal farmers had had their eyes on. The freedom to run their cattle on to fresh land was essential to the Afrikaners' frontier way of life. Since the 1650s they had been able to trek as far as their waggons would go. The frontier was not merely the chance for one's sons to make their living. It was the place to avoid trouble. All the lawyers, imperial rule-makers and gold-diggers could be ignored in the open veld, where a man with a gun was responsible for himself. The British by acquiring Bechuanaland (now Botswana) and Rhodesia (now Zimbabwe) boxed in the Transvaal and put an end to the open frontier. In the face of these challenges, Kruger prudently visited London and did his best to establish contacts with those *uitlanders* who were prepared to recognize the sovereignty of the Transvaal. He even worked closely with some of the mining magnates. But others could see no good in him.

The *uitlander* above all others who was to oppose Kruger was Cecil John Rhodes. For Kruger the centre of the world was a farm in the Transvaal, the purpose of life to serve God and the Afrikaner people. For Rhodes the centre of the world was a college in Oxford, the purpose of life to ensure that the British Empire civilized the less well-endowed peoples, including Afrikaners, Germans, Americans and even, eventually, Africans. Rhodes's career was based on a huge gamble. Like others at Kimberley, he found diamonds in a deep layer of crumbly soil that somewhat resembled Stilton cheese. When that layer was exhausted, prospectors moved on to the next concession, to dig into the Stilton there. Rhodes bought up the empty holes, convinced that the bluish, rock-like earth further below must also contain diamonds. He thus came to own more than anybody else of the deepest and ultimately the richest diamond-mines. He consolidated the entire industry. He then tried, though not nearly so successfully, to do the same on the Rand.

Soon after the frontier farmers of the Transvaal had in 1883 elected Kruger their president, the mixed British and Afrikaner government of Cape Colony had, as coalitions often do, collapsed. Rhodes had recently become a member of the Cape Parliament and was catapulted into the Prime Ministership. He had the charm to win over Cape Afrikaners, British ministers, Queen Victoria, rival speculators and African rulers. He believed that all men had their price and he could find it. One of the few with whom he totally failed was Paul Kruger.

When in 1877 the British had last annexed the Transvaal, Kruger, on horseback with his gun, had helped drive them out. He had no intention of allowing the foreigners to take over again. In 1890 he limited the *uitlander* franchise in Transvaal elections to those who, besides being naturalized citizens, had lived in the republic for fourteen years. This was restrictive, but not unreasonable. The *uitlanders* had come to make money and most of them did not much want the vote.

Rhodes encouraged *uitlanders* in Johannesburg to set up a reform committee, whose purpose was to take over the Transvaal government. If a businessman with no political experience could become Prime Minister in Cape Town, why should not another do the same in Pretoria? In 1896 Rhodes arranged for a colleague, Dr L. S. Jameson, to lead a small, private army to Johannesburg, in support of a prearranged rising of *uitlanders* backing the reform committee. Rhodes informed the British Colonial Secretary in London, Joseph Chamberlain, and the Governor and High Commissioner in Cape Town, Sir Hercules Robinson. Both approved.

Dr Jameson with 500 men marched into Kruger's republic. But the *uitlanders* failed to rise. Rhodes had primed the British press with the story that the disfranchised and abused miners were in spontaneous revolt against the corrupt, tyrannical Kruger regime. The rising had to come first to justify the raid. Jameson carried an undated letter from some of the *uitlanders* begging him to come to their rescue. In the absence of the rising, Chamberlain cabled Rhodes to call the raid off. Rhodes sent Jameson no instruction to this effect, though he had the Colonial Secretary's view passed on. Jameson ignored the message, confident that the arrival of his force would inspire the rising, albeit delayed.

It did not. Kruger's commandos simply rounded up Jameson's men, killing sixty-five, and sending the rest, including Jameson, to London to be tried – to the intense embarrassment of the British government. The heroic rescue of beleaguered Britons, Rhodes's cover story, was replaced by a story far more powerful: a failed attempt at an imperialist invasion to overthrow the Transvaal Afrikaners' popularly elected government. To the British this was a terrible humiliation. To the Afrikaners it finally proved that the British Empire would not allow them to live in peace.

CHAPTER FOUR

The Boer War, 1896–1910

The fiasco of the Jameson Raid put an end to several careers. Rhodes had to resign as Prime Minister of the Cape. A select committee was appointed by the House of Commons in London to find out who had been responsible. It became known as the 'lying-in-state' and led to several civil servants being sacrificed. Their master, Joseph Chamberlain, was thus enabled to survive in office. He appointed a new man, Sir Alfred Milner, to be Governor of the Cape and High Commissioner to the Afrikaner republics.

Milner was the model of an imperial pro-consul. The star of Balliol when Balliol outshone the rest of Oxford, he had been private secretary to the Chancellor of the Exchequer then, after Britain took over Egypt, Director-General of Accounts in Cairo. From there he had written to a friend: 'As England is doing some of her best work in the valley of the Nile, I am glad to be of the company. The more I see of it, the more proud and convinced I become of the great service which jingoism has rendered to humanity in these regions and I touch my hat with confirmed reverence to the Union Jack.' His next job, at the age of thirty-seven, had been back in London as Chairman of the Board of Inland Revenue, which he described as 'hard, important and boring', adding, 'the sober joys of a well-rendered estimate are tame compared with empire-building'. He had turned down the post of Permanent Secretary of the Colonial Office, hoping to be made ruler of one of the imperial jewels – India, Egypt or South Africa. He was pleased to get South Africa, even though, compared with Cairo, he found Cape Town short on both culture and conversation. He saw little good in Afrikaner politicians and demanded that Kruger grant the vote to all *uitlanders* who had lived in the Transvaal republic for five years. Kruger shilly-shallied, as any sensible politician in his situation was bound to do. The majority of his Afrikaner voters were understandably angry about the Jameson Raid. They were in no mood to make concessions to the raiders or their allies. None the less Kruger eventually conceded the bulk of what was asked. Milner persisted in his demand for everything, and broke off the talks. Kruger commented that it was not the franchise but his state that the British were after.

Milner was bent on reasserting British authority, by firm negotiation if possible, otherwise by war. Kruger had visited Germany and reported: 'The Kaiser received me as Head of an important, independent state.' The Kaiser had also decorated him with the Order of the Red Eagle and, following the capture of Jameson, had sent him a cable of congratulation. Not only could Britain not trust the Afrikaner republics to remain quiet allies in the event of a major war between the European powers; Kruger seemed to be climbing into the pocket of one of Britian's potential enemies.

Equally important for Milner was the gold. By the end of the nineteenth century British industry was declining. The earnings of the country were increasingly dependent on the financial activities of the City of London. Gold was essential not only to pay for the supplies needed to fight the empire's distant wars but also to finance the rapid expansion then going on in world trade. Milner, with his Treasury and Inland Revenue background, understood the worries in the City about the inadequacy of sterling's gold base. When he arrived in South Africa, the Transvaal was already the world's largest single producer of gold. This was not an asset he was prepared to see the empire denied.

Some of the big gold-mining companies encouraged him. They needed a state that would be efficient, to keep their large compounds of black workers in order, that would be non-discriminatory, to relieve them of the high costs imposed by Kruger's monopoly-holders, that would be powerful, to protect their product as it was transported over the railways to the sea; above all, a state that would be their customer, buying their gold in large quantities at fixed prices and thus enabling them to recover their huge investment in the Rand's exceptionally deep mines. The largest of the gold-mining companies, Wernher-Beit and Eckstein, made it plain to Milner that Kruger's republic could not provide the conditions their industry required and that they wanted the Transvaal placed under British rule. Such views were music to Milner's ears.

He sent Chamberlain a cable for publication: 'The case for intervention is overwhelming . . . The spectacle of thousands of British subjects kept permanently in the position of helots [these were the gold men on the Rand] calling vainly to Her Majesty's government for redress [Milner had encouraged them to step up their demands] does undermine the reputation of Great Britain and the respect for the British government within the Queen's Dominions.'

Milner got his war. In 1899 the British Cabinet put an army into an armada of ships for the long voyage south, ostensibly in the hope that such a show of determination would make Kruger back down. It had the opposite effect. He began the war while they were still at sea by making pre-emptive strikes into British territory, besieging Mafeking and Kimberley and invading both Natal and Cape Colony.

It was plain to the meanest intelligence that the British must win. They were the greatest power in the world and were eventually to send nearly half a million men to conquer the Afrikaners – equal to the entire Afrikaner population. The British controlled the seas, they had built railways along which they could transport their armies, their skilful diplomacy ensured that neither France nor Germany came to the Afrikaners' aid. It should have been a walk-over.

The Afrikaners, however, were used to forming volunteer commandos and shooting from horseback as they rode across the veld. They could not prevent the huge British army from capturing the towns, notably Johannesburg and Pretoria, and driving old Kruger into exile. But small bands of them could annihilate isolated British units, cut the railway, seize supplies – and ride home for breakfast. Last night's guerilla suspect was this morning's hard-working farmer.

The lumbering British war-machine relieved the towns the Afrikaners had besieged, then in 1900 re-annexed the Transvaal and the Orange Free State. The siege of Kimberley had put a stop to diamond-mining. The prospect of fighting in Johannesburg led *uitlanders* and black workers alike to flee. The huge, new economy of the Rand shuddered almost to a halt. The Afrikaners just kept on fighting. Some, nourished by sympathetic locals, even continued to launch successful raids on the British in Cape Colony.

To confront this tiny new nation in arms, the British had to devise original tactics. When they captured an Afrikaner, they deported him to St Helena, Bermuda, Ceylon or India. That stopped him from getting back on his horse. But they captured few. So they set about systematically removing the guerillas' sources of food and shelter. This was a slow process. They burned Afrikaners' crops and farm buildings and herded their women, children and old people into concentration camps.

The British army decided that Afrikaner women and children must be 'concentrated' (the word of a military bureaucrat) without thinking through the consequences. The measure seemed efficient and cheap. The camps were run on military lines. The inmates were given army rations, but reduced – at first no meat, vegetables, jam or fresh milk, even for babies. The diet alone was poor enough to cause disease. Given inadequate sewerage, typhoid was soon prevalent, children dying. No soap was available, and little medical help. When the governor of the Transvaal launched a public appeal for blankets and clothes, the British commander-in-chief, General Kitchener, objected, on the grounds that to admit shortages would play into the hands of the 'pro-Boers', that the camps were not supposed to be comfortable, that their purpose was to encourage the inmates' menfolk to surrender.

To most Afrikaners, the camps were a mental wound that for generations would not heal – a deliberate British attempt at genocide. Britain's previous actions against the Afrikaners – inconsiderate rule at the Cape, expelling the trekkers from Natal and pursuing them northwards, the shifty seizure of the diamond-mines, even the Jameson Raid – might all have been forgiven and forgotten. The deaths of women, children and old people in concentration camps could not, and created new bitterness about all that had gone before. For the British soldier the camps were just a weapon. For English-speaking South Africans and blacks, against whom the resentment and rage of Afrikaner nationalism were over the next sixty years to be directed, the bodies buried in the camps were to prove dragons' teeth.

In a few months the camps and scorched-earth policies achieved their purpose, weakening the Afrikaner fighters, and reducing their numbers from 50,000 to some 22,000. In 1902 they agreed to negotiate. Milner insisted that the independent republics cease to exist. At the Peace of Vereeniging the Afrikaner fighting units reluctantly acquiesced.

This was a war between white men. Africans served as helpers to both sides – and thousands of them too died in the concentration camps – but their contribution as fighters was not acknowledged. Nor did any of the black nations whom the whites had conquered during the previous thirty years seize the moment of white division to rise. British armies had utterly crushed the black power structures. Now at last they seemed to be in a position to impose their will also on the Afrikaners.

Milner had a plan for reconstruction. The Afrikaner majority among the whites must be outnumbered by Britons, both soldiers who stayed to settle and others who would come in their thousands. Thus he would make South Africa a predominantly British territory, like Canada, Australia and New Zealand. The key was the economy. What he needed was a rapid post-war revival of mining and industry to attract British immigrants and thus make it safe to establish responsible government. He imported the raw material he thought essential to make his ambitious schemes work – brains. Young men with firsts from Oxford joined him to take top jobs in local government, finance, railways and post-war recovery. Afrikaners resented their arrival and called them Milner's kindergarten. Some Afrikaners were particularly angered by the education policy of the kindergarten – anglicization. Milner wrote: 'Dutch should only be used to teach English and English to teach everything else.' Milner called himself 'an Imperialist out and out' and a 'British race patriot'. Such strong views were unusual among the British. (Though of mostly English ancestry, Milner was born and schooled in Germany.)

Soon after the war, Ramsay MacDonald, a rising Labour politician and future British Prime Minister, visited South Africa. Of one village he wrote:

It was as though I had slept among ancient ruins of the desert. Every house, without a single exception, was burnt; the church in the square was burnt . . . Although taken and retaken many times, the place stood practically untouched until February 1902, when a British column entered it unmolested, found it absolutely deserted and proceeded to burn it. The houses are so separated from each other by gardens that the greatest care must be taken to set every one alight. From inquiries I made from our officers and from our host, who was the chief intelligence officer for the district, there was no earthly reason why Lindley should have been touched . . . Grass grew upon broken hearthstones and lizards crawled upon deserted doorsteps . . . The whole journey was through a land of sorrow and destruction, of mourning and hate.

Many other socialists in both Britain and South Africa argued that the war had been launched by Britain on behalf of a few millionaire Jews. 'For the mine-owners it means a large increase in profits,' wrote J. A. Hobson of the *Manchester Guardian*. He called the war a 'Jew-imperialist conspiracy'. (His subsequent book, *Imperialism*, based on his South African reports, is said greatly to have influenced Lenin.) Liberal-minded Britons, always inclined to back the wronged and the underdog, gave their hearts to the Afrikaners.

The war gave the young David Lloyd George the chance to show that he was Britain's most powerful orator. He attacked Joseph Chamberlain with the zeal of a man determined to get to the top, thundering against his deception of Parliament over both the Jameson Raid and the need to go to war. He used the horrifying reports from the concentration camps, where more than 20,000 Afrikaner women and children had died, to question the moral basis of the British Empire. He seized the leadership of Britain's spontaneous pro-Boer movement.

Milner's plan was going wrong. The boom for which he and his kindergarten worked with skill and energy failed to materialize. Even the soldiers who settled began to drift away. Victory had been won at too high a price. The British Liberal Party leader, Sir Henry Campbell-Bannerman, had during the war described the farm-burnings and concentration camps as 'methods of barbarism'. He now saw that the policy of settling enough Britons to swamp the Afrikaners was failing and that further coercion, after the horrors of the war, could not win the backing of British voters. In victory he favoured magnanimity. In 1905 he became Prime Minister.

Campbell-Bannerman's Liberal government set out to win Afrikaner co-operation. This had been British policy through most of the nineteenth century, except for spasms of exasperation or imperialism, and its climax had now come. It was no simple matter. The Afrikaners were unreconciled to British rule. Their cleverest young Boer war hero, Jan Smuts, came to London and submitted a memorandum arguing for complete self-government for the former republics. A Colonial Office civil servant wrote on it: 'Mr Smuts is a Boer and a lawyer . . . His memorandum . . . exhibits all the cunning of his race and calling.' But Smuts had been at Cambridge and knew his way around. He put his case to several Cabinet Ministers, including Campbell-Bannerman himself. They were all greatly impressed by the clarity and force of his arguments: that only by an act of truly 'liberal statesmanship' could the 'wounds and errors of the past' be reconciled. King Edward VII commented: 'After all the blood and treasure we have expended it would [be] terrible indeed if the country were handed over to the Boers.' The House of Lords agreed with the king, so Campbell-Bannerman, knowing he could never get a bill through Parliament, secured his policy by the device of an order-in-council. Within two years the Liberals had returned the Transvaal and the Orange River Colony (as the Free State was called while ruled from London) to Afrikaner control. Formally the king in London was still sovereign; in practice the local electorates, once given responsible government, had the whip hand.

In the short term this policy paid off for Britain. Two of the most successful Boer War guerilla leaders, Smuts and his commander-in-chief General Louis Botha, led a movement for 'conciliation'. Both had been impressed by the millions of pounds Milner had obtained from the British Treasury to revive the South African economy – a novel gesture from a victorious power, even if Milner's purpose was to stoke up a quick boom and thus encourage British immigration. Now Botha and Smuts were even more impressed to find that the responsible government Campbell-Bannerman's Cabinet gave to the Transvaal and the Orange River Colony was without strings.

Since the discovery of diamonds, Britain had been trying to bring these two states into a federation with Natal and the Cape. So long as the federal proposal meant rule by the British Crown, the Afrikaner republics rejected it. Now the Liberals in London and the Afrikaner 'conciliators' revived the idea in a new form: since 1907 all four territories were colonies enjoying internal self-government. Why should they not freely amalgamate? Botha and Smuts urged their fellow-Afrikaners to build on Britain's generosity. They set about forming a united South Africa in which English- and Dutch-speakers would bury their differences. The doubts of many Afrikaners were swept aside by the apparent generosity of the British concession and the activities of key groups. The gold-mining companies and a growing class of Afrikaner large-scale farmers needed a stable, permanent settlement and a large, cheap labour force. To secure a government that would guarantee both, they formed an alliance of gold and maize.

With the British looking on benignly and helping where they could, the leaders of white South Africa assembled. They had many differences, but within three years Afrikaners and British, farmers and mine-owners from the interior, traders and plantation owners from the seaboard, agreed to a merger – not a mere federation but a full union, with overriding powers given to a central government.

Ministers in London welcomed the creation of the Union in 1910 with relief. At last the whole of South Africa would be a secure British ally. The Union provided the guarantee that Britain would be able to keep open the route to India should the Suez Canal be closed by war. This consummation was not entirely delusory. Louis Botha, who became Prime Minister, and Jan Smuts, his deputy, persuaded the electorate that while the Afrikaners could not beat the empire they could gain by a free partnership with it.

Botha had the homely manner of Paul Kruger. He let his fellow-citizens talk themselves out, while he patiently listened and smiled and joked. Like most of them he was a farmer. Milner could never have won the Afrikaners over to trust the British Empire. Botha was willing and able to do it. When a deputation asked him to send Milner's efficient director of agriculture, F. B. Smith, back to England, Botha replied, 'Wait till he has got rid of the cattle-plague, then I may see about it.'

The Anglo-Boer peace-making had a price – paid by the blacks. Since 1835 Britain had been pressing for non-racial constitutions. In Cape Colony blacks, Indians and coloureds could qualify for the vote, though few did. In Natal similar rights were available, though to even fewer. But in the Transvaal and the Orange Free State the vote had been granted only to whites. Britain's Liberal government, in its anxiety to make amends for the army's harsh conduct in the war and in need of Afrikaner support for both the strategy and financing of the empire, abandoned all the principles of liberalism. It was the

British legislature that passed the Act restricting black and coloured voters in Union elections to the Cape alone and providing that no black should be allowed to sit in the South African Parliament.

The South African settlement was Campbell-Bannerman's greatest triumph. To have won over so badly abused an enemy as the Afrikaner people was liberal reconciliation at its best. Concern for the rights of Africans was little voiced. Social Darwinism was a prevalent intellectual fashion – the belief that the fittest races survive and those that fail to prosper must be inferior. To stress equal rights for peoples who are inherently unequal, the theory went on, is mere sentimentality. On these matters, in the euphoria of the Union, most British and Afrikaners saw eye-to-eye.

In 1905 a diamond of 3,025 carats – the Cullinan, the largest ever found then or since – was mined near Pretoria. It was four inches long and its value was beyond computation. Botha and Smuts persuaded the Afrikaner majority in the Transvaal legislature to buy the stone and present it to the British king, Edward VII. Cleaved and polished into nine huge gems, it became part of the crown jewels, worn at the coronation of every subsequent British monarch. For a defeated people it was an act of some style. But many simple Afrikaners, the types who had formerly voted for Kruger, opposed the gesture as spendthrift toadying. They were increasingly worried by what they regarded as their government's pro-British excesses.

CHAPTER FIVE

Two Nationalist Movements
(a) The Afrikaners, 1910–34

The creation of the Union of South Africa was quickly followed by the launching, in 1912, of two political movements. One was the African National Congress (see page 52). The other was the National Party, dedicated to the rejection of the Botha–Smuts conciliation policy, in favour of giving priority to the interests of Afrikaners.

The National Party sprang from the Orange Free State, the only part of South Africa where Afrikaners still formed the overwhelming majority of the white population. Before the discovery of gold, the Free State had fared better than the Transvaal, largely because of its success in sheep-farming. Its burghers resented what they considered the corruption of Cape Town and Kimberley to the west and of Johannesburg to the north. Their political leader was the third Boer War general to seek high office, J. B. M. (Barry) Hertzog.

Hertzog had been fighting the Boer War over again. In 1896 the novelist Olive Schreiner had written: 'In fifty years, fight and struggle against it as we wish, there will be no Boer in South Africa speaking the *Taal* (Afrikaans), save as a curiosity: only the great English-speaking South African people. This movement cannot be hindered, it cannot be stayed, it is inevitable.' Hertzog saw this prospect as genocide of the Afrikaner nation. Louis Botha, the easy-going first Prime Minister of the Union, said that Hertzog's talk 'about the possible treachery of the British' reminded him 'of a man on his honeymoon telling people what he would do if his wife proved unfaithful'.

Before Hertzog would let the Free State delegation join the talks about forming the Union, he insisted on equal standing for Dutch alongside English as the language of Parliament, civil service, courts and schools. Botha, Smuts and the conciliators rejected Milner's

The diamond finds and the conquests that followed

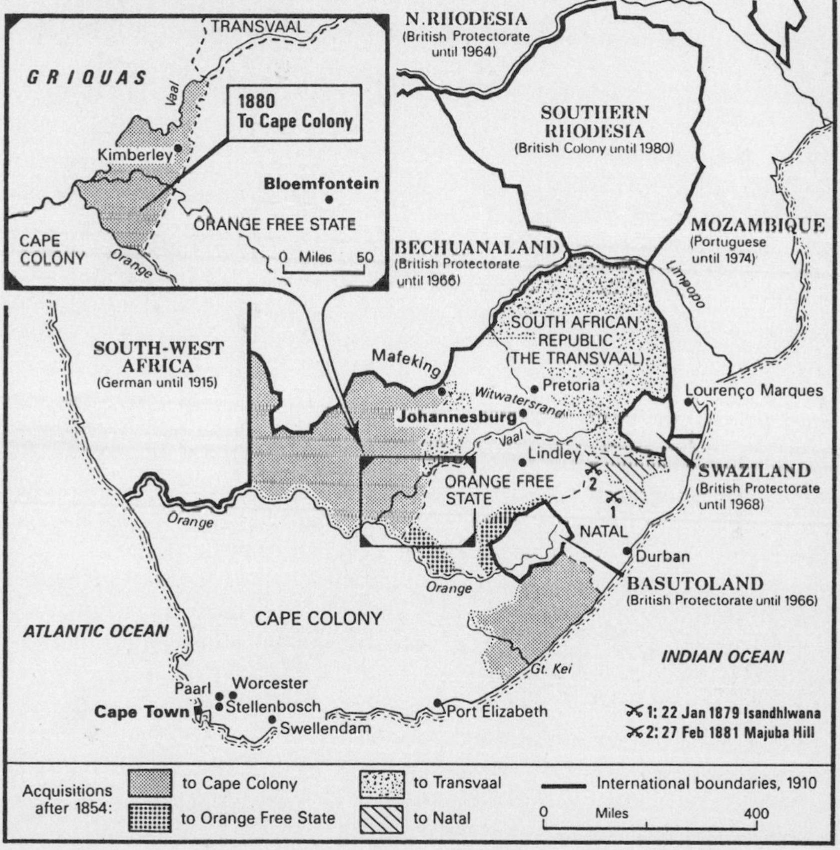
TRANSVAAL
GRIQUAS
Vaal
1880
To Cape Colony
Kimberley
Bloemfontein
ORANGE FREE STATE
CAPE
COLONY
Orange
0 Miles 50
N.RHODESIA
(British Protectorate
until 1964)
SOUTHERN
RHODESIA
(British Colony until 1980)
MOZAMBIQUE
(Portuguese
until 1974)
Limpopo
BECHUANALAND
(British Protectorate
until 1966)
SOUTH AFRICAN
REPUBLIC
(THE TRANSVAAL)
SOUTH-WEST
AFRICA
(German until 1915)
Mafeking
Pretoria
Witwatersrand
Johannesburg
Lourenço Marques
Vaal
Lindley
SWAZILAND
(British Protectorate
until 1968)
ORANGE FREE
STATE
2
1
Orange
NATAL
Durban
BASUTOLAND
(British Protectorate until 1966)
Orange
CAPE COLONY
ATLANTIC OCEAN
INDIAN OCEAN
Gt. Kei
Paarl
Worcester
Stellenbosch
Cape Town
Swellendam
Port Elizabeth
1: 22 Jan 1879 Isandhlwana
2: 27 Feb 1881 Majuba Hill
Acquisitions
after 1854:
to Cape Colony
to Orange Free State
to Transvaal
to Natal
International boundaries, 1910
0 Miles 400

English-only policy, but were happy for parents to choose the language in which their children were educated. Hertzog went further. His father had sent him to Stellenbosch university, near Cape Town, to be taught in English. He feared that others, given free parental choice, would do the same. So he demanded that Afrikaner children be taught in Dutch – compulsorily. The conciliators agreed to this for the first four years at school. Hertzog required that the agreement be entrenched in the constitution – alterable only by a two-thirds majority of both houses of the Union Parliament.

The interest Hertzog was protecting was real. While most Afrikaners in the Cape spoke English, Afrikaner farmers in the Free State and the Transvaal did not. The destruction of their farms by the British during the Boer War and the growth of large-scale agriculture to meet the demands of mining and expanding towns had pushed many of them off the land. They found that jobs in shops, offices and the civil service were open only to English-speakers. This was true even in the capital of the Free State, Bloemfontein, which in 1910 became the seat of the Supreme Court and therefore, for lawyers, the capital of the Union. Here, in the chief city of the province where Afrikanerdom was most dominant, the principal high school was English-speaking. The unfortunates who spoke only Afrikaans needed Hertzog's help to survive. He saw himself as fighting an uphill struggle to protect their rights.

Hertzog insisted on a 'two-stream policy', one English-speaking, one Dutch-speaking, 'each stream with its own language, its own way of life, its own great men, heroic deeds and noble characters'. Hertzog never said he was seeking Afrikaner domination. The British were so powerful that it was better not to say so. Rather he spoke of a kind of federation of English- and Dutch-speakers. But he made it plain that he regarded English-speakers who supported the British Empire as unfit to be regarded as South Africans.

In manner Hertzog was a country solicitor – soft-spoken, mild, studious. According to Smuts he had 'a strange mind, without a spark of humour'. He loved drafting parliamentary bills. When the first Union government was formed in 1910, the conciliators brought him into office and he soon became Minister of Native Affairs. He applied his drafting skill to the race issue. Following the recommendations of a commission appointed by Milner, and with the firm support of most English-speakers in Parliament, his department produced the blueprint for nationwide, state-enforced segregation. The 'natives' would everywhere be compelled to live in reserves where, under white overlordship, they would run their own affairs, being let into white reserved areas only when they were needed as workers. Efficient enforcement of this measure was urgently needed by the gold-mining companies, desperate for labour to dig and crush the ore.

LEFT: Jan van Riebeeck, founder of the Dutch settlement at the Cape, 1652.

BELOW LEFT: Lord Charles Somerset, Governor of the Cape 1814 to 1826, one of the Englishmen most hated by Afrikaners.

BELOW: Dr John Philip, Superintendent at the Cape for the London Missionary Society, 1818 to 1851 – the most hated of all the British 'oppressors' of Afrikanerdom.

LEFT: Piet Retief, Commander of the Great Trek, 1837-8. Statue in the Voortrekker Museum, Pietermaritzburg.

Afrikaner images of the Great Trek, the inspiration of their national ideal.

ABOVE: The camp of Dingaan, King of the Zulu, where Piet Retief and his followers were massacred in February 1838.

RIGHT: Zulu attacking a trekker waggon after Retief's death, painted sixteen years after the event and said to be based on eye-witness accounts.

TOP RIGHT: The Battle of Blood River, 16 December 1838. Three thousand Zulu are said to have been killed, but no trekkers. The event is celebrated each year by the Afrikaners on the Day of the Covenant, 16 December.

ABOVE: Early days at Kimberley – sorting the stones.

TOP RIGHT: Twelve months after the discovery of the big hole:
claims and diggings.

RIGHT: Four years after the discovery: the big hole at Kimberley
in 1874.

The de Beers compound, where black workers lived, photographed from the conning tower, with Kimberley in the background.

INSET: An early compound for black gold-miners on the Rand.

DEBEERS COMPOUND.
FROM THE CONNING TOWER.

TOP: Paul Kruger, President of the South African Republic (the Transvaal) from 1883 to 1902, on the stoep (veranda) of his house in Pretoria.

ABOVE: Sir Alfred Milner, Britain's Governor and High Commissioner, 1897-1905, the man who decided to launch the Boer War.

RIGHT: Cecil John Rhodes, the great charmer.

Given the chance to find other work, South African blacks were declining to live in the mines' labour compounds and work in the disease-inducing dust and heat up to a mile beneath the ground. The mining companies had even been reduced to importing labour from overseas (see page 53). The only way to make black workers come to the mines was to restrict their options. Forced by a competently-run, centralized state to live in reserves, they would turn to the mines' recruitment agencies as the only way to earn cash. In 1913 the scheme Hertzog had helped draft was passed as the Native Land Act, setting aside 7.3 per cent of the land for native reserves. The remaining 92.7 per cent included some mountains and other poor areas, but also the best land and all major towns. The Act received all-party support in the all-white Union Parliament.

Many liberal and humanitarian whites believed that 'parallel institutions' were the best way to secure the interests of blacks, and that unimpeded mixing would totally stifle black culture and political structures. This tradition of thought looked back to Dr John Philip of the London Missionary Society who, when frontier farmers encouraged blacks to settle on their land as a means of obtaining cheap labour, had tried to protect black peoples from white encroachment in any form. The liberal segregationists of 1913 demanded only that a reasonable proportion of the land be made available for the blacks. The reserves could barely hold their existing populations, let alone the hundreds of thousands of evicted squatters due to be returned to them. The majority in Parliament – representing, in 1911, 1.3 million whites (21 per cent of the total population) – agreed and gave an unconditional pledge to 'release' additional areas for 'native purchase' – for the 4 million blacks (67 per cent of the total population). Coloureds (9 per cent) continued to enjoy the legal right to buy land along with Europeans. When successive official commissions made recommendations about the land to be 'released', however, the mood of Parliament, with Hertzog to the fore, was against conceding an inch.

By the time the Native Land Act was passed, Hertzog had provoked a political explosion over the issue that to him mattered most – Briton *v* Afrikaner. He described Smuts as the 'valet of Britain' and in 1912 at de Wildt, a railway halt in the Transvaal, he said: 'I am not one of those who always have their mouths full of conciliation . . . South Africa must be governed by the Afrikaner . . . It can no longer be governed by non-Afrikaners, by people who do not have the right love for South Africa.' For this outspokenness he was dismissed from the government. He responded by setting up the National Party.

Hertzog's line was original. He claimed the right to define who were true South Africans. He was prepared to include British settlers of long standing whom he judged loyal to Afrikanerdom rather than to the empire. But he made it plain that those who failed his loyalty test should not be allowed to share in governing the country. They were *uitlanders*, foreigners.

To most South Africans this view, even though expressed with legalistic moderation, was twisted. It also seemed politically short-sighted. The conciliators dominated the political stage. Thanks to a century of British rule and the immigrants attracted by diamonds and gold, the Afrikaners, though still the majority of the white population, were, at 54 per cent, only just so. If he was to achieve power, Hertzog needed to get nearly all of them to vote for him. It seemed a forlorn hope. By August 1914 he was near to giving up the struggle. He told a friend that if the people did not wish to be saved he would not try further to impose his leadership.

Hertzog was consumed by a nightmare vision of the British Empire dragging South Africa into a war contrary to Afrikaner interests. When, in September 1914, Botha and Smuts offered unstinting support to Britain in the First World War, Hertzog thought his nightmare had come true. Botha and Smuts believed that the Liberal government had since 1905 proved that it paid to co-operate with the world's greatest empire. Liberals, notably the great pro-Afrikaner, Lloyd George, still ran the government in London. For Botha and Smuts to back Britain was a rational political calculation: it promised them a partner's role in what many believed would be the greatest international federation of states ever created – the reformed British Empire. But it had the side-effect of opening the door for Hertzog and his Nationalists.

The telegram from Botha to one of his former Boer War comrades telling him to take up arms drew the reply, 'Certainly, but on which side do we fight?' For many Afrikaners their government's decision to support the British meant spilling the blood of young South Africans in the service of their most menacing foe. The commander-in-chief of the new Union Defence Force resigned and some 7,000 Free Staters and 3,000 Transvaalers rose in rebellion. The Botha–Smuts government sent 40,000 loyal Afrikaner commandos to defeat the rebel army, which broke into fragments. A few leaders were killed in incidents and one, Jopie Fourie, hanged for rebellion, became the last martyr in the Afrikaner pantheon. Hertzog, ever the lawyer, avoided committing his new party to the rebels, but supported their demand for neutrality and pleaded for clemency for those who were captured.

Meetings of the National Party were told: 'The wistful longing of Jopie Fourie was that his blood might awaken the Afrikaner people.' Hertzog made sure that it did, declaring: 'Our blood has been poured out, our money wasted, our markets closed, to forward the interests of Great Britain . . . We are the spittoon of the Empire.' It all helped reinforce his demand for power to be given only to wholehearted Afrikaners.

In 1922 another big windfall came to Hertzog. On the Rand, the workers were organized in the traditional South African way: supervisory jobs were done by highly-paid whites, labouring jobs by low-paid blacks. This had seemed the natural order of things when deep mining began, as skilled men had to be brought from as far afield as the tin-mines of Cornwall and the gold-mines of America and Australia. To avoid loss of life and damage to machinery, it made sense to have supervisors who knew about mine engineering. For digging and carrying it made sense to use cheap labour. By 1922, however, the colour-bar had rigidified. Unskilled Afrikaners had come off the land and taken supervisory jobs. Many Africans had mastered mining skills, but white-only trade unions kept them from doing the work of which they were capable.

After the First World War the price of gold fell sharply. The companies that had invested in equipping the deep mines faced a dilemma. Whites made up about one-ninth of their labour force but took two-thirds of the pay. The only quick way to cut the cost of production was to replace expensive whites by cheap but equally capable blacks.

The predominantly British mine-owners announced that they were going to promote blacks to semi-skilled work, threatening the jobs of 2,000 whites, mostly Afrikaners. In the coal-mines, the British owners gave comparable warnings. The government, led since Botha's death in 1919 by General Smuts, tried to persuade the mining unions to accept the terms. The miners, fearing a conspiracy of bosses and government to replace them with black labour, came out on strike. Soon the strike leaders were asking for the overthrow of Smuts and his replacement by a prime minister who would 'promote the interests of the White Race in South Africa'. A mass meeting of strikers decided to proclaim a people's republic. Armed groups of miners roamed the steets looting, burning and in some cases murdering blacks. During one of many marches through Johannesburg, a communist banner was amended to read 'Workers of the world unite . . . for a white South Africa'.

After efforts at conciliation had failed, Smuts sent troops into Johannesburg. The strikers resisted with fierce street fighting. For nearly a week the town was crippled by civil war. Then Smuts had aircraft and artillery bombard the strikers' headquarters. Most strike leaders capitulated. Two preferred to commit suicide.

Some 200 were killed during the 1922 strike. Of strikers charged with murder, eighteen were sentenced to death and four were eventually hanged. The strikers asked the National Party for its support. Hertzog spoke for the cause, while shrewdly opposing the

use of force. Two years later, in 1924, with backing from the trade
unions and the predominantly English-speaking Labour Party, he
was elected Prime Minister.

The main force that swept Hertzog into power was Afrikaner
nationalism and it was something new. At the time of the Great Trek,
nobody thought of the Afrikaners as a nation. They were frontier
cowboys and pioneers. Kruger, when he first faced Rhodes, was
fighting the cause not of Afrikanerdom but of his republic. He wanted
to strengthen the independence of the Transvaal by directing trade
and arms shipments through Lourenço Marques, thus turning his
back on the Afrikaners of the Cape.

A member of an Afrikaner family from Swellendam, near Cape
Town, recorded: 'Before the [Boer] war our home language was
English and we went to the Anglican church. The children born
before the war were named Sydney, Lancelot, Henry . . . the
post-war group Wilhelmina, Daniel, Aletta . . .' The war inspired the
first major flowering of poetry in Afrikaans. Those who had lost a
husband, a father or a brother, and later the many more who lost a
mother, wife or sister, obtained some solace from reading about their
cause and their country – not in English or Dutch but in the informal
language of the farms where they had lived. Books of war poems in
Afrikaans provided the first boom in Afrikaner publishing. The
language that most British despised and many had tried to suppress
suddenly found that it had a literature.

William Nicol, an Afrikaner clergyman, dated the breakthrough to
the First World War: 'In 1914 it was customary that the better
Afrikaans families used English exclusively as home language. By the
end of the war they had undergone a spiritual and national
revival . . . The most startling revelation of this change was their use
of the Afrikaans language.'

The political fruit of all this was the prime ministership of Hertzog
from 1924 to 1939 – fifteen years of skilful parliamentary work setting
out to ensure that whatever disadvantages Afrikaners suffered,
vis-à-vis the British, the blacks or anybody else, were removed. In
1925, the Parliament that Hertzog now dominated decided that the
second official language of South Africa would no longer be Dutch,
but Afrikaans. The Minister who introduced the measure was Dr
Daniel François Malan.

Hertzog's first task was to bring relief to the poor whites, those
Afrikaners who, workless in the towns as Africans flooded in and
undercut them in the job market, were widely held in lower esteem
than the Cape coloureds. Homeless Afrikaners reduced to beggary
had worried Hertzog's predecessors in government. An official report
in 1923 estimated their number at 160,000 – more than 20 per cent of
the Afrikaner population. During Hertzog's period in office a major

study, in five volumes, of the poor white defined him as 'a person who has become dependent to such an extent, whether from mental, moral, economic or physical causes, that he is unfit, without help from others, to find proper means of livelihood for himself or to procure it directly or indirectly for his children'.

Hertzog's partners, the white trade unions and the South African Labour Party, represented the whites with jobs; Hertzog himself acted for the whites without. He instructed all government departments to recruit 'civilized labour' and replace 'uncivilized'. The circular from the Prime Minister's office, not quite up to his usual standard of legal drafting, explained: 'Civilized labour is to be considered as the labour rendered by persons whose standard of living conforms to the standard generally recognized as tolerable from the usual European standpoint.' He introduced a law to tighten the colour-bar in mines, debarring Africans from engine-driving, blasting, surveying and other skilled occupations. This overruled a recent judgement of the Supreme Court that had found such bars illegal. He offered tariff concessions to firms that created jobs for white workers, usually at the expense of blacks. He created a Wage Board which concentrated on raising the wages of unskilled whites. 'The native cannot blame us,' he said, 'if in the first place we try to find work for our own class.' Partly because of these measures, more substantially because of an economic revival in the mid-1930s, unemployment among the poor whites was held in check.

A residue of the liberalism of British rule in the nineteenth century was the right of Cape blacks to qualify for the vote. Hertzog was determined to remove it. Unless the native franchise is amended, he said, 'It will spread within forty years to the north, and that would be one of the greatest calamities in our history.' However, Cape voting rights, like Afrikaners' language rights, were entrenched in the constitution, requiring a two-thirds majority of both houses of Parliament to amend them. This proved an obstacle.

Many Cape whites, Afrikaners as well as English-speakers, were convinced that the gradual extension of the qualified franchise was the best way to ensure black co-operation with the white man's plans. Gradual was the word. By 1934, after eighty years of the native franchise, only in four of the Cape's sixty-one Union constituencies was the native vote more than 10 per cent of the total (though in some elections 10 per cent had proved decisive).

Jan Hofmeyr, a leading Cape politician and an Afrikaner, pleaded in the Union Parliament that it would be a disaster to deprive black men of the vote, as it would 'drive them back in hostility and disgruntlement and make educated natives . . . the leaders of their own people in disaffection and revolt'. Hofmeyr, like Smuts, believed that the electoral door should be kept open, to admit the black vanguard into white politics. Hertzog rejected this argument and, after ten years of parliamentary battles and major changes in the composition of his government (see pages 62 to 72), got most of his way.

The 1934 general election was the last in which black and white in the Cape voted together at the polling booth. Thereafter qualified Cape blacks were placed on a separate roll that enabled them to elect three Europeans to the Union House of Assembly. Though millions of Cape natives might become educated and highly qualified, Hertzog's amendment to the constitution effectively disenfranchised them. They would have no more than their three representatives in Parliament – all white.

Hofmeyr said of Hertzog's measure: 'It starts out from fear and its underlying conception is the interests of the stronger . . . When I hear the Christian principle of self-preservation invoked in connection with this Bill' – Hertzog had invoked it – 'I am reminded of the eternal paradox that whoever shall save his life shall lose it.'

Despite Hertzog's persistent legal and administrative inventiveness, the growing claims of Afrikaner nationalism remained unsatisfied. In 1926 Hertzog had been to London, anxious to receive recognition by the British Empire of South Africa's 'national autonomy'. He got all he asked for – a declaration by the British government that South Africa, Canada, Australia, New Zealand and Britain were 'autonomous communities within the British Empire, equal in status'. For Hertzog this spelled out South Africa's right, should Britain again go to war, to stand neutral. Membership of the empire offered advantages, especially commercial ones. Hertzog was now satisfied that these were bought at no cost in Afrikaner autonomy. He returned to tell those in his party who believed that to secure independence they must leave the empire and form a republic that they were wrong: 'We are just as free as the English people, and he who seeks more freedom seeks the impossible. With respect to the empire . . . it is in our interest to remain within it. We should be stupid to withdraw.'

Hertzog went further. Since 'the great question of our freedom and independence' had been decided, there was 'not the least reason' for Afrikaans- and English-speaking South Africans not to 'work together in all respects'. Such statements were consistent with Hertzog's 'two streams' strategy: once the Afrikaners had shown that in South African politics they were fully the equals of the English-speakers, their concerns could never again be ignored. But some of his followers thought he had gone soft. They felt dangerously exposed on two fronts. The British bosses of the mining and industrial companies, ruthless and deceitful as ever, remained smugly on top. And the blacks, the overwhelming majority of the population, must in time threaten them from below.

Worse, they did not altogether believe Hertzog when he said that, should Britain go to war, South Africa would be able to stay neutral. It had not happened in the First World War. While the top jobs in the civil service, army, universities, banks and mining companies remained overwhelmingly in the hands of English-speakers, Afrikaner political activists feared that the establishment would still, in a moment of crisis, overrule the will of the people. And for many, even if Hertzog was right, neutrality was not good enough. A growing number of Afrikaners believed their country's interests would be best served by backing any country that was Britain's enemy, ideally Kruger's one-time supporter, Germany. So long as the King of England was also King of South Africa, that freedom – the ultimate expression of a truly independent Afrikaner state – was denied them.

CHAPTER SIX

Two Nationalist Movements

(b) The Africans, 1910–36

By the end of the nineteenth century most of the black clans and states of southern Africa had been defeated in war. The rest had wisely entered protection agreements with Britain, leaving them subject to four governments, two British, two Afrikaner. Across the vastness of South Africa no cohesive force existed to create African political unity.

In the Cape, the largest population group, 59 per cent of the total, were Xhosa-speakers. Most of them lived in the Transkei, a 'native' reserve where land tenure was largely communal. Like the other African peoples of the Cape, they were permitted to own or rent land outside their reserve. They could also qualify for the vote, but the financial requirements were so high and the number who qualified so low (in 1909 a mere 6,633 out of an African population of 400,000) that the Cape African franchise had not fostered any kind of popular political movement. On the contrary the tiny enfranchised élite – journalists, teachers, churchmen, clerks – were drawn into the white political parties and unable to bring much benefit to the mass of their fellow-Africans. Only one African, Rev. Walter B. Rubusana, was ever – at the turn of the century – elected to the Cape Provincial Council.

In Natal, also governed by a theoretically non-discriminatory constitution, almost 80 per cent of the total population were Zulu. Their kingdom had been dismembered and most of them were obliged to live in reserves. The British settlers had no intention of letting them recover by the vote what they had recently lost on the battlefield and so fixed the educational and property qualifications for the franchise that in 1909, in Natal's population of 1.2 million, the total number of African voters was six.

The constitutions of Transvaal and the Orange Free State, by contrast, discriminated openly. Africans there, however well qualified, would never be allowed to vote. In the Free State they could not even own land. Most of the Tswana, Sotho and Pedi peoples in these former Afrikaner republics lived and worked as squatters on white men's farms. Native reserves were few and small (largely because the Afrikaner republics had been too weak to conquer their African neighbours).

To bring all the separate – and often rival – African peoples into a single nationalist movement required time, hard work, luck and external provocation. Since the 1880s congresses, vigilance associations and welfare societies had been springing up here and there, and some had even briefly joined forces. But the first nationalist resistance organization to make a notable impact had nothing to do with Africans. It was created by a genius from India, M. K. Gandhi.

British settlers in Natal had from the 1860s been importing Indians to work their sugar plantations. Soon Indians set up in business and in 1893 one of them needed a barrister. Gandhi was recommended. He was the son of the Prime Minister of a small Indian state, had recently qualified at the Bar in London, had started to practise in Bombay but was not doing well. He proved an adequate lawyer and an outstanding political leader.

He arrived in South Africa when the whites of Natal were feeling threatened by the success of Indian businessmen. It was in 1893 that the Colonial Office in London granted Natal representative government, and the colonial assembly, overwhelmingly British in composition, promptly enacted laws to make Indians carry passes and pay an annual tax equal to six months of a plantation worker's wages. Further inland, Transvaal forbade Indians to enter its territory. Gandhi's reply was to use the techniques of non-violent resistance that, when later applied in India, were to make him one of the most significant and original figures of the twentieth century. He relied on the British to obey their own laws and repeatedly, when local officials overrode him, proved that he knew the law better than they did. The British Empire, he argued, was a major force for good in the world and would stop its underlings from behaving unjustly, once it was aware what they were up to. He briefed reporters to make sure news of his campaigns reached London and Delhi, whence he repeatedly received support.

But he stayed too long. Once British authority was withdrawn in 1910, the appeal to London and to liberal principles could not long continue to work. By then African nationalist leaders in South Africa had quite independently created a national movement to follow a path closely resembling Gandhi's. But that path had become blocked. As

Gandhi had in 1894 set up the Indian Congress of Natal along the lines of the Indian National Congress in his homeland, so they in 1912 set up an African National Congress. Like him they emphasized non-violence and obedience to the law and built their movement from among the wealthier and more educated of their people. He, however, devoting himself to his Indian compatriots, showed no interest in the rights of Africans. In 1915 he returned to India.

African nationalism in South Africa started among Christians. Mission schools, notably Lovedale in the eastern Cape founded in 1841, not only educated the young blacks who later became political leaders but also proved to them that some whites were true believers in racial toleration. Consequently the African who wanted to bring his people the benefits of European technology and government – and ultimately the European type of nation state – often set out by teaching in a mission school or working in a European church, spreading the idea that black and white were brothers. Reacting against the missions, others founded thousands of independent churches, many of them fiercely opposed to the idea of black-white brotherhood. The missions fostered a belief in London as the final place to appeal for justice. After the London Missionary Society under John Philip had petitioned Parliament in the 1820s and 1830s, some frontier excesses had been overruled. In 1906 Gandhi led a delegation to London after which the British government reversed the Transvaal Asiatic Law Amendment Ordinance (the last such intervention before the Liberal government relinquished Britain's powers). To show faith in the brotherhood of man – and in London – was, at the turn of the twentieth century in South Africa, not necessarily naive.

Sol Plaatje, the first Secretary of the African National Congress, was from the Tswana tribe or family of Smiths (the Baralong) whose trade dates back to the fourteenth century. He was brought up and educated on a German mission. Plaatje means flat in Dutch, and according to family tradition Sol Plaatje's grandfather had a flat head, was nicknamed Plaatje by a Dutch farmer on whose land he lived, and the name stuck. Sol Plaatje obtained work with the government, rising to the post of court interpreter in Mafeking, where he was a valued public servant during the siege of the town by the Afrikaners at the start of the Boer War. His boss, the Civil Commissioner and Magistrate, reported that the 'faithful interpreter shifted about with his typewriter in order to meet the requirements of the big gun and the Mauser bullets, and varied his accuracy according to the activity of the Boer fire'. After the war Plaatje resigned to edit a newspaper. The Civil Commissioner presided at its launching ceremony. When the Colonial Secretary, Joseph Chamberlain, came from London and visited Baralong chiefs at Mafeking, Plaatje interpreted.

Plaatje was one of a group of Africans who had in 1898 brought a famous law case, R. *v* Mankazana. The Pass Laws, designed to keep 'unauthorized' Africans out of the towns, were often harshly administered. In Kimberley the police stopped any African they felt like challenging and demanded to see his pass. If he did not have one, they threw him into prison, with magistrates regularly backing their action. A respectable citizen of Kimberley, Mr S. Mankazana, chairman of the Eccentrics Cricket Club, suffered such harassment. When Plaatje and others retained a white lawyer to appeal on his behalf, they won a ruling from the High Court that to justify an arrest 'it was not enough for a native to have no pass'; further, before demanding to see his pass, the police must have reason to believe he had committed an offence. The ruling was, of course, binding on magistrates and police alike and, at least in Kimberley, was obeyed. Plaatje, like Gandhi, was influenced throughout his political career by such triumphs.

In the Boer War most educated black South Africans supported Britain. They hoped that a British victory would lead to the Cape franchise being extended northwards. Plaatje wrote in 1904 in his newspaper in Mafeking that the Cape Africans 'have that expensive little asset, the franchise . . . We are too few to do anything with it, but knowing that we possess it, the colonists treat our people very well'. By 'very well' Plaatje did not mean as equals. Indeed he did not demand social equality. What he meant was unusually generously compared to most conquerors.

Educated Africans could not believe that Britain had become converted to segregation and was encouraging the Afrikaner republics to keep blacks disfranchised and to extend discriminatory laws. Through his newspapers, first in Mafeking and later in Kimberley, Plaatje had contact with blacks from other parts of South Africa. Editors posted their papers to each other and copied striking reports. As the British concession of self-government to the former Afrikaner republics was followed by steps towards union, these newspapers reported widespread protests by black groups. They complained of Britain's failure to extend the Cape franchise northwards and of the clauses the British Parliament had written into the South Africa Act to legalize the colour-bar and to ban blacks, even in the Cape, from becoming MPs.

A delegation of Africans travelled to London in 1909 to appeal to the British government. A former Afrikaner Prime Minister of Cape Colony, W. P. Schreiner, went with them to see the Colonial Secretary. They were told Britain could not interfere in what were now the internal affairs of South Africa. However, the government in London, suffering some pangs of conscience, announced that the protectorates of Bechuanaland, Basutoland and Swaziland, much though South Africa wanted to incorporate them, would continue under the control of the Colonial Office until the Union's native policies conformed to imperial ideals.

In January 1912 a small group of educated blacks invited others from all over southern Africa to a meeting in the Bloemfontein African location. Formally dressed in suits, frock coats, top hats and carrying umbrellas, they heard Pixley ka Izaka Seme, a member by marriage of the Zulu royal family in Natal, sent by American missionaries to Columbia University, Jesus College, Oxford, and the Middle Temple in London, say:

> The white people of this country have formed what is known as the Union of South Africa – a union in which we have no voice in the making of laws and no part in their administration. We have called you therefore to this conference so that we can together devise ways and means of forming our national union for the purpose of creating national unity and defending our rights.

They agreed to set up the South African Native National Congress and elected Rev. John L. Dube, a teacher and editor from Natal, as their President. In his first policy statement, Dube stressed 'reliance in the sense of common justice and love of freedom so innate in the British character' and put his faith in patience and reasonableness to 'break down the adamantine wall of colour prejudice and even force our enemies to be our admirers and friends'. The African National Congress (ANC; in 1923 it was to drop both 'South African' and 'Native' from its title) quickly established links, not always close, with the African Political Organization of Cape Coloureds.

The first challenge faced by the ANC was the Native Land Act, passed by the Union Parliament in 1913. Africans in large numbers were moving into the towns. Only those recruited by the native labour authorities to work in the mines or those for whom a white employer had vouched were given passes. But where money was available to be earned, others flocked in. By 1910 more than 100,000 lived in Johannesburg alone. The ability of whites there to keep themselves to themselves, was threatened.

A stronger motive drove the new Union government as its first major measure to intensify restrictions on blacks. Many Afrikaner farmers, particularly in the Orange Free State, had acquired more land than they could use. For generations they had allowed Africans to occupy small areas as squatters. Now, with the expansion of gold-mining and the beginnings of industry, all fertile land could show a profit. White farmers wanted to evict the squatters and employ some of them as wage-labourers.

Even more unacceptable was a movement among some Africans who had become commercial farmers to buy land in white areas.

The decisive reason for the Native Land Act was the labour need of the mines. Exporting gold was the key to making the whole of South Africa wealthy. But the new, deep mines were not a pleasant place to work. When, at the end of the Boer War, Milner had wanted to haul the South African economy into profit, the urgent need to get the mines back to full production, given the interruption of war and the reluctance of local Africans to go down them, had led him to import 60,000 Chinese. Only the great international power of the imperial government could move entire populations in this way. The grateful mine-owners saw profits rise, but the influx of Chinese struck the voters in South Africa and their new friends the Liberal Party in England as introducing the 'yellow peril'. In 1906, as soon as the Liberals came to power in England, they banned the recruitment of Chinese indentured labour. Within five years all the Chinese were sent home.

This had faced the Botha–Smuts government that came to office in Pretoria in 1910 with its most vital challenge. To maintain the peace between Boer and Briton, to make the Union work, to bind South Africa in a mutually supportive relationship with the British Empire, the mines must lay their golden eggs. They must have a reliable, steady supply of labour.

When Sol Plaatje led delegations to Cape Town to meet lawyers, politicians and civil servants who had previously helped him in his campaigns, they did not explain that all the liberal principles that Britain professed had been overruled by the labour needs of the gold-mines. But it was so. Because of gold the imperial government in London had first adopted the 'native' policies of the Afrikaner republics and then handed over the power to apply those policies more widely and intensively.

The new Union government set about extending the policies into a nationwide system of segregation. Its first step was the Native Land Act of 1913, which allocated land as follows:

	Total area (in morgen*)	Native reserves	%
Cape	83,700,000	6,217,037	7·5
Transvaal	33,400,000	1,159,296	3·5
Natal	10,650,000	2,972,312	29·7
OFS	14,800,000	74,290	0·5
Total	142,550,000	10,422,935	7·3

* One morgen = slightly more than 2 acres.

This meant that 67 per cent of the population was allowed to buy or rent property in only 7.3 per cent of the land area (although the courts promptly ruled that the Act could not apply in the Cape, as it conflicted with African franchise rights there, which were entrenched in the constitution).

Some effects of the Act were immediately visible. Plaatje, travelling on his bicycle in the Orange Free State, saw families whom farmers had evicted 'living on the roads, their attenuated flocks emaciated by lack of fodder, many of them dying while the wandering owners ran the risk of prosecution for travelling with unhealthy stock'. These families did not know where they were going. They had no idea that once they reached the reserves the overcrowding there would drive thousands of their men to queue at the native labour office and, if lucky enough to be recruited, to walk to the Rand, there to live in barrack compounds and go down the mines.

The ANC petitioned the Union Parliament to repeal the Act and, making no impression, decided to send a delegation to London. Theoretically the king in Parliament had the power to disallow an Act of the South African legislature. General Louis Botha, Prime Minister of South Africa, concerned at the impact the ANC delegates might make, saw them twice to urge them not to go.

He need not have worried. In London the Colonial Secretary would not even guarantee the South African government's promise to make more land available for the reserves. He told the delegation that to guarantee General Botha's word would be to insult him. The king, after correspondence with Botha, refused to see the delegation.

All Plaatje and his colleagues in London could do was appeal to the public. They addressed many meetings. Newspapers reported their complaints about the Act. MPs raised the issue, provoking the Colonial Secretary to tell the House of Commons what he had already told the delegation: that Britain had washed its hands of the matter. He added that the Natives' Land Act was not a Dutch-inspired wickedness but a continuation of recent British policy.

This was true and the ANC went halfway towards accepting the Act. While some ANC leaders opposed all of it, many were willing to acquiesce in rural segregation if a fair quantity of land was set aside for native reserves and the Cape common roll was maintained. The delegation to London actually signed a submission to the British government accepting the principle of segregation. They were advised that this was the best way to get British help. But the tactic – which Plaatje promptly repudiated – did them no good.

The ANC's diminishing hopes now rested on the Beaumont commission, set up after the passage of the Act to advise what areas should be added to the natives' 7.3 per cent. The commission toured South Africa looking for land that could be bought for native use without creating an outcry from white farmers. In 1916 it recommended the release of a further 8 million morgen and a bill was brought before Parliament to give this effect. The National Party opposed the measure passionately and the government decided to shelve it. The land allocated to native reserves remained 7.3 per cent of the total for another twenty years.

The ANC delegation was still in London when the First World War broke out. Their governing body, meeting in Bloemfontein, decided 'to hang up native grievances against the South African Parliament till a better time and to tender the authorities assistance'. ANC leaders wrote to the Defence Minister, Smuts, offering to raise 5,000 troops. Smuts replied that the government had no desire to use the services 'in a combat capacity of citizens not of European descent'. He did not want to arm Africans. However, the government raised a native labour contingent of 10,000 for support duties in France, and the ANC played an active part in recruiting them. General Botha told Sol Plaatje that his backing the recruitment campaign 'would help the native people better than any propaganda work'. By 1918, 865 black South Africans had lost their lives on war service.

This loyalty brought no reward. The new National Party, which opposed the very existence of the native labour contingent, was becoming increasingly powerful. While Botha and Smuts intended to concede little to the Africans, the pressure from Hertzog and his supporters forced them to concede nothing at all. In 1917 Smuts made a speech at the Savoy Hotel in London. It was useless, he said, to try to govern blacks and whites in the same way. The 'Native' population had to be kept 'apart as much as possible in our institutions and in land ownership'. Natives would come to work in white areas, 'but as far as possible the forms of political government will be such that each will be satisfied and developed according to his own proper lines'. Nobody rose to argue with Smuts. In London as in Pretoria his view was regarded as sensible by the vast majority of whites.

After the war Sol Plaatje led a last, desperate effort to raise support in Britain. He achieved one remarkable success. In spite of the strong opposition of the Colonial Office, he obtained a meeting for his delegation with the Prime Minister, the former supporter of the Afrikaners, David Lloyd George. According to the shorthand note of the Prime Minister's secretary, Plaatje said:

Great Britain, with whom our fathers bargained in the earliest days to take our country under her protection, has thrown us away . . . If ever there was a case which called for protection, it is the case of the natives in South Africa who are told that they have no right to buy or lease land in their own country . . . Our one crime is not that we want to be the equals of the Dutch but that we are loyal to a foreign flag, the Union Jack. If it offers us no protection then our case is indeed hopeless.

Lloyd George, always a maverick, was impressed. 'Your case,' he told the delegation, 'certainly ought to be taken into the consideration of the South African government and I shall take the earliest opportunity of presenting the whole of the facts to General Smuts.' This was an amazing promise. Lloyd George knew that the attachment of South Africa to Britain was based on both countries' complete self-government. Had Hertzog and his National Party known that the British Prime Minister was trying to tell the South African how to conduct his internal affairs, they would have claimed it as proof that Smuts was indeed 'the valet of Britain'.

Nevertheless, fifty years after the event, an English historian, Brian Willan, discovered files in the Colonial Office proving that Lloyd George was as good as his word. He wrote two long letters to Smuts, giving details of the arguments about the Land Act, the Pass Laws and the colour-bar that had been put to him by the delegation. He added: 'They said they had been told not to ventilate their grievances outside South Africa . . . But, they asked, what was the use of calling upon them to observe constitutional methods if they are given no adequate constitutional means for doing so? If this is a correct statement of the facts it seems to me a very powerful point.' Smuts replied that many of the delegation's facts were wrong and his government was trying to create 'improved machinery for voicing the needs of the Natives'.

Plaatje never learned of Lloyd George's letters. He would no doubt have been pleased by an incidental remark in one of them: 'It is evident that among the natives of South Africa are men possessed of very considerable oratorical gifts. The contrast between the case made by these black men and by the deputation headed by General Hertzog was very striking.'

Fine words did the Congress no good. Plaatje and the other ANC leaders were proving ineffective, and the initiative in confronting the authorities was to be taken from them. In Johannesburg black workers observed closely and learned from their white colleagues' method of exerting pressure.

The first major African strike, in 1918, was by the 'night soil boys'. Few houses in Johannesburg yet had water-borne sewerage, so the sanitation department employed Africans to empty and disinfect the buckets each night. Their strike, in quest of a pay increase, quickly subjected the city's wealthy areas to a great stench. The 152 strikers were arrested and sent to jail by a magistrate who told them they would have to carry on their work under the strict supervision of prison officers. Black workers in Johannesburg immediately threatened a general strike. The government, anxious to avoid worsening trouble, intervened and the Supreme Court reversed the magistrate's decision. The 152 night soil boys were released – though without their pay increase. Plaatje, in a letter to de Beers diamond corporation, referred dismissively to 'these black Bolsheviks of Johannesburg'.

A succession of other strikes followed, in mines and docks. Congress leaders helped organize some of them, but most of the ANC took Plaatje's view. They were educated men, in touch with tribal chiefs and white liberals, and they believed that the fragments of power they enjoyed through newspapers, the courts, the churches and the Cape franchise, while they might not be extended as they had hoped, were at least safe, and worth protecting. They refused to back mass action, particularly if it might be unconstitutional.

While Plaatje had been travelling abroad for the ANC his newspaper went bankrupt and the press was sold. Funds to launch a paper were, on his return, his greatest desire. Mine-owners were worried by the growing militancy among their black workers and a group of them decided to launch a newspaper in Johannesburg to report black politics. They hoped it would help calm a dangerous turbulence and invited Plaatje to be editor. Knowing that the mine-owners would have the final say, and therefore that to edit such a paper could lose him his standing among Africans, Plaatje regretfully turned the offer down. Twice in the past he had raised money from chiefs to found newspapers, but now he could not. He continued writing as a freelance journalist, his articles widely printed in newspapers for both blacks and whites. He translated *Julius Caesar*, *Othello* and *The Comedy of Errors* into Setswana and devoted himself to the temperance movement. By 1920 his political influence and that of the ANC were in decline.

More militant Africans tried to exercise power through the growing ranks of black industrial workers. In 1919 a black union movement, the Industrial and Commercial Union (ICU) was founded. An adviser from the British Labour Party came to help organize it and to deliver speeches. Advice flowed freely from negro movements in the West Indies and the United States (whose representatives were not admitted to South Africa). But where the government of General Smuts brought in the army to put down strikes by black and white workers alike, after 1924, when General Hertzog came to power, the forces of the state, with the support of white trade unions, were directed against black workers alone. The ICU leaders were divided by both theoretical and personal quarrels. Some local strikes were effective, but nationally the ICU's mobilization of the workers, both urban and rural, was to prove as impotent as the petitions and delegations of Congress.

In 1927 the President of Congress, James Gumede, was invited to Moscow and brought back the message that Russia under communism was the 'new Jerusalem'. His vision failed to inspire the ANC. Its members were mostly Christians who respected their tribal chiefs. Gumede was removed from office. But some European communists came to South Africa to recruit and organize the blacks. They were among the few Europeans actively to throw themselves into African politics, and they had some success, both in winning recruits to their party and in encouraging trade-union militancy. They also provoked a widespread white fear of black communism.

An ANC leader in the Cape, Elliot Tonjeni, began regularly to distribute communist leaflets at his meetings. In 1930 in Worcester a white civilian was arrested for shooting at natives. When he explained to the magistrate that he was trying to shoot Tonjeni, he was fined five shillings for being in possession of a rifle without a licence. Africans commented that he was fined because he missed.

Hertzog pressed on steadily in Parliament with his catalogue of measures restricting African rights. His Native Administration Act of 1927 made the governor-general (the head of state under the British Crown) supreme chief over all Africans, with the power to appoint and depose chiefs and to create a separate administration and legal system for natives. The same Act made it a punishable offence to promote 'any feeling of hostility between natives and Europeans', a neutral-sounding law that was used exclusively against Africans and their white allies, never against those whites who promoted hostility towards blacks.

Gandhi, in the 1890s, had held meetings in Natal at which he led Indians in burning their passes. He had got away with it. In 1930 the ANC sent a delegation to tell the Native Affairs Minister of the impact of the Pass Laws on the 40,000 Africans who were being convicted under them each year. The Minister showing little response, the ANC launched a pass-burning campaign. In most towns Africans were too cowed to take part. In Durban a large meeting assembled and nearly 4,000 passes were collected. The police then opened fire, killing the leader of the protest, Johannes Nkosi, and two others. A further twenty-six Africans were sentenced to hard labour for 'incitement to violence'. The campaign collapsed.

In 1930 the government invited selected Africans to a conference to discuss its latest innovation, the Native Service Contract Bill, designed to increase farmers' control over their black workers. As its method of enforcement the bill contained a 'whipping clause', applicable only to Africans in Transvaal and Natal. Sol Plaatje, normally voluble with detailed criticisms and evidence, revealed his sense of helplessness by speaking only once, and briefly. Why, he asked, did the clause apply only to Transvaal and Natal: 'Are not the natives of the Cape and Orange Free State cheeky?'

By the 1930s African leadership was fragmented, African political organization moribund. On one issue, however, most African leaders stood together: the abolition of the Cape native franchise. General Hertzog offered the measure as part of a package that included more land for native reserves. Africans in the northern provinces stood to lose nothing and to gain land. Had Hertzog by this shrewd device split off the Cape Africans, he could have told Parliament that the majority of natives supported his package. His chance of winning the two-thirds parliamentary majority he needed might thereby have been strengthened. On this issue, the Africans failed him.

He kept trying. In 1936, ten years after his first attempt, his much-amended package at last seemed about to secure its two-thirds majority. To help him swing a few extra parliamentary votes, Hertzog again tried to enlist the support of leading Africans. A group came to Cape Town to meet him. 'It is not that we hate you,' he told them, 'but if we give you the right to vote, within a very short space of time the whole Parliament will be controlled by Natives. I must tell you point blank, I am not prepared for this.'

Some of those who came to see him were prepared to accept what he offered: in return for their acquiescence in the loss of the Cape native vote on the common roll in elections to the Union Parliament, the government would raise the proportion of land allocated to native reserves under the 1913 Act from 7.3 per cent of the total to 13 per cent. After much argument among themselves, his African visitors turned him down. Nevertheless he secured his two-thirds majority in Parliament.

One of the Africans who had met him explained to the press what Hertzog had been doing. A chicken-farmer, he said, sent word he wanted to consult his fowls. They were astonished, as it was not his custom. He said: 'My children, I want to consult you on an important matter. I want to make soup of you – a great deal of soup. I have therefore come to ask you: into what kind of soup would you like to be made?'

CHAPTER SEVEN

Two Leaders, 1934–8

(a) A Superior Person

Jan Christian Smuts was austere and solitary, a mountain climber with a habit of looking down on his fellow-men. 'When I think of Italy,' he wrote once to a friend, 'Hannibal and his glorious march come before my mind's eyes. You see cathedrals. I see battlefields of the past.'

Born in 1870 of an Afrikaner farming family in the Cape, Smuts showed his intellectual superiority at Cambridge in 1895 when he took parts 1 and 2 of the law tripos in the same year and got firsts in both. Soon afterwards Kruger asked him to go to the Transvaal to eradicate corruption from the state attorney's department. During the Boer War, Smuts led the most daring of all the guerilla commandos, into the heartland of British power, Cape Colony – and was never captured. His saddle-bag contained Xenophon's *Anabasis* in Greek and Kant's *Critique of Pure Reason* – his means of relaxation. After the war he devised the schemes that persuaded the four British colonies in South Africa to form the Union.

During the 1914–18 war, Smuts commanded South African and empire armies against the Germans in Kenya and Tanganyika – the ex-Boer general adroitly winning himself large credit for some small imperial victories. The British people cheered him, since at the time most of their troops were bogged down in the mud of northern France. In 1917, sent as Botha's deputy prime minister to London, he was made a member of the Imperial War Cabinet, advising Lloyd George, Churchill and other British leaders.

These were Smuts's greatest years. He quickly grasped the arguments of generals and politicians and was able, in 1917–18, to help formulate Allied military plans. After the war, he was equally effective in turning the hopes of the victorious countries' leaders into proposals on which they could agree. As an honest outsider whose clear exposition of complex issues all parties respected, he acquired a unique standing. President Woodrow Wilson told the United States' Senate that his scheme for the League of Nations was drafted 'in the light of a paper by General Smuts', and in 1919 at Versailles Smuts helped found the League. He wrote the preamble to its charter. Throughout Britain, politicians, universities and the public showered him with honours.

South Africans appreciated him less. When he was offered a seat in the British House of Commons, he turned it down, on Botha's advice, to avoid his fellow-Afrikaners thinking him wholly English. He became Prime Minister on Botha's death, not because he was popular but because he was so deft at handling the business of government. Hertzog was a lawyer and politician of above average competence, but Smuts could master all sides of an argument before Hertzog had finished reading the papers. An anonymous versifier wrote:

> He longs to be an autocrat, does Smuts,
> To rise above all party tiffs
> And rule without annoying 'Ifs'
> Or 'Buts'.

Smuts's attitudes worried many of his fellow-Afrikaners. Once a Boer hero against the British, he seemed to have changed sides. His clear mind appreciated the case of the British millionaires who presented him with figures proving that if they were forced to go on employing unnecessarily large numbers of expensive white workers in their gold-mining companies, their contribution to the South African economy would have to be cut. His backing of the bosses against their white workers did not, of course, mean that he supported the black workers. For Smuts that would have been unthinkable. In race relations he was a man of his time and place. Those Afrikaners who suspected him of being soft on blacks were misled, partly by his haughty manner, more substantially by the deliberate distortions of his political opponents, above all Hertzog. Smuts saw himself as a liberal, a man of integrity and a philosopher (he wrote a book on 'holism' during a quiet phase in politics), but it never entered his head to see black men as his equals. He considered the evidence to be against the proposition. Nevertheless, he could never bring himself to utter a crude slogan like 'Whites First', not even to win an election.

Milner and his kindergarten had argued for a federal parliament in London to govern the empire. Smuts, after his experience in the 1914–18 war, was one of those who led the argument for reshaping

the empire into a commonwealth – a free association of states, each
independent but bound by common interests and values. This idea
appealed to Smuts partly because it was the only way he and South
Africa could continue to be a major influence on world affairs, but also
because he was genuinely impressed by the liberal humanism of
British culture. He saw it as vital for the Afrikaners not to creep into
the shell of a narrow nationalism. He wanted to build not an
Afrikaner nation but a white South African nation – and if that meant
that Shakespeare and Walt Whitman played a larger part in
education than the great Dutch and Afrikaner poets, he did not mind.

The educated classes, especially in Cape Town and Johannesburg,
recognised that in Smuts they had a leader of quality. The wealthier
English-speaking voters came to trust him and, after 1920, large
numbers of them, having held back for ten years, joined the political
party Botha and he had founded. Afrikaners were more divided.
Those with large farms, secure businesses or successful professional
practices – and who feared the mob, be it white or black – saw Smuts
as the man to protect them. But he had no idea how to win the hearts
of the mass of poor Afrikaners. After Hertzog had broken away to
form the National Party in 1912 and Louis Botha had died in 1919,
Smuts was able to muster support from the majority of his own
people only fleetingly.

When in 1924 the electorate put Hertzog's National Party into
power, largely inspired by dislike of the English-speaking mine-
owners and the empire-loving plantation-owners who still seemed
able to dominate South African affairs, Smuts continued to see his
main political task as uniting Afrikaners and English-speakers into a
single white South African nation. His next opportunity did not come
until the great crash, the financial collapse that hit all western
markets in 1929–31. Hertzog's government lacked the skill to ride a
total dislocation of world trade. Smuts, whose party might have
exploited the government's discomfiture in order to obtain sole
power, instead offered to form a coalition. He became Hertzog's
deputy prime minister, helping him turn the economic upset to
advantage.

The relationship mellowed Hertzog, who in 1934 agreed to a 'fusion'
of the rival parties in an effort to secure the long-term co-operation of
the Afrikaners and British – the 'two races'. They set up the United
Party. It restored in substantial measure the coalition spirit that
Smuts had sought and Hertzog opposed before the First World War.
Hertzog had some regard for Smuts. They had both fought in the
1899–1902 war against the British and they both, although lawyers,
liked to think of themselves as Boer farmers. They often chatted
about the comparative nutritive qualities of different grasses.

The most dangerous opponents of their revived movement for

conciliation between the two white 'races' were to be those extreme Afrikaner nationalists who refused to follow Hertzog. They rejected 'fusion' and relaunched the National Party without him. Even though their leaders had been members of his government since 1924, had helped him introduce the colour-bar into Union law and advance the position of the poor whites, they felt that as Afrikaners they were not yet in control of their own country.

Fusion, when in 1934 it was carried into effect, was their signal for action. More Hertzogite than Hertzog, a small group of them had been quietly building up their strength since 1918. The First World War had convinced them that for Afrikanerdom to survive South Africa must cut itself off completely from Britain and its empire. They set up a secret movement called the Broederbond (Band of Brothers), organized in cells like a revolutionary Communist Party. They were trying to refight the Boer War in local councils and committees, and this was not a respectable thing to do. The Broeders invited into membership those they thought likely to be influential – future politicians, army officers, civil servants, local officials, teachers – who, on joining, swore to keep the organization secret and to devote their lives to strengthening Afrikanerdom.

The Broeders set up Afrikaner scout groups (the Voortrekkers), student leagues, teachers' and women's federations. They arranged for the Bible, which had always been read in Dutch, to be translated into Afrikaans, and they recruited the Dutch Church – which in 1837 had opposed the Great Trek – into the front rank of their campaign. They warned businessmen of trouble unless company letters were written in Afrikaans, which of course meant recruiting Afrikaner employees. They set up charitable and self-help committees to find jobs for Afrikaners or to help them improve their farms. Eventually Broeders ran an investment bank to finance Afrikaner businessmen, a building society to help Afrikaners buy homes and an Afrikaner chain of stores.

When Hertzog agreed to fuse the National Party into the new United Party, with Smuts as deputy leader, the Broederbond swelled in significance. The conviction spread among the Broeders that Hertzog, their own Prime Minister, was a traitor. He responded fiercely, denouncing their secrecy and excesses and, above all, their religious determination to split the white community. 'The Broeder-bond,' he said, 'is a serious threat to the peace and order of the Union . . . Whenever will certain people give up the foolish and fatal idea that they are the ones chosen by the gods to rule over the rest?' Later Smuts was to call the Broederbond 'a dangerous, cunning, Fascist organisation'.

Dr Daniel Francois Malan, who took over the leadership of the rump of Broederbonders and Afrikaner zealots who resurrected the

National Party, refusing to follow Hertzog into fusion, was a
Broeder. He was a fat, crumpled ex-clergyman who looked like Mr
Pickwick. Since 1924 he had been a minister in Hertzog's
government, where he did not so much argue with his critics as
thunder – as though he were the Day of Judgement made flesh.
Hertzog contemptuously rejected the notion that God had anything to
do with Afrikaner politics. His speeches had the cautious style and
phrasing of a solicitor's letter. Malan, a Doctor of Divinity of the
Dutch Church, made every speech sound like a sermon:

> Back to your people; back to the highest ideals of your people; back
> to the pledge which has been entrusted to your keeping; back to
> the altar of the people on which you must lay your sacrifice, and, if
> it is required of you, also yourself as sacrifice; back to the sanctity
> and inviolability of family life; back to the Christian way of life;
> back to the Christian faith; back to your church; back to your God.

Smuts thought such a windbag could never reach the top in politics.

Malan renamed the residue of Hertzog's party the Purified
National Party. For him the most important objective on earth was
to keep Afrikanerdom pure. When the Broederbond and its
associated movements encouraged teachers to indoctrinate their
classes with a version of South African history distorted for
nationalist purposes and a religious ideology that identified the
Afrikaners as God's chosen people, Malan backed them enthusiastically. Hertzog supported the charge of parents that such teachers were
improperly influencing their children. 'No party in this country,'
Hertzog said, 'can be built upon a foundation of hate towards its
fellow-citizens simply because they are English-speaking.'

It was much like a repeat of 1912. Then Botha and Smuts, the
conciliators, had so dominated politics as to make Hertzog's National
Party seem a hopeless cause. Now Smuts and Hertzog, the fusionists,
set about doing the same to Malan. Hertzog managed to secure most
of the party organization and newspapers, leaving Malan little more
than a claque of poor whites in Cape Province. In the Transvaal, only
one MP, J. G. Strijdom, followed Malan into the Purified Party, and
he had to pay a large part of the party's provincial expenses out of his
own pocket.

Malan fought on regardless. The issue on which he had split from
Hertzog was republicanism. Malan insisted that South Africa break
completely from the British Empire and declare itself an independent
republic – the fulfilment of the ideals of the trekkers and of Kruger.
That republic, he insisted, must have one citizenship (South Africans
enjoyed both Union and British citizenship, which he considered
anomalous), one flag (an uncomfortable two-flags compromise had

been put through Parliament by Hertzog in 1927) and one national anthem. He wanted no more of the Union Jack atop South African flagpoles or of Afrikaners owing allegiance to a king in London.

The Prime Minister, by skilful ducking and weaving, tried to prevent such issues from enlarging Malan's support. At the opening of Parliament in 1938 Hertzog ordered that, in addition to the British national anthem, 'God Save the King', the band should play 'Die Stem van Suid-Afrika' ('The Voice of South Africa'), a patriotic song popular among Afrikaners. When some English-speaking MPs protested, Hertzog explained that the Union had no generally accepted or officially recognized national anthem of its own. 'God Save the King', he said, was only 'a solemn invocation to the Almighty for his protection to our King'. It would continue to be played on all 'appropriate occasions', but 'Die Stem' would also be played, in recognition of the 'special esteem' in which it was held by Afrikaners.

Such compromises gave pleasure to Hertzog – who continued to prize a good piece of drafting – but to few others. They were, however, the mechanism by which Hertzog and Smuts made sure that the United Party maintained its electoral support. Of the two, Smuts, gazing calmly over the heads of the petty, quarrelsome people around him and successfully ignoring even the irreconcilable conflict in his own psyche, was the more attached to liberal principles. He found some of Hertzog's measures, like the removal of Cape Africans from the common voters' roll, hard to take. But he was deputy prime minister and committed to the slow task of binding Afrikaners and English-speakers into a single white South African nation. So he swallowed hard and digested what Hertzog placed before him.

The mighty alliance of the two generals, bitter political opponents for twenty years, gave Hertzog control of the detail of government. In return Smuts secured what he most cared for: the welding into the British Empire of a united, white South Africa. He believed that European civilization and law could be maintained into the indefinite future only if Afrikaners and English-speakers were prevented from falling into a renewal of their war, that a revival of 'inter-racial' – Afrikaner-English – strife could lose them everything. For Smuts, the need to heal the wounds the whites had inflicted on each other always had first priority. That was why his considerable intellect was never fully applied to what he considered a secondary problem – the need to bring blacks into South African public life.

Hertzog stood by his policy of 'two streams'. He fought for the rights of Afrikaners and taxed the mining companies and the English commercial community heavily as a way to finance relief for the poor whites, to build up state industries and create the beginnings of an Afrikaner manufacturing sector. He forced English companies to employ expensive white workers and to accept the colour-bar on the employment of blacks, even though many of them resisted these policies as inefficient. But he did not risk driving the British out of business. Once he had done what he could for the Afrikaners, he agreed to conciliation.

Dr Malan's view was more messianic. He declared that the suffering the trekkers and their successors had endured as they grimly challenged both the elements and the British imperialists had been a holy purification, an agony through which they had proved themselves worthy of God's favour. With aid from on high they would cut themselves off totally from the British Empire, re-establish their sovereignty, form a republic dedicated to their contract with God, and alone rule South Africa. Where Hertzog was prepared to seek the alliance of the English and even of the coloureds, where Smuts, like the English Whigs of 1832, favoured absorbing and embracing troublesome critics, Malan was driven by a spirit like that of the Inquisition. Since the British and the blacks had stood in the way of God's will, it was the duty of God's chosen instrument to sweep them aside.

(b) A Man of God

Dr Malan, the crumpled ex-clergyman, was determined to secure for the Children of Israel the promised land that had been stolen from them. He declared:

> We hold this nationhood as our due, for it was given us by the architect of the universe. His aim was the formation of a new nation. The last hundred years have witnessed a miracle behind which must lie a divine plan. Afrikanerdom is not the work of men but the creation of God.

A professor at the Potchefstroom University for Christian Higher Education, H. G. Stoker, wrote in 1941:

> If we had had to predict what would happen to the Voortrekkers in 1838, if we had noticed the Black peril, the wilderness and barbarism of the interior, the danger of bastardization and anglicization, each of us would have prophesied that our little People were doomed to extinction. And yet that little People remains. Not because we Afrikaners are tremendously good people, but because God, the Disposer of the lot of the nations, has a future task for our People.

God, according to this view, had punished His people with oppression by the British, the hangings of Slachter's Nek and the death of Piet Retief. Then He had raised them up by letting them found the Transvaal and Orange Free State as independent republics. He had then chastized them again with a series of blows that included the Boer War, as punishment for their failure to keep the Covenant allegedly made with God in 1838, on the day before the Battle of Blood River. The trekker commander on that occasion, Andries Pretorius, wrote a report two weeks afterwards saying the trekkers had 'promised in a public prayer' that, if they were victorious, they would build 'a house to the Lord in memory of his name'. A modest barn-like church had indeed been built at Pietermaritzburg, capital of the short-lived Republic of Natalia, but it was soon put to commercial purposes, including waggon workshop, mineral-water factory, tea-room and blacksmith's. According to what became the authorized version of the Covenant, written thirty-three years after the event by Sarel Cilliers, a former church elder and occasional celebrant of prayers for the trekkers, the promise made before the battle was that in return for victory they would commemorate the day each year as a sabbath and enjoin their children to do the same. This promise, if it was ever made, was for several decades forgotten.

At the centenary of the Trek, the leaders of Afrikaner nationalism set out to compensate for such backsliding. They not only promulgated Sarel Cilliers's version of the Covenant, they rededicated themselves and all their followers to keep it. Henning Klopper, founder of the Broederbond, said:

We believe the Afrikaner will again under the guidance of God arise from the debris and ashes of his defeats, shake them off and finally become powerful and victorious. His sense of freedom is too strong to be extinguished. It lives in his heart like the burning bramble bush, unextinguishable, kept burning by God.

Dr Malan's style of speaking was not an eccentricity. His was the most prominent voice in a burgeoning movement. In serious discourse with each other, and even sometimes with outsiders, he and his followers repeatedly stated that they were God's chosen people. They built many shrines to honour the memory of their people's suffering. The Vrouemonument near Bloemfontein bears a dedication to 'the memory of the 26,370 women and children who died in the concentration camps . . . as a result of the war of 1899–1902'. From its unveiling in 1913 it attracted pilgrims and a constant stream of organized groups of Afrikaner schoolchildren.

The greatest of the memorials was to the trekkers. In centenary year, 1938, the high priests of Afrikaner nationalism organized a pageant. It began with the building of a replica: an ox-waggon of stinkwood. The plan to drive it from Cape Town to Pretoria lit fuses of enthusiasm in the Voortrekkers (the Afrikaners' own Boy Scout movement, set up because they found it hard to like Baden Powell's scouts; he had been a British officer in the Boer War and the Scout movement he had launched insisted on singing 'God Save the King'). So numerous were the young Voortrekkers who applied to join the ox-waggon on its trek into the interior that one waggon was not enough. Eventually volunteers built nine. For outdoor lads – of all ages and both sexes – it was the treat of a lifetime. The girls were to dress up in the bonnets and long skirts of the 1830s and the men, those who could manage it, were to grow beards. The Broederbond urged clergymen of the Dutch Church in villages along the way to set up committees to provide the trekkers with food and fresh teams of oxen. Busy enthusiasts set to everywhere, obliging the organizers to send each waggon on a different route, so that they ended up calling at almost every town and hamlet in the Union.

Their destination was a ridge above Pretoria, visible for miles around, where the foundation-stone was to be laid for a vast granite monument to commemorate the exodus from the land the British Pharaohs had made intolerable. Pictures and diagrams of the proposed monument appeared in all Afrikaans newspapers. A large part of the Afrikaner population of the Union took part in the event, by sewing clothes, giving food, walking beside the waggons as they trundled through the villages and the new Afrikaner suburbs, singing psalms and Dutch folk-songs with the trekkers at their nightly camp-fires, laying wreaths on the graves of Afrikaner heroes, or – for 100,000 or so – witnessing the dedication ceremony.

The Voortrekkers' teams of oxen dragged eight of the nine waggons to Pretoria, where amid the vast crowd they heard speaker after speaker tell the stories of Slachter's Nek, the Great Trek, the Covenant, Blood River; the sacrifices, the dedication to God, the determination that now at last they would resume control over the land of their forefathers. The Prime Minister, J. B. M. Hertzog, had been invited to lay the monument's foundation-stone, but he was left in no doubt that it would be a celebration of Afrikanerdom at a time when he was leader of a 'fusion' government of Afrikaners and English-speakers. The notion that God had blessed only the Afrikaners was offensive to Hertzog and threatening to some of his colleagues in office. He declined to be used to help propagate it. The absence from the platform of his precise, legal tones did nothing to reduce the occasion's fervour.

The trekkers drove the ninth waggon over the Drakensberg mountains and down into Natal, to the site of their most celebrated victory, where Malan aroused his congregation with a new idea: the Second Great Trek.

Here at Blood River [he said] you stand on holy ground . . . The trekkers heard the voice of South Africa. They received their task from God's hand . . . Their task is completed. Your Blood River is not here. Your Blood River lies in the city . . . Afrikanerdom is on trek again. It is not a trek away from the centres of civilization, as it was one hundred years ago, but a trek back, from the country to the city . . . In that new Blood River, black and white meet together in much closer contact and much more binding struggle than one hundred years ago . . . Today black and white jostle together in the labour market.

In the litany of Afrikaner historical memories, the blacks had never been the main foe. They might cause trouble by treachery – as when Dingaan killed Piet Retief – but the resolute Afrikaners always defeated and subjugated them. The deep-rooted fear that black men might desire and be desired by white women had been calmed by a law of 1927 making sexual relations between black and white a punishable offence. The oratory of the movement was partly anti-black, but its central thrust was against the British, the ruthless imperialists and capitalists who were still in possession of the Afrikaners' birthright, making them servants in their own country. To Malan, the blacks were like oxen, lowly creatures that could be dangerous if not kept in their place; but the British Empire was like Assyria in the Book of Isaiah, the incarnation of evil and the foil against which God would reveal His power.

Such religious inspiration had taken over Afrikaner nationalism only recently. The Calvinism that the Dutch had brought from Holland in the seventeenth century disposed them to believe in predestination and the chosen people, but those who claimed that the religious tone of their nationalism had its roots in van Riebeeck's time were exaggerating. Unlike the Pilgrim Fathers who sailed to America, the original seventy colonists were not inspired by religious motives. The Dutch East India Company had purely commercial purposes and no evidence has been produced to show that the men it paid to colonize the Cape were any different.

The reports of travellers and other contemporary observers until at least the middle of the nineteenth century describe, on the contrary, a society in which godliness was conspicuously absent. Afrikaner farmers read the Bible – in many of their homes it was the only book – but the most important lesson they derived from Christianity (like some Catholics in Latin America) was that non-Christians, i.e. non-whites, could be treated as chattels. John Barrow's *Account of Travels into the Interior of Southern Africa* published in 1801 describes the Boers as 'an inhuman and unfeeling peasantry, who, having discovered themselves to be removed to too great a distance from the seat of their former government to be awed by its authority, have exercised, in the most wanton and barbarous manner, an absolute power over these poor wretches [the Khoikhoi]'. A sympathetic traveller, George Thompson, writing in 1827, ascribed Afrikaners' irreligious and immoral ways to

. . . the many disadvantageous circumstances under which they are placed: to their being thinly scattered over an immense territory, out of reach of religious instruction or moral restraint, to the vicious and corrupt character of the old Dutch government, to the inefficient police, which encouraged a system of unrighteous aggression against the native tribes, and last to the influence of slavery, which inevitably pollutes society.

Paul Kruger when he was President of the Transvaal Republic had often, like Malan, confused the platform and the pulpit. He was without doubt a deeply religious man. But he did not claim that the Afrikaners were God's chosen people. In short, the marriage of Afrikaner nationalism and Calvinist Christianity buttressed by the myth of a sanctified history did not develop until the twentieth century. Then, particularly in the years after the Boer War, large numbers of Afrikaners were forced off the land, ghettoes of poor Afrikaners sprang up at town fringes, and Afrikaner clergymen became aware that the poverty of their flocks required them to do more than pray. To revive the morale of down-trodden and broken communities, some idealization of their past was essential. If the Ancient Greeks and the Israelites could do it, if the British themselves with all that fuss about the Spanish Armada could do it, why not the Afrikaners?

Malan when he was a young dominee (vicar) had himself seen the suffering of the many of his fellow-Afrikaners who had sunk to the despised class of 'poor whites'. In 1910 he told a church congress:

I have observed the children of Afrikaner families running around as naked as kaffirs in Congoland. We have knowledge today of Afrikaner girls so poor they work for coolies and Chinese. We know of white men and women who live married and unmarried with coloureds. These unfortunates are all our flesh and blood; they carry our names; they are Afrikaners, all of them.

Afrikaner children in government schools were at that time suffering the effects of Milnerism. Teachers spoke English. Children who could not do so were liable to be mocked or punished. One justification for this policy was that it gave the children full access to modern science, technology and the world's cheapest and best textbooks. But to a defeated, impoverished people it felt like wanton humiliation. It led to the demand for separate schools for Afrikaners. Dominees established a Christian National Education Movement in the Transvaal and the Free State to provide them. Many of the teachers were Afrikaner clergymen who had watched their congregations losing their livelihoods, their language and their national identity. Knowing how the Dutch in the United States had first been anglicized and had then vanished, many came to believe that as a distinct Afrikaner people their parishioners too faced extinction.

By the time of Dr Malan's speech at Blood River in 1938, the risk of extinction had become remote. Hertzog's years in office had seen to that. But most of the Afrikaners were still economically a depressed class. Many schoolchildren were still forced to sing the British national anthem every morning, though Afrikaners among them – and no doubt some British – made it tolerable by changing the words to:

> God Save our noble King,
> Wash him in paraffin
> And put fire on him.

The wicked deeds of the British Empire still provided the stories with which Malan and his fellow-preachers liked to spellbind their flocks. But Hertzog's claim that the British Empire had now granted South Africa complete independence was difficult to disprove. Malan, the former government minister addressing the assembled Afrikaners at Blood River, needed something extra to transform his audience and himself from a nostalgic, religious group, excluded from power, into the dominant force that would rule the nation. He made the attempt with as ambitious – or as ridiculous – a claim as any politician has ever made: that God's destiny for the Afrikaner people, the reason he had chosen them, punished them, saved them, was to preserve the white race.

To rational observers at the time, it seemed the hyperbole of a religious fanatic. No sensible analyst of South Africa in 1938 thought the white race there was endangered. Hertzog, Smuts and Malan had for two generations been in total agreement that the white race and white civilization had to be protected – and would be – by policies of racial segregation. Each year these grew more oppressive, yet the Africans seemed to accept them, behaving like the English sportsman's ideal, the good loser. Even though Malan's call for racial purity echoed the words of Hitler and his increasingly powerful Nazi movement in Germany, even though his audience was large and enthusiastic, the tide of history did not seem to be behind him.

Seven months earlier, in May 1938, an overwhelming majority had returned the Hertzog-Smuts United Party to power, with 111 seats in the House of Assembly. Malan's Purified Nationalists had won only twenty-seven. Smuts wrote, 'I almost feel as if we are at last through our racial troubles [i.e. British *v* Afrikaner]. I am glad [of] this internal settling down and fusion.' The conciliation policy of 1910, the policy of Louis Botha and Jan Smuts, had finally, by winning over J. B. M. Hertzog, secured firm electoral support from the majority of both Afrikaans- and English-speaking South Africans. Neither by his attacks on the British imperial connection nor by his Wagnerian orchestration of the *swart gevaar*, the fear of blacks, had Malan managed to turn his brand of Afrikaner nationalism into the mood of the majority.

ABOVE: Johannesburg in 1886, the year the first gold was mined.

LEFT: Johannesburg in 1888.

BELOW: Commissioner Street, Johannesburg, in the 1890s.

General Louis Botha (leading horseman on the left), returning from an engagement, May 1900. In 1910, he became first Prime Minister of the Union of South Africa.

ABOVE: The British march through Pretoria, former capital of Kruger's South African Republic, 1899.

RIGHT: General Kitchener, who argued for making life in the concentration camps hard, seen in Johannesburg.

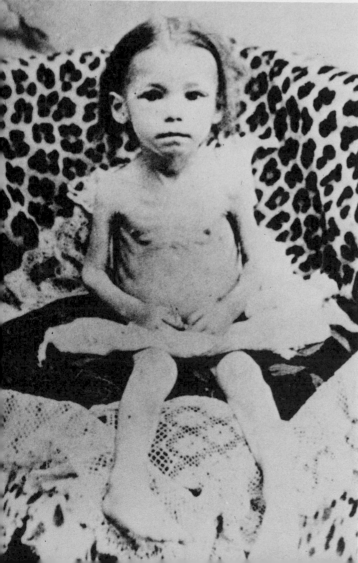

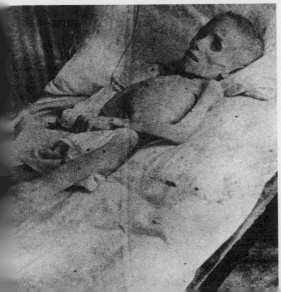

ABOVE: Afrikaner women being taken with their furniture to a concentration camp.

ABOVE LEFT: A concentration camp. At first the inmates were housed in wooden huts. Later only bell tents were available.

LEFT: Sick and dying Afrikaners in a British concentration camp, 1901.

TOP: African National Congress delegation to London, 1914. Sol Plaatje, top right; Walter Rubusana, the only African ever elected to the Cape provincial council, seated centre.

ABOVE LEFT: Sol Plaatje, the ANC delegate who caused the British Prime Minister, Lloyd George, to question Smuts on racial policy.

ABOVE: 'Hoggenheimer', the 'English-Jewish capitalist' whom Afrikaner cartoonists constantly depicted getting his way over the Union government.

LEFT: Gandhi, master of non-violent protest, outside his Durban office.

CHAPTER EIGHT

By-products of War, 1939–45

As in 1914, it was a war in which Britain opposed Germany – the Second World War – that changed everything. September 4 1939 was the day the wounds were reopened. General Hertzog rose to tell the South African Parliament that there appeared to be 'a serious difference . . . an unbridgeable division' in his Cabinet. He went on, 'We are concerned here in a war in which the Union has not the slightest interest . . . England has certain obligations towards Poland. We have no such obligations.' Were South Africa to join the war on the British side, he said, she would do so because a section of her people cared more for British than for South African interests. Such an outlook was incompatible with South Africa's independence. If it prevailed it would destroy South Africa's unity. 'It is urged,' he went on, 'that we should take part in the war because the German Chancellor has demonstrated that he is out to obtain world domination . . . Where can we find proof?' Hertzog explained that the German government under Hitler had annexed the Rhineland, Austria, Czechoslovakia and Danzig only because it had to. He argued that the government of South Africa should maintain its 'existing relations with . . . the various belligerent countries as if no war is being waged'.

The deputy prime minister, General Smuts, rose next. He said that Hitler had repeatedly broken his promises and expanded his ambitions. Germany would soon be seeking the return of its African colonies – including South-West Africa, which South Africa had conquered in 1915 and since administered under a League of Nations' mandate. Once Germany recaptured South-West Africa, the security of South Africa itself would not be worth much. The time to defend the Union's independence was now, while the war was far away. He urged Parliament to sever relations with the German Reich and carry out its undertakings to the British Commonwealth. Otherwise South Africa would soon find itself isolated.

The Cabinet had split 7–6 in favour of declaring war on Germany. Hertzog was confident that Parliament would overrule this decision. But his defence of Hitler's actions went too far for a small group of MPs, who began to waver. Malan defended Hitler unreservedly and pushed the waverers further. Smuts won the vote by eighty to sixty-seven. Hertzog resigned. Smuts took over as Prime Minister, committed to wholehearted support for Britain.

For Hertzog this was a fatal blow. For the remains of his former party, too, it was a blow. But it was also something more: confirmation that they had been right all along. Against Hertzog's prediction, Britain was once again, for its own imperialist-capitalist purposes, inducing South Africa to pour out Afrikaner blood.

Hertzog knew that entering the war on Britain's side would reawaken the Afrikaner xenophobia that had swept him to power after the 1914-18 war. His failure to keep South Africa neutral brought to an end not only his fifteen years' prime ministership but also his ability to hold down Afrikanerdom's wilder elements. A year after the parliamentary vote against neutrality, finding himself overruled on one side by Smuts and the British and on the other by nationalists even more extreme than Malan, he retired from public life. Smuts, knowing that Hertzog had never used office to line his pockets and that he was in financial straits, led Parliament in voting him a pension. Soon afterwards Hertzog died.

The challenge facing Malan was similar to that which had faced Hertzog in 1914–18. He had to try to unite rebellious and fragmented Afrikaner nationalists behind his party so that he would be in a position to muster votes should an election, rather than a German victory, prove the route to power. But the Afrikaners were not an easy community to unite. When Smuts took command of their country for the war against Germany, many of them rejected the parliamentary system and turned to violence. Smuts ordered the police to confiscate all privately licensed fire-arms. It was a necessary precaution.

The government's recruitment campaign for volunteers to fight in the war provoked one Broederbond offshoot, the *Ossewa-Brandwag* (Ox-Waggon Guard, OB) to launch its own recruitment drive and set up a corps of *Stormjaers* (storm troopers), who trained at secret manoeuvres for the ostensible purpose of keeping order at meetings. The OB had been founded to take part in the centenary celebrations of the Great Trek. By 1940, when the government had raised 137,000 men for the war, the OB claimed 250,000, openly dedicated to Nazi policies and the end of democracy. They adopted the Swastika badge, gave the Hitler salute, threatened death to the Jews and provoked fights with army volunteers. Their leaders assumed a military form of organization, like a shadow defence force, ready to take over the country in the event of a German victory.

The OB and other bodies of Nazi or neo-Nazi Afrikaners – the Grey Shirts, the New Order – gave Malan as much trouble as they gave the government. Malan was not just an inspiring religious orator, he was also a dedicated and skilled manager of party and parliamentary committees. They had little time for such niceties. They understood that Hitler's war aims for Africa included the capture of all French and British colonies in alliance with Germany's only friends on the continent, the Afrikaners, fellow-members of the 'master race'. In the first two years of the war, when Germany and Japan were ascendant, Afrikaner muscle-men seemed poised to assume power.

Malan and his small group of parliamentary supporters, although more committed to constitutional methods, also felt warmly towards Germany. Many of them considered Hitler's theory about the innate superiority of the Aryan race over all others, especially blacks and Jews, to be the voice of sanity – and a blueprint for South Africa. Purified nationalists had long used Hitler's words when they attributed the policies of the South African government to 'British-Jewish capitalist' forces. They revived a cartoon figure, 'Hoggenheimer', who had become famous in the Boer War as the Afrikaners' enemy number one, a fat Anglo-Jewish financier.

In 1942, Malan published a draft constitution for the republic. Afrikaans would be the first official language, English second or supplemental; a State President, chosen by the all-white electorate, would be 'responsible only to God'; a Community Council would help tackle 'important problems' like 'Indian penetration and the surplus Jewish population'; public life would be 'Christian-National'. It was Malan's way of seizing the initiative in readiness for the arrival of the German armies. A committee of Afrikaner political organizations, chaired by a Broederbond member who was also a professor of philosophy, accorded Dr Malan the title of *Volksleier*, leader of the people, echoing Hitler's title, *Der Führer*, the leader.

Smuts tried to avoid provoking Afrikaner extremists. He had several hundred interned – including an OB general named Balthazar Johannes Vorster, who was later to become Prime Minister – but he did not allow even those found guilty of the most blatant acts of treason to be hanged. Few governments have handled threats to the state in wartime with such restraint. He avoided conscripting Afrikaners into the army, limiting recruitment to volunteers – a typical piece of Smuts subtlety which led to many Afrikaners volunteering. He promised that South African troops would serve only in Africa. He chose a Cabinet half English-speaking and half Afrikaans. It was all a last, desperate attempt to keep Afrikaner consent for the link with Britain.

The early course of the war was encouraging for the nationalists. German armies swept triumphantly across Europe and North Africa, and Germany's ally, Japan, seemed likely to liberate South Africa itself from Britain's financial and military embrace. By mid-1942 Japan had destroyed the American Pacific fleet at Pearl Harbor, sunk the British Far Eastern fleet, conquered the British colonies of Malaya, Singapore and Burma, and the Dutch East Indies, as well as the Philippines and French Indo-China. The Dutch and British had developed Cape Colony in order to help hold their eastern possessions. With most of these conquered, it made strategic sense for Japan to capture the staging-post, especially as German control of the Mediterranean had made the Cape again vital for British access to India. With the political leaders of Afrikaner nationalism so openly in favour of their government's enemies, this was the moment if ever there was one for ministers to seek the support of the African population.

Smuts did his best. In a debate in Parliament in 1942, Malan, leader of the opposition, said that Japan was justified in seeking Lebensraum. For him any ally who would help remove British control was to be welcomed. The Prime Minister replied that if Japan tried to conquer South Africa he would 'see to it that every native and coloured man who can be armed will be armed'. Armed blacks! To Malan the idea was unthinkable. Some served in the army, but only in such roles as drivers, diggers and potato-peelers.

An outbreak of liberal thinking in the South African government in 1942 was partly attributable to the danger of war. It was also partly the result of Smuts replacing Hertzog as Prime Minister, of Hofmeyr and others of a liberal inclination coming into office, and of a realization within the Native Affairs Department that the growing communities of urban Africans had needs which, if not attended to, would soon grow into problems. In 1942 the Minister of Labour opened the Congress of Non-European Trade Unions and seriously considered the inclusion of Africans in official collective-bargaining procedures. The Secretary of the Department of Native Affairs, Douglas Smit, chaired a committee on the social, health and economic conditions of urban natives. It heard evidence from Africans about the locations in which they lived – insanitary, overcrowded, far from the factories in which they worked – and about African wages, often as low as £3 a month when the government's own experts said the minimum needed for survival was more than £7. The committee confirmed much of this evidence. Among the reforms it proposed were the relaxation of the Pass Laws, setting up labour exchanges and subsidising the travel costs of black workers. Douglas Smit said publicly that restrictive laws and artificial barriers to the African's progress were 'unjust, and we should take courage in our hands and abolish them all'.

Smuts himself told a meeting of the South African Institute of Race Relations in 1942:

A revolutionary change is taking place among the native peoples – the movement from the old reserves to the big European centres of population. Segregation tried to stop it. It has, however, not stopped it in the least. The process has been accelerated. You might as well try to sweep the ocean back with a broom.

For forty years he had backed segregation as essential to protect the white man and his civilization. Now not only was segregation being overwhelmed by the flood of Africans into industrial jobs, it was threatening his ability to defend his country. Smuts was not converted by this intellectual awareness to a fundamental change in his attitude towards Africans. He was too old for that. His speech to the Institute of Race Relations went on: 'If [the African] is not much more, he is the beast of burden; he is the worker and you need him. He is carrying the country on his back.' Smuts found western-educated Africans an embarrassment and preferred to see blacks in the settings to which he was accustomed, as chiefs in native areas or as 'the beast of burden'. He complained about the time wasted in Parliament debating the 'native' issue. He wanted the matter out of the way, to enable him to devote himself to his primary concerns: international strategy and managing the war.

So he allowed those who were administering the home front for him to turn a liberal face towards the blacks. It was only in 1938 that, helped by the introduction of petrol-driven pick-up vans, the enforcement of influx control had become systematic and nationwide. Just as the war industries began to build up their demand for black labour, the Department of Justice took delivery of its vans, and newly-motorized policemen were delighted to find an influx of able-bodied black workers without passes whom they could arrest and drive out of the towns. It took until May 1942 for the officials responsible for boosting the output of war industries to demonstrate that the trouble they were having in meeting their targets was caused by other officials who were administering the Pass Laws. The Cabinet instructed the police to stop arresting blacks for technical Pass Law infringements. The number of arrests fell sharply.

After 1942, as the Americans entered the war and the allies grew stronger worldwide, normal politics resumed command in South Africa – and the police resumed the rigorous enforcement of the Pass

Laws. Smuts had to face a general election in 1943 and could not afford to be accused of being soft on blacks. He won, thanks to support from the overwhelming majority of English-speakers and those Afrikaners who chose to back the side that now looked like winning, to the fact that many Afrikaners were repelled by the Nazi tendencies of their own more extreme nationalists, and to the full employment brought by the war (money in the voter's pocket always helps the party in power). The Broederbond tried to build an alliance between Malan's National Party and the various extra-parliamentary and Nazi groups that opposed the war, but those Afrikaners who had been hoping for German arms to help them seize power were not willing to fall in behind Malan. They attacked him and each other. Many Afrikaner voters abstained. Nevertheless, Malan's party came second, winning forty-three seats against eighty-nine for Smuts's United Party. Malan had laid down a marker for the future.

The contribution of Smuts and South Africa to the war effort was substantial. South African troops drove the Italians from Ethiopia, helped oppose Rommel's German army in North Africa and later – after Smuts had obtained parliamentary approval – took part in the re-conquest of Italy. Smuts turned the entire South African economy to war production, making bullets, bombs, gun-carriages, uniforms. To free resources, he introduced controls on raw materials and profits. South Africa exported so much food for Allied troops that the government had to introduce a rationing scheme for flour and the Minister of Agriculture to announce 'meatless days.'

Such measures were unpopular. Even more disliked by Afrikaner nationalists and poor whites was the influx of more than half a million blacks whom the war industries had by 1945 drawn into the cities. They lived in shanty-towns, behaved boisterously and threatened, once the war-time boom was over, to compete with Afrikaners for jobs.

Smuts wrote to a friend:

I have been giving my attention to the next moves to be made in our Native and Indian questions – both at present in a jam which must be broken . . . The fact is that both Native and Indian leaders want status. Mrs Ballinger [one of the Native Representatives] said in Parliament that in social and economic advances we have a strong case. But the Natives want rights and not improvements. There we bump up against the claim for equality . . . Small doses will not satisfy the leaders. I have so far done my best to follow the other line [of improvements] as less open to white prejudice and opposition. I must try again.

Smuts did not really have a race policy – just a vague paternalism subordinated to an unshakable conviction that white interests must come first. The heavy war-time demand for labour had led to increases in African wages, to school feeding schemes for Africans, to pensions for some categories of African employees and increased government spending on African schools in towns. In 1944, Smuts instructed government departments to address non-whites in letters as 'Sir' or 'Madam' (with Mr or Mrs on the envelope) – i.e. to stop addressing them by their first names and to treat them in this respect like whites. The concession provoked loud protests. The necessities of war – and his government's willingness to adjust to the changing needs of the economy and of urban blacks – seemed to be leading Smuts in an unexpected and politically hazardous direction.

CHAPTER NINE

The End of Acquiescence, 1936–46

The Cape common-roll franchise, which Sol Plaatje and other Congress leaders of his generation had so desperately hoped to extend northwards, was in 1936 finally abolished. The blacks protested noisily and then gave in, since they had no means with which to fight. Afrikaner newspaper placards proclaimed 'Naturelle bly stil' ('Natives stay quiet').

The most effective opponents of J. B. M. Hertzog's measure, a group of white liberals, secured the Africans some compensation. To muster the two-thirds majority in Parliament that a change in the franchise required, Hertzog had to concede that the proportion of South Africa's land to be set aside for native reserves be raised from 7.3 to 13 per cent. The Act that ended the common-roll franchise also created a trust to buy the land as quickly as it could persuade the government to give it the necessary money and introduced new forms of African representation. Black voters for the first time elected three white Members of Parliament (from the Cape) and four white Senators (from the country as a whole).

These seven 'native representatives' made more impact in the legislature than Hertzog expected. The first elections in 1937 were contested (by qualified franchise in the Cape, by chiefs' nomination elsewhere) and aroused some interest. And one of the MPs, Margaret Ballinger, proved a brave and persistent critic of the government. The African National Congress provided detailed information about living and working conditions which Mrs Ballinger and her colleagues, all needing to win re-election, supplemented by visits to native areas. The MPs and senators, it was widely agreed, used their knowledge skilfully to make the case for improvements in housing, employment, health and education. Mrs Ballinger went further and called for the Africans to be properly represented in Parliament by means of a common-roll franchise, like that recently abolished. It says something about the poor state of African organizations that the most effective voice of African interests was for some years the system of white representation set up by Hertzog.

As a further item of compensation for the loss of the Cape common-roll franchise, Hertzog conceded a Natives' Representative Council. To this body the Africans elected twelve of their leaders, whom the government undertook to consult on native issues. Again the Congress did its best to take advantage of the concession, and its members won several seats on the council. Here they met the Minister for Native Affairs, who would listen politely to their complaints and explain that what they asked required study by officials; then, at the next meeting, he would announce the beginning of consultations with all parties likely to be affected; and then, some months later, he would give the reasons, often convincing, why the proposed action was difficult. Usually the government was unable to provide the required funds. Douglas Smit, Secretary for Native Affairs, 1934–45, regularly did his best to meet African demands. Jan Hofmeyr, Finance Minister under Smuts, prided himself on the ingenuity with which he found money for native purposes in the face of competing demands from his Cabinet colleagues. But the sums found were always small, the improvements limited.

In 1941 the Africans spotted an encouraging signal. The British Prime Minister, Winston Churchill, and the United States' President, Franklin Roosevelt, signed an agreement, known as the Atlantic Charter, announcing the aims for which the Second World War was being fought. The Charter was part of Roosevelt's publicity campaign to persuade American voters to join the war, so it emphasized freedom, democracy and the right of people to self-determination. Nothing was further from Churchill's intentions than that these sentiments should be taken seriously in Africa.

When the Congress supporters on the Natives' Representative Council quoted the Atlantic Charter, the Minister for Native Affairs told them that the freedoms envisaged were indeed for Africans as well as white men, but he defined them narrowly, emphasizing freedom from fear, want and oppression. The Africans argued that the Charter must mean the replacement of the council itself by a proportionate place for Africans in Parliament and their acceptance 'as co-partners in this country'.

That was asking too much. The declared policy of Smuts's government was, where necessary, to improve African social conditions – at the price of vehement attacks from Malan's nationalists. After the 1943 elections, the President of Congress, Dr

A. B. Xuma, wrote to Smuts offering 'humble congratulations' and asking again for the basic freedoms outlined in the Atlantic Charter. Xuma led a committee of Congress in preparing a pamphlet, 'African Claims', which spelled out in detail what blacks in South Africa understood the Charter to promise them. It went way beyond previous Congress policy and included the abolition of the Natives' Representative Council and the extension of the vote to all adults. Before publication, before it had even been adopted as Congress policy, Xuma sent a copy to Smuts, asking for a meeting to discuss it. The Prime Minister refused to see him. As in 1912, Congress was submitting petitions, phrased in the moderate language of western liberals, to a government that put white interests first.

But something had changed. Between the 1936 and 1951 censuses, the number of Africans recorded as living in towns more than doubled, from 1.1 million to 2.3 million. Their concentration in industry was becoming sufficient to form the base for a mass movement. A group of Congress supporters decided that this opportunity must be exploited. In 1944 they formed a ginger group which they called the Youth League.

The man who gave the Youth League its ideas was a young Zulu, Anton Lembede. Where most of the ANC establishment came from wealthy African families who had paid for their education and often sent them abroad, Lembede was the son of a farm labourer. Largely self-educated, he earned his three university degrees by correspondence courses, while working to keep himself. Like many Africans, he had read about the Italian invasion of Ethiopia in 1935–6 and seen pictures both of Ethiopian soldiers bearing arms and of the Emperor Haile Selassie preparing to drive off the white aggressors. The sales of African newspapers that carried the stories had briefly boomed. In all of Africa, only two independent black states survived, and Haile Selassie led one of them. But the European army of Mussolini had conquered, and the liberal powers, for all their promises to protect Ethiopia by sanctions, had let it happen.

Lembede concluded that there was no hope for Africans so long as they relied on white men to win their battles for them. The old men of Congress nearly all wanted the esteem of white liberals and aspired to join them in the governing élite. Appalled by the idea of rabble-rousing among illiterate black workers, they were, in the words of the Youth League manifesto of 1944, 'a body of gentlemen with clean hands'. Lembede set about converting Congress to rabble-rousing. He was impressed by the discipline and determination of the National Party of the Afrikaners. He judged that what crippled most Congress leaders was a sense of their own inferiority, causing constant deference to whites. What they needed, he believed, was an Afrikaner-style ideology, based on pride in their own national past, confidence in their future and a burning love for their own God-given blackness. 'Look at my skin,' he used to say. 'It is black like the soil of Mother Africa.'

Unconsciously Lembede echoed Malan. He wrote:

We must verily believe that we are inferior to no other race on earth; that Africa and ourselves are one; that we have a divine mission of unifying and liberating Africa. We must develop race pride . . . We have to go out as apostles to preach the new gospel of Africanism . . . Minor, insignificant differences of language and customs . . . will not hinder the irresistible onward surge of the African spirit . . . Foreigners of whatever brand and hue can never properly and correctly interpret this spirit, owing to its uniqueness, peculiarity and particularity.

All nationalist movements seem to need such rhetoric.

Most previous Congress leaders had been careful to avoid encouraging anti-white or anti-Indian feelings. Lembede and his colleagues in the Youth League were less scrupulous. Again resembling Malan, Lembede was willing to arouse racism against others if that was the way to bring his own people to political awareness and action. He writings repeatedly depicted whites as evil in their behaviour towards Africans and condemned white liberals as purveyors of eyewash to deceive the outside world and lull Africans into a false sense of hope.

The Congress leaders greeted the new group with caution. The Youth League seemed determined to mobilize forces that might be impossible to control – but that might be the wave of the future. The young men's decision to operate in Congress rather than against it was a relief. But many of Congress's 5,000 members hoped that the war would change things for the better, that the vital contribution of Africans to industry would be recognized (as Smuts had hinted), that wounded, white soldiers would be grateful to the black stretcher-bearers who had carried them (and many of whom had won bravery awards), that collaboration would at last be rewarded.

The Youth League's belief that non-collaboration was the better policy was supported by a rash of spontaneous actions. Groups of workers showed that in the right circumstances black solidarity could win the day. In August 1943, in the township of Alexandra beside the Johannesburg–Pretoria road, the local bus company provoked the first proof. The fare for the daily journey to work was 4d. The company raised it to 5d. It was more than the Africans could afford. Some 15,000 clerks, messengers, cleaners and washerwomen chose to walk the nine miles to Johannesburg and back. For some this involved getting up at 3 a.m. and arriving home after 9 p.m.

Congress promptly set up a bus committee, but the initiative lay with the workers. They carried on walking until, after nine days, the company cancelled the rise.

That was act one of the Alexandra bus boycott. Fifteen months later, in November 1944, the bus company again tried to raise fares by 1d. This time the boycott lasted seven weeks. The township-dwellers borrowed cars from friendly Europeans and used horses, mule-carts, taxis, lorries and bicycles. And again the majority walked. The city council became involved and eventually set up a utility company, financed by a levy on employers, to provide the service at the old fare. For the first time, Africans had conducted a peaceful boycott and completely succeeded in their objective.

At Orlando, another location of grey, uniform boxes near Johannesburg, African workers surprised themselves by their collective power. The demands of manufacturing industry for labour, increased by the war, had led to over-crowding and insanitary conditions. In April 1944, a group left Orlando and built shacks of maize stalks, sacking and old crates on nearby municipal land. Soon thousands of homeless Africans from other locations around Johannesburg joined them, quickly creating a shanty-town. This was illegal and the trespassers knew it. They expected the Johannesburg authorities to throw them off, probably with force. They named their movement 'Sofazonke', Zulu for 'We shall all die'. But the council did not send guns against them. Instead it released funds to build weather-proof, breeze-block shelters for the shack-dwellers and arranged to lift the colour-bar on construction sites to enable black workers to get the dwellings built.

Orlando was one of the townships to the south-west of Johannesburg that were later given the joint name Soweto (short for south-western townships). Here some of the Youth League leaders, including Nelson Mandela and Walter Sisulu, lived, and here many of the meetings with Lembede, the movement's chief thinker, Oliver Tambo, and others were held. The total membership of the Youth League was about sixty. Most were young lawyers, teachers and doctors working in Johannesburg. They set out not to take over the leadership of Congress but to persuade the existing leaders to steer the movement in a new direction.

Success did not come quickly. Throughout 1944–6 the old Congress leaders devoted much of their time to organizing an anti-pass campaign, with the purpose of securing a million signatures on a petition. Surely with so many behind them they could not be ignored? The issue was never tested. Most blacks no longer believed, if they ever had, that passing round forms to gather signatures would do them any good. The climax of the campaign – handing the petition to Parliament and presenting their case to the Prime Minister – was repeatedly deferred to allow time to reach the million. Eventually the petition was delivered with many fewer signatures than promised and the Prime Minister and his deputy refused to meet the organisers.

In September 1945, following the Allied victory over both Germany and Japan, a 'Thank you General Smuts Day' was organized. Smuts was to speak at Johannesburg City Hall. Hours beforehand many Africans gathered to glimpse their country's leader and listen to him. As the time for his arrival approached, white military police drove the Africans away. Blacks had served in the war, but the victory celebration was for whites only.

In both Congress and the Natives' Representative Council frustration mounted. In August 1946, the willingness of the NRC to go on behaving as though the government was the Africans' potential benefactor was undermined. Some 50,000 African mine-workers went on strike in Johannesburg. Living cut off in compounds, present only for the duration of a short contract, so badly paid they were not expected to keep their families, let alone pay union dues, black mine-workers were among the most difficult groups for trade unions to organize. This time, after the Chamber of Mines had repeatedly refused to discuss a pay rise, a sixth of the labour force in the gold-mines stopped work. It was the biggest strike in South Africa's history. Police and armed guards soon sealed off the compounds and, faced with determined resistance, opened fire. In the subsequent disorder six blacks were crushed to death.

A few days later, while the strike was still going on, the NRC met. They had since 1938 been petitioning the government for a meeting-place of their own. Their request was repeatedly set aside, and they had taken to meeting in some comfort in Pretoria City Hall. In 1946 the nationalist majority on Pretoria Council refused any longer to let the NRC hire its premises. So the natives' representatives found themselves shepherded into cramped quarters in the Department of Labour, where the only lavatories were behind doors marked 'Whites Only'. The delegates had to leave the building to find non-white lavatories.

For ten years the Natives' Representative Council had done their best to play the role assigned to them. But the government's consultation of them was a farce. None of their main requests or recommendations had been implemented. Even their minor ones usually became stuck in administrative or financial mud. Smuts, since becoming Prime Minister, had never found the time to attend their sessions. In August 1946, the black members assembled under the chairmanship not of the Minister nor even the Secretary for Native Affairs, but a young under-secretary. When they asked for a board of arbitration to look into the miners' dispute, he told them he could not accept their resolution. When they asked to go to Johannesburg – a mere twenty-five miles away – to see what was happening for themselves, he again refused. Their impotence thus made manifest, they unanimously voted that 'the government forthwith abolish all discriminatory legislation affecting non-Europeans in this country' and adjourned the council indefinitely. One of them described their journeys to Pretoria as 'just a waste of time'. Another called the council 'a toy telephone'.

This was a turning-point. Since the foundation of Congress in 1912, its leaders had held back from outright confrontation with the government. They had criticized and grumbled, petitioned and appealed, but had always kept open the door to future co-operation. The August 1946 resolution demanding that Parliament repeal half the main laws it had passed in the previous thirty-six years closed that door. The chairman would have liked to refuse it as procedurally incorrect, but the twelve elected councillors all insisted and even the three government-appointed chiefs voted for it. No nationwide African political organization would ever again ask for less. The vote to adjourn indefinitely, ten years after Parliament had set them up, brought a long phase in the history of South Africa to an 'end: the last in a series of instruments through which black acquiescence had been secured had finally refused to work.

Hofmeyr, the deputy prime minister, wrote to Smuts: 'It means that the moderate intellectuals are now committed to an extreme line against colour discrimination and have carried the chiefs with them. We can't afford to allow them to be swept into the extremist camp, but I don't see what we can do to satisfy them, which would be tolerated by European public opinion.' Smuts replied that the government would have to liberalize its social policy and somehow carry the electorate along with it. He did not say how this could be done. He did not know. On policy towards the Africans – the majority of the population of the country – Smuts and his ministers were now completely baffled. The liberal principles they professed plainly told them to do what the makers of the American constitution had done in 1788 and the Whig grandees in Britain in 1832: open the doors of the franchise wide enough to win over the leaders of any potential challenge. But the courage to make such concessions comes to governments only in times of crisis and Smuts, while he could see what needed to be done, could not see how to shake his party or his electorate into doing it. Nor did he, in his late seventies, have the will.

CHAPTER TEN

The Apartheid Election, 1946–8

Alaric's sack of Rome in A.D. **410** or Lenin's arrival at the Finland station in 1917 are recognized as turning-points in history. Elections rarely provide such clear markers, but the 1948 election in South Africa has come to be seen as more like the sack of Rome than a normal election. It is generally believed that it led to the introduction of apartheid as the system governing relations between blacks and whites. It was certainly the occasion when Dr Malan put the word 'apartheid' into the world's political vocabulary.

Yet concerning black-white relations, the champions of the two main parties that fought the election, Smuts and Malan, had much in common. They had known each other since they were children in the little town of Riebeeck West in Cape Province. 'Jannie' Smuts, four years the older, sometimes took Sunday school, with 'Dannie' Malan in his class. Every fortnight, the Smuts family, wearing their best clothes, went to the Malans for dinner. At Stellenbosch University Smuts introduced Malan, his fellow student and protégé, to the debating society. When in 1947 Smuts wrote in a private letter, 'I am a South African European proud of our heritage and proud of the clean European society we have built up which I am determined not to see lost in the black pool of Africa,' he voiced both his own feelings and those of the man who was now his chief opponent.

The two had for decades supported the policy of segregation and saw no way it could be replaced. They were proud to be Afrikaners and found educated blacks puzzling. If this was 'the election that introduced apartheid', how was it that most of the laws that were to constitute apartheid had been introduced decades earlier, some when Malan was a member of Hertzog's Cabinet, busily making government and industry give jobs to whites at the expense of blacks, and others when Smuts and Hertzog served together, introducing Native Land Acts and removing blacks from the Cape common-roll franchise?

The answer is that what Malan and his party were seeking was not so much a new way to suppress the blacks, as the triumph of the Afrikaners over the British. They wanted to displace English-speaking South Africans from control of the main levers of power in the state. Apartheid, in the run-up to the 1948 election, was primarily a slogan for winning votes. Malan had no idea how it might be implemented in practice, or if so ambitious and wide-ranging a concept – the total removal of blacks from the towns and from any rights in 'white areas' – could be implemented at all. His party, in so far as they had thought about the matter, were fundamentally divided about what apartheid meant. They agreed, however, that it was the one issue that could arouse poor whites and farmers, between them the majority of the Afrikaner population, to political passion – that could unite Afrikanerdom behind the party.

Two of the drawbacks to apartheid had become evident in the years 1946–8, but neither of them worried Malan or his nationalists. The first was that the outside world began in these years to take an intrusive interest in South Africa's race relations policies, giving notice that the newly-created United Nations – the fruit of the Atlantic Charter – could create embarrassment and political problems for a democratic state that flouted its principles. The second was that highly qualified South Africans, after long and careful study of recent social changes in their country, reported that further to rigidify the existing pattern of segregation was not practical: it would not work. The years 1946–8 mark a sea-change because South Africa was in this period to steer away from the current of world opinion on a course that even its own chart-makers showed had become impassable.

In 1945, Smuts in South Africa was like Churchill in Britain, a victorious leader. The war had enhanced his reputation as a world statesman and, in recognition of the creative role he had played in 1919 in founding the League of Nations, he was appointed chairman of the commission that in 1945 drafted the constitution of the United Nations' General Assembly. Ironically it was in that very assembly soon afterwards that South Africa's race policies caused the country – and Smuts himself – to be placed for the first time in the world's pillory.

Once the stir created in the 1830s by Dr John Philip and his London Missionary Society colleagues had died down, the segregationist practices of whites in southern Africa, though oppressive, had come to be internationally accepted or, more commonly, ignored. The course on which the British Liberal government had launched the Union in 1910 and along which Smuts, the philosopher-statesman, had guided it ever since had been approved as within international norms. Smuts had been able to speak as a liberal abroad without suffering much criticism for being simultaneously a conservative at home.

In 1946 at the United Nations, India launched the first attack. The complaint did not concern South Africa's treatment of blacks, but of Natal Indians. Gandhi, who had led them in civil disobedience at the turn of the century, was now about to celebrate the independence of India. He had taken a continuing interest in his South African former clients and protégés and was dismayed when Smuts, whom he considered a friend, tightened legal discrimination against them.

Trouble had arisen in Durban, the capital of Natal. In the nineteenth century, Indian traders had bought premises and market-gardens there, and the expansion of the city turned these into Indian 'islands' surrounded by whites. In the 1930s, with the islands becoming overcrowded, some Indians bought property in white areas. As the purchases increased, the whites of Natal – nearly all English-speaking and Smuts's allies against the Afrikaner nationalists in supporting the war – demanded that the Indians be stopped from 'polluting' their areas. Smuts, remembering how Gandhi had stirred up public opinion in Britain against him more than thirty years earlier, adopted the cautious policy of a bill to 'peg' the situation in Durban, hoping to allow time for conciliation and review. By 1946 his time was up. The Natal whites demanded restrictions throughout the province on the Indian right to buy or occupy land. In India, newspapers and the Congress took up the pleas of the Natal Indians and denounced the proposal.

Malan had expressed himself publicly on the question: 'The Indian as a race in this country is an alien element.' The overwhelming majority of the whites in Natal, and probably throughout the Union, agreed with him. Smuts had, in a private letter, been equally forthright. 'What taunts flung at me,' he had written, 'and all because some utterly selfish wealthy Indians choose to spend their ill-gotten gains . . . in buying up the properties of whites and thus raising fears for the future of European civilization in South Africa.' Smuts kept up his efforts to secure a compromise that would forestall attacks from Gandhi. But when the British and Indians in Natal proved unwilling to agree terms, he saw no choice but permanently to restrict the Natal Indians' rights. In an attempt to silence his critics, he included in the bill provisions to give South African Indians for the first time representatives (who would be white) in the Natal provincial councils and in Parliament. The Natal Indians rejected this attempt to buy them off. They went on demanding the right to buy

property and live where they wanted, and denounced Smuts's
measure as the 'Ghetto Bill'.

In December 1946 the government of India placed the issue on the
agenda for the first session of the United Nations General Assembly.
Smuts flew to New York to answer the criticisms himself. Victory in
the public confrontation went to the Indian delegate, Mrs V. L.
Pandit. By appealing to fundamental principles of justice, she damned
South Africa's undeniably discriminatory new law. Smuts's reply –
that under the United Nations' own rules the matter belonged to the
internal jurisdiction of South Africa and should therefore be ruled out
of order – may have been legally correct, but it made little impact.
The General Assembly decided by a two-thirds majority that South
Africa's treatment of its Indian citizens threatened friendly relations
between two member states and requested their governments to seek
an agreed solution – the last thing that Smuts's electorate would
tolerate.

Smuts, badly mauled, sat in the UN delegates' lounge when Mrs
Pandit came over to him. Gandhi, she said, had told her 'that I should
shake your hand'. Smuts replied, according to Mrs Pandit's memoirs,
'My child, you have won a hollow victory. This vote will put me out of
power in our next elections, but you will have gained nothing.'

Smuts's words were no doubt soured by the humiliation of being
defeated by an Indian woman almost young enough to be his
granddaughter in a forum he had himself helped to create. The vote
was by itself not nearly as decisive as he told her. But in the Union it
did damage him. That his own much-vaunted United Nations had
kicked him in the teeth could hardly increase respect for his
judgement. Indeed, many South Africans thought he had for years
spent too much time out of the country, meddling in world affairs,
when he ought to have been dealing with their local problems. The UN
rebuff not only reinforced that view, it also contributed to a hardening of
European attitudes on race policy. Some whites demanded that all
285,000 Indians in South Africa be expelled. In the Transvaal, Europeans
boycotted Indian traders.

Smuts's difficulties were compounded by his deputy prime
minister, Jan Hofmeyr, the eloquent opponent of Hertzog's 1936 bill
to abolish the Cape common-roll franchise. Hofmeyr, the only other
South African politician in the same intellectual class as Smuts, was
short and fat and wore pebble glasses. He was one of those whom life
wounds. His health was poor, he never married, and he lived with his
mother until he died. For years Smuts had relied on Hofmeyr – on his
masterly debating to win difficult points in Parliament, on his loyal
supervision of government business to make possible those journeys
to meet allied war leaders and discuss strategy that were the
general's favourite pastime. Like Smuts, Hofmeyr felt it important to

satisfy himself that the policies he was currently pursuing were consistent with his liberal principles. Over the Asiatic Land Tenure and Indian Representation Bill, he did not find this easy.

Hofmeyr considered the property clauses in the bill a 'surrender to European prejudice' and the colour-bar the bill introduced into the Natal franchise a further surrender of principle. He wrote tortured letters to Smuts, before eventually accepting what he recognized as the price of political survival. Perhaps it was partly to salve his conscience that shortly afterwards he made a remarkable speech.

The University of the Witwatersrand was already the most cosmopolitan and richly endowed centre of academic excellence in southern Africa. Hofmeyr was its Chancellor and used its 1946 graduation ceremony as his platform to appeal for freedom from prejudice.

> Surely it is a mockery for us to talk of ourselves as a free people, while we are as a nation to so large an extent the slaves of prejudice, while we allow our dislike of the colour of our fellow South Africans to stand in the way of dealing with them . . . As long as we continue to apply a dual standard in South Africa, to assign to Christian doctrine a significance that varies with the colour of men's skins, we shall suffer as a nation from what Plato called the lie in the soul . . . May you be prepared to say with Thomas Jefferson, 'I have sworn upon the altar of God eternal hostility against every form of tyranny over the mind of man.'

The thunderous applause of the university – where he that day handed degrees to the first two black students to graduate from the medical school – helped buoy up Hofmeyr's spirits when he returned to Parliament. He told the House that he supported the 'Ghetto Bill' because it uplifted 'the at present still unrepresented Indian community'. As for the colour-bar franchise provisions, 'I take my stand for the ultimate removal of that colour-bar from our constitution.' J. G. Strijdom, the leader of the Transvaal nationalists and Malan's chief lieutenant, challenged Hofmeyr to endorse the maxim that the white man must be master. Hofmeyr replied that there could be no lasting relationship on that basis. His remark provoked, over the next few months, enough jeering to blight his life – and ruined the chance he appeared to have earned of becoming Prime Minister.

A slogan adopted for the election by some nationalists was 'Hofmeyr must be destroyed'. During a by-election meeting in January 1947 in the Cape constituency of Hottentots Holland, he was asked a question about the franchise and confirmed his earlier position: 'Natives will eventually be represented in Parliament by

Natives and Indians by Indians.' When the United Party candidate
for whom Hofmeyr had spoken was defeated in what had previously
been a safe seat, one newspaper commented that Hofmeyr had made
'a gift of the seat to the Nationalists'. Whether this was true or not,
he had certainly given them ammunition.

In Parliament the nationalists launched a barrage against him. One
MP said he was digging the grave of a European South Africa,
another that he was pursuing the downfall of 'white civilization'. J. G.
Strijdom was particularly sneering. Hofmeyr's conscience, he said,
'should be preserved for generations': how could the minister sleep
while 200,000 women in native areas were separated from their
husbands, brothers and lovers? The National Party produced a
pamphlet called 'Meet Mr Hofmeyr', quoting every statement that
seemed to show him as a supporter of black rights, black votes,
removal of colour-bars and the creation of 'a coffee-coloured race'.

Hofmeyr's defenders pointed to the handbook of the United Party:
'Our policy is to grant political rights gradually to those who prove
they are capable of meeting the corresponding obligations.' Hofmeyr
explained his views clearly:

> I am not in favour of a policy of assimilation. I have repeatedly
> stated that the essential differences between Europeans and
> non-Europeans must be taken into consideration. The policy of
> Christian trusteeship I have in mind does not mean suppression,
> nor does it mean equality. It means the realization of our
> responsibility not to ignore the interest of people of whom we are
> the guardians.

Hofmeyr had merely reasserted the case for qualified but
colour-blind franchise provisions and for humane trusteeship. But the
nationalists succeeded in portraying him as bent on opening the
floodgates to black rule. 'A vote for Smuts,' Malan warned the
electorate, 'is a vote for Hofmeyr.'

Early in 1947 George VI, King of South Africa as well as of Britain,
toured the Union accompanied by his Queen and their children. Malan
and some of his leading National Party colleagues attended parts of
the royal progress, but boycotted others. Smuts danced almost
constant attendance on the visitors throughout their tour, to the
contempt of some nationalists (and the annoyance of Hofmeyr, who,
as usual, had to deal with all the prime ministerial paper-work during
Smuts's travels).

The royal visit was partly a tribute to Smuts, an Afrikaner who
had become one of the great men of the British Empire, but it was
also a successful exercise in propaganda. Malan and his party were at
heart republicans. They wanted to break all links with Britain and its
king. But the royals were popular, Afrikaners turned out in thousands to

see them, were charmed by the young princesses, the future Queen Elizabeth and her sister Margaret, and many of them found themselves cheering.

In deciding his election tactics, Malan now faced a difficulty. The single issue that had united his nationalist supporters ever since his break with Hertzog in 1934 had been republicanism. And opposition to the war had fired a renewed determination to shake off British overlordship. But with the war won, and in the aftermath of the royal visit, it seemed out of tune with the public mood to emphasize the long oppression at the hands of the evil British and the importance of rejecting the monarchy. Instead, Malan and his colleagues did their best to rouse fear of communism, portraying Smuts as a communist and drawing attention to his praise for Stalin as a war-time ally. 'A vote for Smuts,' nationalists announced, 'is a vote for Joe Stalin.' But Churchill, Roosevelt and de Gaulle had been just as grateful to have communist Russia on their side, so this charge carried little conviction. As the election approached, only one issue seemed capable of swinging voters to Malan, the issue that underlay both the nationalists' Hofmeyr-baiting and the widespread resentment among whites at UN intervention in South African affairs – the black peril, *swart gevaar*.

Once before it had worked as an election-winner. In the 1929 election Hertzog had accused Smuts of being soft on the blacks. Hertzog had known it was not true, but it could be made to seem so because Smuts had opposed Hertzog's 'civilized labour' policies and his early efforts to abolish the Cape African franchise. The philosopher-statesman's liberal principles had then prevented him from entering the competition to utter the most racist slogans – and Hertzog had won the election.

This time Malan had an even better case for raising the *swart gevaar*. Not only could he point to selected quotations from Hofmeyr and to the interference of the United Nations in South Africa's domestic affairs, but he could also legitimately draw attention to the growing number of blacks working in the towns, to the farmers who had lost their black labour-force, to the many Afrikaners who were without jobs, to the softness of Smuts's war-time administration in enforcing the Pass Laws, to Smuts's 1942 Institute of Race Relations speech, to the Smit report, to the government's proposals – though little money had been spent on them – for improving the health, housing and education of urban Africans. The charge that Smuts's government was more concerned with the interests of blacks than of whites was untrue. But to many white voters it was plausible, particularly when, in January 1948, three months before the election, Smuts appointed Hofmeyr deputy prime minister, and thus heir apparent.

Smuts and Hofmeyr saw no choice but to grapple with the changing
reality of the economy and consequently of race relations. Smuts for
one did not like some of the changes that were happening, but he
recognized that it was impossible to ignore them. Strijdom said that
what the National Party wanted was white supremacy, *baaskap*,
with the blacks kicked out of the towns and returned to their proper
place, the native reserves: 'I say that in a bus I will not sit alongside
a Native.' To Smuts, such simple-mindedness in tackling a complex
problem was childish. To help clarify what he recognized as the most
divisive political issue his country had ever faced, and in the hope of
removing it from the forefront of politics, he appointed an
independent commission.

The whole subsequent story of apartheid needs to be seen in the
light of the findings of the Native Laws Commission. Its chairman,
Mr Justice H. A. Fagan, had once been a Nationalist MP and was
later to become Chief Justice of the Union. Appointed by Smuts in
August 1946, he delivered his report in March 1948, in time both to
influence the election and, if the incoming government chose to listen,
to help shape its policies.

The Fagan commission found that about 60 per cent of the natives
lived in so-called European areas and only 40 per cent in native areas.
Total segregation, therefore, required sufficient extension of the
native areas to enable them to house, feed and employ more than
twice the number then living in them. Furthermore, total segregation
required Europeans to stop using black workers. The commission
commented:

> We have seen no sign whatever in the country of a readiness to
> dispense with native labour. The best example is farming . . .
> Nowhere did we find the farmer considering the replacement of
> natives by European labourers as practical . . . On the contrary
> [farmers wanted] native labourers to remain on, or return to, the
> farms.

The commission found the arrangement by which most natives
living in towns were treated as temporary sojourners,

> a system which in the long run cannot be maintained other than on
> a limited scale . . . There may in every generation be a number of
> men and a few women who go forth without their families to work
> for a while and then return to their homes. If only a relatively
> small number of young people do that, well and good. But the
> greater the number who leave – and the more marriageable and
> married men among them – the greater is the economic, social and
> moral dislocation in the tribe where the broken families are left

behind: and the greater also the . . . consequent licentiousness, immorality and crime in the places to which they will go. Even if we lull our consciences and risk our safety in the tolerance of these evils, only a limited number of people will offer themselves for migratory labour and . . . they [will] be at work for only part of their lives.

The commission concluded:

Firstly that the idea of total segregation is utterly impracticable – in the words of a clergyman of the Dutch church who gave evidence: We need them and they need us; secondly that the movement of natives from country to town [is based on] economic necessity . . . and cannot be stopped or turned back; and thirdly that in our urban areas . . . there is a settled, permanent native population. These are simply facts we have to face . . . The old cry 'Send them back' . . . no longer offers a solution. The policy based on the proposition that the natives in the towns are all temporary migrants . . . has proved to be false . . . [This] admission, forced upon us by hard facts, makes it necessary for us to find a new formula for revision of existing legislation.

On behalf of the United Party, Smuts accepted both the principles and the proposals of the Fagan report.

While the Fagan commission was at work, the National Party set up a rival body, under the chairmanship of Paul Sauer MP, to draw up its race policy for the coming election. The Sauer report stated that South Africa's 'eventual ideal and goal' must be 'total apartheid between whites and natives', and called for 'a plan for the gradual reduction of the number of natives in the urban areas'. Its aim was 'the gradual extraction of natives from industries in white areas'. But its commitment to these objectives was weakened by the finding that Afrikaner businessmen and farmers needed their black workers. So 'total apartheid' would 'as far as it was practicably possible, be pursued gradually, and with the necessary care to avoid the disruption of the country's agriculture and industries.' Indeed, the report spelled out the need for 'labour bureaux' to recruit African workers to fill the growing number of vacancies advertised by white employers.

For party thinkers about to fight a general election in which their central campaigning issue was to be the need to save white civilization by means of apartheid, this was a disappointing conclusion. They handled the problem with some political acumen. The report's authors had done their best to speak with two voices without anyone noticing. They had outlined 'two stages' of apartheid.

In the first, blacks would be allowed to work in white areas, in the second they would not. But how long stage one would last and how industry would survive when it ended, the Sauer committee left totally unclear. The party thinkers took this fogginess one step further. They kept the Sauer report strictly to themselves. Few copies were made, and scarcely anybody outside the top ranks of the party obtained one.

On one crucial point the Fagan and Sauer reports agreed: that, if South Africa's manufacturing industry was to survive, total apartheid was a non-starter. To many in the National Party the conclusion was unacceptable. A group of them set up a body named SABRA (South Africa Bureau of Racial Affairs) to try to argue their way out of the dilemma. They were determined to prove apartheid viable. They put forward schemes for intensive immigration from the Netherlands and Germany to provide white workers, intensive mechanization to displace blacks. It was all highly intellectual – invented in universities and discussed in party committees – but it did not appeal to businessmen, even Afrikaner businessmen.

Consequently, the National Party entered the 1948 election campaign with a platform its leaders knew to be fatally flawed. Discussion at election meetings was sometimes difficult. When businessmen asked questions about the long-term prospects for the labour-force, or women voters asked if they would be allowed to keep their black cooks, housemaids and nannies, the answers had to be about the lengthy cushioning period offered by apartheid stage one. When unemployed or low-paid whites asked when their black rivals in the job market would be driven out of town, the answers had to raise hopes of the speedy arrival of apartheid stage two. The National Party in 1948 was not the first political party in a democracy, nor would it be the last, to enter an election committed to a policy that defied the facts of life in the real world.

The pamphlet it issued for the election, 'Race Relations Policy of the National Party', stated:

The choice before us is one of these two divergent courses: either that of integration, which would in the long run amount to national suicide on the part of the Whites; or that of apartheid, which professes to safeguard the future of every race . . . The fundamental guiding principle of National Party policy is preserving and safeguarding the White race . . . Churches and missions which frustrate the policy of apartheid will not be tolerated . . . Educational institutions and social services for blacks should be situated in the reserves, instead of the present practice of providing them in urban locations . . . Blacks in urban areas should be regarded as migratory citizens not entitled to political or social rights equal to those of the Whites . . . More land for the blacks in terms of the 1936 Act will be granted only after judicious consideration, but determined efforts will be made to encourage soil improvement and conservation . . . We have in mind the repatriation of as many Indians as possible . . . No Indian immigrants are henceforth to be admitted to the country . . . Our party will not tolerate subversive propaganda among the non-whites against the whites.

The oppressive tone of this document belonged to an Afrikaner tradition dating back to the early trekker republics. It matched Strijdom's frank statement that his purpose and the party's was white supremacy, *baaskap*. It was the tone of the poor whites in the towns, the small farmers in the countryside, men who felt vulnerable and feared that the rich English-speakers would negligently ruin them by making liberal concessions to the blacks. It was the bitter tone of a people who had tried unsuccessfully for more than a hundred years to secure Afrikaner ascendancy in an Afrikaner nation.

The liberal tradition, to which such Afrikaners as Smuts and Hofmeyr adhered, professed to be seeking to uplift the blacks. Secure in their superiority, backed by business and professional links with a still powerful empire, by a sense of having a right to dine at the world's top table, their language when discussing race relations was that of people with nothing to fear. Smuts and his party spoke for those, English- and Afrikaans-speakers alike, whose homes and careers and bank balances protected them from danger. They knew that no conceivable black advance that Hofmeyr and Fagan might propose could disrupt the even tenor of their ways.

Whether a widespread sense of insecurity, and of the need for apartheid to overcome it, was decisive in winning the National Party the election cannot be known. The result was an anomaly. Of the total vote, Smuts's United Party and its allies won 547,437, or 50.9 per cent, and Malan's National Party and its allies 443,278, or 41.2 per cent. But the Nationalists won many country seats where the electorate was small, while the United Party found itself winning wastefully large majorities in the towns. In the new Parliament Dr Malan commanded seventy-nine seats to General Smuts's seventy-one. The National Party in its 'purified', most extreme form, had at last got its hands on the levers of power.

CHAPTER ELEVEN

Baaskap, 1948–58

(a) . . . over the English-speakers

To Malan the opportunity was given to avenge his people's defeat in the Boer War. In the words of a character in Christopher Hope's novel, *Kruger's Alp*, 'If you couldn't out-gun the English, you could out-vote the bastards.' Malan was the first Prime Minister of South Africa not to have taken up arms against the British by serving in the Boer commandos. His three predecessors, Louis Botha, Barry Hertzog and Jan Smuts, had all emerged from the 1899–1902 war as generals. In the 1930s Hertzog had poured scorn on Malan because, at a time when they had risked everything, he had pleaded the need to continue his studies in theology. Now Malan's moment had come. Not only could he shake off the national humiliation of 1902, he could outdo the generals who had treated him with such disdain. Whereas they had all come to terms with the British and appointed English-speakers to their cabinets, he would have none. In May 1948, when he became Prime Minister, his cabinet was the first in the history of the Union to be composed entirely of Afrikaners and to conduct its business entirely in Afrikaans. He set out to secure Afrikaner mastery over all the arms of the state.

His government's first priority was not to introduce apartheid and thus further subjugate the blacks, but to secure Afrikaner supremacy over the English-speaking whites. The proof lies in his immigration policy. Smuts, during his last years in office, had encouraged white immigration, and tens of thousands had arrived, mostly from Britain. Such an inflow, if sustained, would have raised the proportion of whites to blacks in the population, an obvious gain for a government motivated by the *swart gevaar*. Malan's government, however, promptly put a stop to it. Immigrant ships due to sail from Britain were cancelled. Malan described Smuts's mass immigration scheme as 'opening the nation's doors to the riff-raff of Europe'. His government set about preparing a 'selective immigration' policy, whose purpose was to attract immigrants from Germany and Holland and, when that proved unsuccessful, to restrict new British arrivals so that they would not reduce the Afrikaners' 60–40 majority in the electorate.

To ensure that Afrikaner control would be unchallengeable, the Nationalists set about putting their own men – especially Broeders – into top posts. Their will was strengthened by an action Smuts had taken in 1945. He had argued that the Broederbond was a secret political movement and therefore membership was incompatible with the duty of officials to keep government secrets: loyalty had to be to the Broederbond or to the state. He therefore ordered any civil servant who was a member of the Bond to resign from it or face dismissal; 1,094 people resigned from the Bond (of whom more than 800 rejoined when the National Party came to power), a small number resigned from the civil service, and two were dismissed by Smuts for refusing to take either course of action. One of the two, Wentzel du Plessis, stood for the National Party in the 1948 election in Smuts's own constituency of Standerton. 'I am not a field marshal in the British army,' he told the voters, 'and I can't pick up the phone to Churchill. But I'll be the better representative of your interests.' He won the seat and Afrikaner Nationalists danced with glee at the rejection of the great war leader and friend of Britain – or, as they saw it, the great quisling. Soon afterwards Smuts retired from public life. In such circumstances, it was only to be expected that the new government would promote large numbers of Broederbond members at the expense of English-speakers.

Most of these promotions followed the death or retirement of officials. But the new ministers sometimes felt unable to wait. Little more than a month after the election, Major-General Evered Poole, who had successfully commanded South African troops during the Allied conquest of Italy and who was the clear front runner to become Chief of the Defence Force, was the subject of an announcement by the new Minister of Defence: General Poole had 'vacated' his post. In reality, as an English-speaker, he was shunted into a minor diplomatic job to enable the top army post to go to an Afrikaner.

In 1945, South African Railways, state-owned and the country's largest employer, had appointed its youngest-ever general manager, W. Marshall Clark. He resisted what he described as 'the repeated and earnest requests of the Prime Minister', Dr Malan, that he should retire at forty-five. Eventually he agreed to do so only on payment of £80,000 compensation – more than forty years' salary. Clark's ability was never questioned and he moved on to a successful career in business. His successor at the railways was a 58-year-old member of the Broederbond who, on retiring two years later, was followed by another Broeder.

The bench of judges, long accustomed to the British manner of promotion – by discreet soundings, longevity and mutual approval – were startled to find the new government promoting Afrikaners over the heads of senior English-speakers. The law libraries echoed with the outraged whispers of English-speaking barristers who suddenly found themselves pleading before Afrikaner judges many years their junior.

It was even more important for the Nationalists and the Broederbond to sew up Parliament. The government, with its tiny majority in the assembly, felt the need to be protected from the fickleness of the voters. The first step was to extend from two to five years the time-qualification for citizenship. This ensured that recent British immigrants would not be able to vote in the next election. The Prime Minister went on to secure himself a reliable six extra seats in the assembly and four in the senate by an Act, passed in 1949, to give South-West Africa representation in the South African Parliament. This was of doubtful legal validity, since South-West was not part of South Africa but had merely been 'mandated' into the Union's temporary care by the League of Nations, with a view to its being advanced towards independence. By providing for South-West to have MPs at Cape Town, Malan showed his contempt for the United Nations (which had taken over the League's role as overseer of mandates) and took a step towards incorporating the territory into the Union. Both were popular measures with his voters. Further, confident that the Germans and Afrikaners who lived there would support the National Party (nobody contemplated enfranchising the territory's black majority), Malan allotted South-West Africa a disproportionate number of seats. Where constituencies in South Africa contained between 9,000 and 12,000 voters, those he created in South-West had only 4,000. The National Party's majority in the assembly was doubled at a stroke. Malan remarked: 'This means that we can stay in power for another fifteen or twenty years.' It was an electoral cheat worthy of Cook County.

Next Malan set about removing the coloured voters from the common roll in Cape Province's fifty-five parliamentary seats. In the 1948 election, most of the coloureds had voted for Smuts's United Party. Their vote was significant in half the Cape constituencies, may have been decisive in seven, and could have been again in the future. So they had to be disenfranchised.

The method by which the government achieved this objective was significant. The constitution required a two-thirds majority in a joint sitting of both houses to amend the franchise. Lacking such numbers, the government got the measure passed in each house separately by a simple, though narrow majority. Four coloured voters challenged the resulting Act in the courts. A unanimous appellate division ruled that, as the Act had not been passed in the way laid down by the constitution, it was null and void.

The government tried again. It introduced a bill to create a committee of MPs that would be called the High Court of Parliament and would be empowered to overrule the Appeal Court. The same four coloured voters went to court to challenge this measure, and again they were upheld by the appellate division. By now it was 1954, and Malan, who was more than eighty years old and had qualms about browbeating the courts, had retired as Prime Minister. His successor was the unyielding leader of the Transvaal Nationalists, J. G. Strijdom, who resolved the issue by using procedures that did not need a two-thirds majority. Strijdom carried an Act raising to eleven the number of judges required to hear any case about the validity of an Act of Parliament. He also appointed five new appeal court judges, thus ensuring that a majority favoured the government's cause.

Further, to make doubly sure, Strijdom had the Nationalist majority in Parliament pass an Act enlarging the Senate from 48 to 89 members and changing the principle of selection. Instead of equal representation for each province, with senators chosen in proportion to the votes cast by provincial electoral colleges, the larger provinces (where Afrikaner Nationalists were narrowly in the majority) were given additional senators, and the new law provided that a majority of one in an electoral college was sufficient to elect all the senators for that province. English-language newspapers responded by regularly describing the upper house as 'the packed Senate', until the Speaker ruled it improper and unparliamentary language. Thereafter the English press amended the adjective, calling the house 'the enlarged Senate' and its members 'enlarged senators'. Such insults did no damage. Cook County's bosses had met their match.

Thus, after a six-year struggle, the Nationalist government removed the coloured voters from the Cape common roll. In the 1920s and 1930s, when seeking the disenfranchisement of Cape blacks, Hertzog had insisted that the 25,000 registered coloureds should retain the vote. He had wanted to give other coloureds throughout the Union equal status with whites. They nearly all spoke Afrikaans and had Afrikaner blood in them. Hertzog believed they could be relied on to stay close to the whites and reinforce them in any future conflict with the blacks. Malan took the opposite view, not only to punish the coloureds for their perversity in voting for Smuts, but also because he saw voting rights for coloureds as a possible advance guard for the blacks, and therefore to be eliminated.

The heights of the economy were harder for Afrikaners to scale. In 1948, some 90 per cent of South Africa's taxes were paid by English-speakers and their businesses. The great mining companies such as de Beers and the Anglo-American Corporation were among the world's largest companies, with shareholders in Britain and America and no disposition to appoint senior managers from among Afrikaners, most of whom they regarded as peasants. The main finance houses, insurance companies and international traders were likewise still British-owned, with few Afrikaners in top jobs. When an Afrikaner walked down his local high street, the shop-fronts left him in no doubt that nearly all the department stores, banks, petrol stations, cinemas, building societies and agricultural wholesalers were still controlled by the hated British. And those that weren't British were mostly Jewish or Indian.

The National Party had a strong socialist streak and some of its leaders were disposed to nationalize British assets. The state-owned steel corporation, ISCOR, set up by Hertzog's government in 1927, like the railways, showed how nationalization afforded the opportunity to promote Afrikaners. But taking control over mines and manufacturing, if it was not to disrupt profitable sectors, was bound to be slow work. In many fields of business, English-speakers complained that, after 1948, the government replaced the former practice of open tenders for official contracts by invitations to Afrikaner companies to tender privately.

The National Party government was aggressive towards English-speakers because its supporters, the Afrikaners, felt downtrodden and under threat. Only for the poorest among them did the threat come from the blacks. If Afrikaners took no action, the culture, language, banking system and international connections of their main historical enemies would almost certainly anglicize them. Contrariwise, to afrikanerize South Africa meant overcoming the most powerful alliance in the world of language, technology and investment – since Americans were the partners of the British in ownership of the strategic heights of the economy and consequently reinforced the English-speaking tendency. The sense that they were a beleaguered people fighting an uphill struggle constantly preoccupied National Party leaders. It sometimes made them seem a little humourless.

Their intense feeling of vulnerability to the British is vital to an understanding of the deliberate blindness of National Party leaders to the changing needs of Africans. Embattled against the British enemy in front of them, they responded to the economic advance of blacks as though it were a flanking movement threatening their rear. Most National Party voters – and consequently politicians – lacked the magnanimity that comes from self-confidence.

When, during their first two decades in office, they forced through their policy of apartheid, the National Party had to override some of the biggest financial, commercial and industrial interests in the state. In the years after 1948, the leaders of the fast-growing manufacturing sector of industry argued that what the country needed was an adaptable labour force, black as well as white, educated to the levels that were essential for efficiency. Equally important, they maintained, was growth of the internal consumer market, which could be most rapidly achieved by letting blacks climb the economic ladder. Both needs, the manufacturers insisted, called for the expansion of industry at existing growth points, i.e. where businessmen judged profitable. There they maintained the largely black labour force should be allowed to settle with their families, thus building up both skills and industrial stability. In 1943, for the first time, the contribution of manufacturing to the gross national product outstripped that of mining. For the new industries then developing, migrant labour was no longer adequate. Mine managers – still the country's principal earners of foreign exchange – found that it paid them to recruit a raw, new, cheap labour force every six months. Managers of more complex manufacturing plants could not cope with such a high rate of labour turnover.

The National Party government was prepared to overrule the demands of manufacturers because it saw itself as a revolutionary – almost an invading – force. Its purpose was to reverse the advances English-speakers had made since 1815 and resume the kind of control over *uitlanders* that had been exercised, the new republicans liked to think, by Paul Kruger, advancing Afrikaners into every possible seat of power, as he had tried to do, by taking advantage of the developing economic structure and finding within it *baantjies vir boeties*, jobs for the boys.

However, it was equally important for the new government to keep Afrikanerdom united. That was the vital prerequisite for winning the next election. Overruling the bosses, the 'capitalists', as both the National Party and the communists liked to call them, was popular with the party faithful. And the largest number of Afrikaner voters, the poorest section of the electorate, were truly worried by the competition and proximity of blacks. What they had voted for and expected their government to deliver was apartheid. Faced with, on the one hand, evidence that the introduction of total apartheid was likely to damage the fastest-growing sector of the economy – indeed, that some loosening of segregation was the only way to ensure the growth of manufacturing industry – and, on the other hand, the certain knowledge that failure to introduce apartheid would anger their most enthusiastic party activists, Malan and his ministers dithered and scratched their heads.

(b) . . . over the Blacks

As soon as Malan took office, the opposition began to taunt him, 'Tell
us, what is apartheid?' His replies were designed to reassure his
supporters and were presented in his usual determined style. But Malan
had little interest in 'native policy' (a topic that he curiously neglected
in his memoirs). *Swart gevaar* had done its job so far as he was
concerned, by helping him unite the Afrikaner voters behind his
party and thus gain power. He did not apply his mind to the
mechanisms by which apartheid might be made to work but was
content to tighten up the screws of the already proven system of
segregation and introduce a few dramatic-seeming measures to please
the voters.

The man he appointed Minister of Native Affairs, Dr E. G. Jansen,
was no ideologue but a lawyer so uncontentious that he had for some
years been Speaker of the House of Assembly. Jansen's policy
statements in the Senate were almost empty of the jargon of
apartheid and he worked happily with his department's senior
officials, all appointed in the Smuts years, mostly English-speakers
and by and large followers of the Hofmeyr-Smit school of meliorist
administration. Together they pursued a flexible approach, trying to
tackle practical problems such as soil erosion in the reserves and the
shortage of housing in the townships. They decided to set up a
commission of inquiry to advise how apartheid might be made to work.

The politics of the National Party demanded something different.
South Africa had reached a turning-point in black-white relations.
For fifty years government practice had been guided by an unstated
but consistent set of priorities: that whatever was required by the
mining industry, by the farmers and by the need to win white votes
should be done. Now manufacturing industry was demanding an
increased supply of permanent black workers. And the hardcore
members of the National Party had demanded that black workers be
removed from the towns. White trade unionists, mostly Afrikaners,
wanted to deprive their employers of cheap African labour, partly to
secure their own jobs, partly to remove the possibility of blacks
moving into their neighbourhoods, and partly to do down what they
liked to think of as the 'English-Jewish capitalist conspiracy'.
Farmers with small to medium holdings, most of whom were
Afrikaners, wanted black workers driven from the towns to increase
the supply of cheap labour on the land. In the face of such demands, a
scholarly rethink of 'native' policy by a commission of inquiry was not
good enough.

To several questions nobody knew the answers. Would the new
government resist the pressure from manufacturers that Marxists
had said could be resisted only by a revolution? Would they erect

ABOVE: J.B.M. Hertzog, first
leader of the National Party,
Prime Minister 1924-39 and,
like Smuts and Louis Botha, an
ex-Boer War general.

LEFT: Jan Christian Smuts,
Prime Minister, during the
1922 miners' strike. Nobody
was surprised when he sent
troops against black
dissidents, but his use of them
against white miners (below)
was a major cause of his defeat
in the 1924 election.

ABOVE: Black and coloured troops in the Second World War. Note: no weapons.

BELOW: Dr A.B. Xuma, President of the African National Congress, 1940 to 1949. The model of an old-style Congress leader.

RIGHT: Smuts photographing the royal family, Cape Town, 1947.

FAR LEFT: Dr Daniel Malan, high priest of Afrikaner nationalism and Prime Minister 1948-54, with his wife.

LEFT: Jan Hofmeyr, South Africa's leading white liberal who became deputy Prime Minister just before the 1948 election.

BELOW: The first all-Afrikaner cabinet, 1948. Seated, second from left, E.G. Jansen, Minister of Native Affairs 1948-50 (the man who was replaced by Verwoerd); third from left, Malan.

The Voortrekker Monument near Pretoria, formally opened in 1949
by Dr Malan: the shrine of the Afrikaner volk.

Passive resistance: the Indian campaign in Durban, 1946, (right) and the joint Congresses' Defiance Campaign against 'unjust laws', 1952.

barricades against the black tide? Would they go so far as to expel the blacks who were already in the towns? Even though the leaders of the National Party had known that the solution they proffered was over-simple, their election promise had seemed clear. Now they were in power, would they dare to act?

In their first two years, Dr Malan's government failed to answer these questions. They passed several measures of what came to be known as 'petty apartheid'. Suburban railway lines in the Cape region had been free of the colour bar. Parliament laid down that portions of all trains would in future be reserved for whites only. Since 1927, extramarital sexual intercourse between a European and a 'native' had been a punishable offence. The new government extended the offence to intercourse with any non-European, i.e. coloureds and Asians, making it necessary for the captains of ships calling at South African ports to warn their crews of new and surprising dangers in casual liaisons. Likewise marriage between white and black had long been illegal, and the ban was extended to marriage between a white and any non-white.

Malan also had Parliament pass the two enabling laws that were essential preconditions for 'grand apartheid', in whatever form it was eventually implemented. The first was the Population Registration Act, which required all citizens to be classified by race and the result stamped in their identity passes. Boards, set up to decide if borderline cases were white, coloured or native, caused great distress, particularly among coloureds; 100,000 people appealed against their classification. Some who were downgraded lost their jobs or had to move home. Some found they were married to spouses with whom continued habitation made them liable to arrest.

The second enabling law was the Group Areas Act. In some towns people of all colours lived side by side. The Act empowered the government to mark off areas for residence, occupation and trade by the different 'races' and then to move each race into its 'own' area, by force if necessary. While this opened the way for 'grand apartheid', its immediate purpose was to settle the National Party's debt to its poor white voters, many of whom lived in racially mixed areas and wanted coloureds, blacks or Asians moved out. They would vote for the party next time if it carried out the evictions. Otherwise they might turn to an even more extreme saviour. When native representatives, MPs and churches (though not the Dutch church) opposed the measure, Malan told them that the question they should really be asking was: 'Why did the Creator make the mistake of creating countries, nations and languages? He should not have done so . . . and in addition the Creator also proceeded to create different colours. I say that [opposition to the measure] is a charge against Creation and the Creator.'

In spite of his continuing eloquence and political deftness, a section of the National Party voiced dissatisfaction at Malan's sloth in introducing total apartheid. They saw the potential command-post of change as the Native Affairs Department and they wanted Jansen and the moderate-minded senior officials removed. The leaders of this group included a young party organizer newly elected to Parliament, P. W. Botha. In October 1950, Malan acted. He appointed Dr Hendrik Frensch Verwoerd to be Minister of Native Affairs. This was the real turning-point. A man with an unusually powerful intellect and an absolute determination to make apartheid work was at last in charge of the crucial ministry. If anybody could reshape the facts of economic and social life to fit his party's theories, Verwoerd could.

Converts often make the strongest believers. By birth Verwoerd was not an Afrikaner. He was born in Holland in 1901 and, when he was two, emigrated with his parents to Cape Town where he was sent to an English school. When he was nine, the family moved to Southern Rhodesia where, again, he went to a school that taught in English. Young Hendrik was a rebel. At the start of the First World War, he shocked the imperialist British headmaster at the Milton Boys School, Bulawayo, by speaking up for the Afrikaners a few hundred miles to the south who were resisting South Africa's participation on Britain's side in the war. Then, in 1915, the Verwoerds moved again. Hendrik's father took up work selling bibles and religious tracts in the Orange Free State, the heartland of Afrikanerdom. Here in 1912 J. B. M. Hertzog had established the political base of his rapidly growing National Party and in 1913 Afrikaner leaders had unveiled the *Vrouemonument*, commemorating the 26,370 women and children who had died in British concentration camps in the Boer War.

On graduating from Stellenbosch University, Verwoerd was offered a scholarship of £300 a year, then a princely sum, to go to Oxford. He turned it down, choosing instead to stay at Stellenbosch and prepare the first Ph.D. thesis in psychology to be written in Afrikaans. Only after its completion did he accept a foreign travel bursary. It was worth half the Oxford one and enabled him to continue his studies in Germany, that other victim of British power.

On his return, Stellenbosch appointed Verwoerd Professor of Sociology and in 1934 he was asked to help organize a conference on poverty among whites. He told the delegates that the provision of jobs for whites in towns 'can succeed only if the Native is provided for elsewhere . . . even if this is less attractive to him . . . for example through improved economic development of the re-serves . . .' Thus, sixteen years before he became Minister of Native Affairs, the policy that he was later to implement as 'separate development' was fermenting in his mind.

In 1935, the Purified National Party chose Verwoerd to edit the
newspaper that it planned to start in the Transvaal. He gave up his
professorship and moved his family to Johannesburg. He launched
the new paper, *Die Transvaler*, with, in his own words, 'a mission to
serve the volk by making the voice of true and sublime nationalism
resound'. The paper regularly disparaged the English, Jews and
blacks – though Verwoerd avoided the verbal crudities of the Nazis
that he had recently seen in Germany. For example, he argued that
Jews should be refused admission to South Africa mainly for their
own good. Doing things to people 'of other races' and 'for their own good'
was to become the dominating theme of his life.

His most remarkable feat as editor came in 1947. When all other
South African newspapers were filled with news and photographs of
the royal tour by King George VI and Queen Elizabeth, when
hundreds of thousands of Afrikaners came onto the streets to glimpse
their king and queen and many stayed to cheer, when the Prime
Minister and his cabinet and mayors, businessmen and civic leaders
welcomed the royal family, when the king opened Parliament in Cape
Town, Dr Verwoerd did not allow *Die Transvaler* to mention the
royal presence once. In the ten weeks from their arrival in southern
Africa until their departure, not a word.

The next year, when the Nationalists won power, Malan had
Verwoerd appointed to a seat in the upper house of Parliament, the
Senate. There he reinforced his reputation for always having
ingenious arguments ready to support party policy. Verwoerd
treated the Senate, as he did all audiences, like a class awaiting his
social science lecture. His speeches were never short, or amusing, or
designed to beguile. He knew he had important things to say, often
complicated and analytical, and he was determined to utter every last
syllable. Where Malan could inspire with his religious conviction,
where Strijdom spoke with a rasping determination to put Afrikaners
on top, Verwoerd revealed slowly, in convoluted paragraphs which
only those in the party appreciated, that he had thought through
their policies more fully than anyone else. Above all, he had planned
how to introduce apartheid. Where for Malan it was a great
vote-winner but a possible threat to the economy, for Verwoerd it
was an intellectual and administrative challenge that had to be met.
When, in 1950, he was appointed Minister of Native Affairs he
became the Great Induna, chief of chiefs, ruler of all the Africans in
South Africa, i.e. of ten million people, almost 70 per cent of the total
population. He set about his task of reform with the drive, vitality
and self-confidence of Napoleon leading his armies to war.

As a minister, Verwoerd was able to address the elected House of
Assembly, and in his first year he delivered five long speeches there.
When opposition members yawned loudly, he told them that the

ruder they were the longer he would speak – and resumed the explanation of his master-plan. Verwoerd revived all the arguments of the liberal segregationists of the early twentieth century: separate development was in the interests of the blacks, their traditional institutions would be restored and respected in homelands where they could to a substantial extent govern themselves, saving them from losing their distinct and valuable cultural heritage in the European-dominated mêlée of the cities. Eventually, separate development would lead to the establishment of a number of African homelands, responsible for their own local government, which would be able to form a confederation with their great protector and friend, white South Africa.

To the Sauer report's dilemma of a present and foreseeable future during which blacks were needed to work in the towns, followed by an unspecified future date after which they would be excluded, Verwoerd offered a verbally elegant solution. In between, he explained, would come the saturation point, when the labour needs of white-owned industry would be fully met, the black inflow would stop, white workers would increasingly displace blacks, the black outflow would begin, and the ideal of total apartheid could at last start to be realized. Meanwhile, he set his department to work to control the inflow immediately, intervening to make sure that in every town throughout the Union blacks who did not have jobs with white companies were hunted out and sent to the reserves.

The key to Verwoerd's policy was tribalism. Under the Minister of Native Affairs, conservative chiefs in the reserves must be encouraged to reassert their dwindling tribal authority, to win back control over those of their people who had gone to the cities and to restore the traditional beliefs and practices that contact with whites – especially with white education – had undermined. Naturally the Africans who bore the burden of reviving their largely moribund tribal traditions had to be rewarded for their efforts. Salaries and privileges were provided for chiefs and headmen in the first step towards Verwoerd's grand design, the Bantu Authorities Act of 1951.

Verwoerd himself paid a succession of visits to African kraals, or villages. His local officials ensured in every case that the traditional ceremonies for welcoming a great chief were re-enacted in all their ancient splendour, with such cries as 'Rapula!' (the rain bringer) or 'Sebeloke!' (the patron). The formal and verbose exchanging of gifts was followed by a meal in which Verwoerd and his civil servants joined their hosts in a circle round a pot of mealie-porridge. Sometimes an ox would be roasted on a nearby spit, to be eaten with handfuls of the porridge and washed down with Kaffir beer. Verwoerd would then make his speech as the Great Induna, the protector of tribal customs, explaining how he understood and sympathized with the plight of the chiefs, their young men not only going away to the cities to work but returning puffed up with radical white men's ideas that threatened the centuries-old dignity and honour of the chieftainship. He also had to sit listening to long speeches from the chiefs which, for a man of his temperament, was no easy task. To help the chiefs and headmen, the Native Affairs Department arranged training courses. These taught the techniques of modern administration as well as procedures to ensure that the Department's officials kept ultimate control.

For the academic and precise Verwoerd, this enthusiastic championing of traditional tribal authority was in one respect odd: it was a procedure which the most eminent expert on such matters had a decade earlier pronounced dead. In 1938 one of the British Empire's top colonial administrators, Lord Hailey, had written his famous, massive *African Survey*, a report on government throughout the whole of Africa, in which he had concluded that 'indirect rule' – by which white governments had used headmen and chiefs to conduct local administration – could not long survive. Educated young Africans, Hailey had reported, would not put up with it, and they were the people whose support had to be mobilized if their societies were to progress.

Verwoerd was undeterred by such arguments or by the fact that South Africa had more city-dwelling, educated Africans than any other part of the continent. He was determined that the chiefs would be his allies in imposing a system built on what survived of ancient tradition and forcing the majority of Africans to live within it. He enjoyed some striking successes. In 1955 his Bantu Education Act was passed. This transferred control of schools for Africans from provincial councils to the Department of Native Affairs, in order to counter the influence of missionaries and others whose attitude to education was too liberal. Verwoerd explained why the measure was needed:

> My department's policy is that Bantu education should stand with both feet in the reserves and have its roots in the spirit and being of Bantu society . . . There is no place for [the Bantu] in the European community above the level of certain forms of labour . . . What is the use of teaching the Bantu child mathematics when it cannot use it in practice? That is quite absurd. Education must train people in accordance with their opportunities in life, according to the sphere in which they live.

The new apartheid syllabus that Verwoerd's department introduced stressed teaching in native languages – a particularly poor basis, it was found, for further study in maths or physics. Teachers who objected were posted to remote parts of the country; 116 of them were sacked. Black parents were told that, if their children did not attend the reformed schools, they would not be admitted to any form of state-assisted education. Verwoerd proved he meant it by having 7,000 children removed from school registers. He withdrew government grants from church schools that tried to defy his instructions. Where missions or groups of blacks tried to start new schools, he used the power the Act gave him to refuse them permission to open.

Soon afterwards his department's journal, *Bantu*, sent free to tribal administrators and school principals, carried a poem entitled 'Dr Verwoerd, Minister of Native Affairs' by an African named H. Kharibe. Part of it reads (in translation):

Dr Verwoerd, thou art with us! Glory unto thee our redeemer,
Praises be unto Dr Verwoerd, the defender of the Bantu,
He that helped the chiefs by giving them good laws,
He that gave our schools proper education,
Because he knew what we needed and we could not manage.

Verwoerd subsequently said that the poem was published without his consent, that it was just one example out of many 'given of their own free will by Bantu' of their warm feelings towards the government and its policy.

A more important success was Verwoerd's victory over the Transkei Bunga. Under the old system of government in Cape Province, the Transkeian Territories General Council, usually called the Bunga, had been the most important native authority in the country. Its 103 members, two-thirds of them elected, exercised some local authority powers over a million and a half blacks. In 1952 they refused to accept Verwoerd's introduction of a system of local government that they regarded as based on a false traditional tribalism. He came to put his case to them, persuaded them that his Bantu Authorities Act increased the scope for them to raise money for betterment schemes and, in 1955, as a direct result of his visit, the Bunga, after fifty years' existence, voted to abolish itself, making way for tribal administration under the new Act.

Since tribal government and education were to be the wave of the future, Verwoerd set about removing all traces of the system by which Africans had elected representatives to put their views to the administration in Pretoria. In 1946, after the Natives' Representative Council had voted to adjourn indefinitely, Smuts had invited some of its black members to consider a proposal to enlarge the number of elected members and to give the Council some legislative powers. The members had rejected Smuts's proposal as inadequate, so

Verwoerd knew they would find even less acceptable his proposal that in future all representation of Africans would be through their chiefs. He summoned the Council to Pretoria and told them they were to be formally abolished. Verwoerd asked them:

Must the future development of the Bantu and White societies take place together, or separated as far as possible? If together, then rivalry and clashes will take place everywhere. In such clashes, the whites will come off best, at least for a long time . . . This will inevitably cause growing resistance and resentment. For neither the White nor the Bantu can such a situation offer an ideal future . . . The only possible way out is that both accept development apart from each other . . . The present government believes in the domination [*baaskap*] of whites in their own areas [and] of Bantu in their areas.

Such statements brought Verwoerd trouble from some National Party MPs. The idea of creating truly self-governing institutions for blacks and of investing heavily in the reserves – as was essential if blacks were to be drawn out of the cities – was to many whites unacceptable. So in Verwoerd's scheme both steps – and the eventual need to buy enough land to make the homelands viable – were set aside until the final phase of his apartheid timetable:

Always we have said that the road of apartheid is a long road . . . a party is not concerned with fulfilling what is to take place along the entire road . . . People assert that if, at the end of the next fifty years, six million natives will still be in the white areas, that proves we have jettisoned our policy of apartheid. It is untrue . . . The year 2,000 is one of the stations on the road to our ideal. It is not the end . . .

While Verwoerd toured the country persuading black traditionalists to co-operate and argued day and night with fellow ministers, civil servants and party colleagues that he had the key to the future and the complete moral, practical and political answer to every question, the official commission of inquiry, set up in 1949, shortly before he became a minister, went painstakingly on with its work. Malan had appointed an agricultural economist, Professor F. R. Tomlinson of Pretoria University, to chair the inquiry because agricultural development in the native reserves was thought the most likely way to make apartheid work. Verwoerd had made it clear he had no need of the commission. He knew what to do. And Tomlinson, after five years' study, produced a report that in Verwoerd's view was overloaded with irrelevant facts.

Unless economic development can be diverted from its present geographical concentration [the commission reported in 1955], the Bantu share of the urban population will increase . . . Bantu are leaving the reserves in ever-greater numbers to settle permanently in non-Bantu areas [because of]:

1. The undeveloped and backward state of the Bantu areas;
2. The slow rate of progress in the purchase of land [to bring the reserves up to 13 per cent of the total area] under the 1936 Act;
3. The large-scale economic integration of the past decade;
4. The slow and half-hearted manner in which administrative powers were conferred on the Bantu in the Bantu areas.

The commission concluded: 'The policy of separate development is the only means by which the Europeans can ensure their future unfettered existence, by which increasing race tensions and clashes can be avoided, and by means of which the Europeans will be able fully to meet their responsibilities as guardians of the Bantu population. The European population should therefore be willing to take the necessary steps to put this policy into effect.' This meant 'large-scale sustained development of the Bantu areas'. To have any hope of becoming economically viable, the 260 separate, scattered native reserves had to be consolidated into seven blocks. Given the present rate of growth of existing manufacturing centres, some industry must immediately be developed in the reserves or there was no hope for them. The commission estimated that, in the next ten years, development in the reserves would require £104 million.

The money was a problem. The government agreed that the return of the blacks to the reserves was the right policy, but it was not prepared to spend the sums needed to make the reserves viable. The government even agreed with the commission's finding that the scattered land of the reserves must be consolidated, but added: 'It is however unrealistic to indicate . . . boundaries . . . which involve European land, the acquisition of which cannot possibly now be considered.'

Tomlinson, many of the civil servants who worked with Verwoerd and the Afrikaner intellectuals in SABRA – the South African Bureau of Racial Affairs – were sincere in demanding total apartheid. They were prepared to campaign for the large financial sacrifice by the white community that would be required, knowing that the gold and diamond mines were earning well and the economy could bear the cost. Most of them supported the policy because they believed it was the only way to ensure the long-term survival of the whites.

Verwoerd himself, however, was far too canny a politician to be unaware of his policy's two glaring inconsistencies. The first was that the reserves could be made to accommodate the blacks only at a price in investment that the South African electorate would never make available. The second was that the urban blacks were to be immediately deprived of all rights, on the promise that at some time in the future they would acquire rights in reserves, but of a kind that their political leaders – and independent evidence – indicated they did not want. What the blacks wanted, according to those who spoke for them, was to be allowed to stay in the cities, where the demand for their labour was growing, and to be granted the normal rights of citizens – to live with their families and to influence their own circumstances by use of the vote.

Tomlinson had confirmed the Fagan report's finding that 60 per cent of Africans lived in 'white' areas. Many of them had been born and brought up far from the tribal homelands where their parents or grandparents were born. Some were children of mixed marriages (of couples from different tribes) and were so completely detribalized they had never seen their parents' home areas and had no remaining links with them. How was apartheid to deal with those among them who had lived all their lives in 'white' towns? Verwoerd answered:

> The Bantu in the cities are not distinct from the Bantu in the Native Reserves. They belong to one another . . . Bantu are visitors in the white areas . . . for their own economic benefit. Their roots are in the Native Reserves. The opportunities for them to enjoy rights, whether they be social or political rights, are available in their home areas.

By the mid-1950s the hope of the liberal segregationists was at an end. When the government refused to spend the sums the Tomlinson report said were urgently needed and refused to recognize that apartheid ignored the legitimate concerns of the urban blacks, its policy had to be acknowledged as one of naked domination. Malan never said so publicly, nor did Verwoerd. Both made much of their adherence to Christian principles. But in April 1955 Malan's successor as Prime Minister, J. G. Strijdom, gave Parliament his own authoritative version of the truth about apartheid:

> Call it paramountcy, *baaskap* or what you will, it is still domination. I am being as blunt as I can. I am making no excuses. Either the White man dominates or the Black takes over. I say that the non-European will not accept leadership – if he has a choice. The only way the Europeans can maintain supremacy is by domination . . . And the only way they can maintain domination is by withholding the vote from the non-Europeans. If it were not for that we would not be here in Parliament today. It is because the

voting power is in the hands of the White man that the White man is able to govern South Africa today. Under existing law it is not possible for the Natives, through merit or any other means, to get the government into their hands. The government of the country is in the hands of the White man as the result of the franchise laws, and for that reason the White man is *baas* in South Africa . . . To suggest that the White man can maintain leadership purely on the grounds of his greater competency is unrealistic. The greater competency of the White man can never weigh against numbers if Natives and Europeans enjoy equal voting rights.

CHAPTER TWELVE

Defiance, 1946–56

The election of 1948 did not at first greatly affect the African nationalist movement. Chief Albert Luthuli, who was soon to become ANC President and later, to the disgust of most South African whites, to receive the Nobel Peace Prize for the pacifism and restraint of his leadership, wrote: 'The election seemed largely irrelevant. We had endured Botha, Hertzog and Smuts. It did not seem of much importance whether the whites gave us more Smuts or switched to Malan. Our lot had grown steadily harder, and no election seemed likely to alter the direction in which we were being forced.'

The question for the African nationalists was whether they were at last going to pull themselves together and confront the government effectively. Regional and tribal divisions and a chronic predisposition to give the white man the benefit of the doubt had long impeded their effectiveness. Now these were made worse by bitter arguments about theory. Should the black bourgeoisie be treated as natural allies of the white oppressors? Should the ANC continue to move only at a pace acceptable to chiefs and headmen? Should a black vanguard commit the movement to Africanism and reject the proffered help of Indians, white liberals and communists? Was the problem they faced one of race or one of class? When their hour of triumph arrived, what would they do about white people's property?

The 1948 election was to help them answer some of these questions. In Luthuli's words: 'I doubt whether many of us realized at the time that the very intensity of Nationalist oppression would do what we had so far failed to achieve – awake the mass of Africans to political awareness, goad us finally out of resigned endurance.'

Under Smuts's United Party government, Jan Hofmeyr, Douglas Smit and others – even Smuts himself when he gave African affairs his attention – had been prepared to listen to the representations of leading blacks and, within limits, do what they could to prevent trouble. Once Malan became Prime Minister – and particularly once Verwoerd became Minister of Native Affairs – willingness to listen was at an end. Afrikaner Nationalists, people who were members of his own party and his supporters, found Verwoerd a bad listener. If he invited them for a chat, this often proved a three-hour monologue – and uninterruptible. To nationalist-minded blacks he was not even prepared to speak, let alone listen. It was largely in response to his deaf pursuit of increased segregation that Congress and the African nationalist movement, for so long a babble of contradictory voices, at last became to some extent united. At least they agreed in saying: 'We do not consent.'

In conveying this message, Indians and their ideas became important. The reason was the great impression they had made in 1946 by their resistance to the Asiatic Land Tenure and Indian Representation Bill. The pillorying of Smuts at the United Nations, which they had brought about, was a spectacular achievement. No African protest had ever made so much impact. It had certainly shaken the Prime Minister and provoked a strong reaction from whites. It may even have played a significant role in causing the United Party's election defeat.

Nor had the Indian community rested on their laurels. When the bill they had resisted became law, they boycotted the concession it gave them – the chance to vote for a few whites to sit in all-white councils. Their impressively unanimous refusal to use the segregated franchise was backed by a two-year campaign of civil disobedience. They occupied sites in white areas of Durban and illegally crossed provincial borders. More than two thousand of them were arrested. Gandhi, with more urgent matters preoccupying him in India, was proud of them. What impressed ANC leaders was not that these activities changed the government's policy, which they did not, but that they showed how skilful organization of the people could make the world aware of the government's pettiness.

The ANC had already begun to enjoy support from Indians. In 1946, the Indian government and the South African Indian Congress had helped the then President of the ANC, Dr A. B. Xuma, a respected medical practitioner in Johannesburg, to put the Africans' case at the first session of the United Nations in New York. Xuma attended a reception at which Smuts was present. The two had never met, and Smuts's secretary brought them together. 'Xuma, my dear man,' said the field-marshal, 'what are you doing here?' 'Well, sir,' replied the doctor, 'I have had to fly ten thousand miles to meet my Prime Minister. He talks about us but he won't talk to us.' 'Man alive!' said Smuts, 'let's get together. You know, Xuma, I am a most misunderstood man.' Smuts was then drawn away to speak to another delegate – and never took up the chance to tell Xuma why he was misunderstood (though he is said to have been surprised and pleased to meet a South African black who was so cultured).

Indians from Natal became active helpers of the ANC in spite of growing support in Congress for Anton Lembede's Africanism, with its call for blacks to fight alone. Lembede died unexpectedly in 1947, and even his Youth League colleagues, Nelson Mandela, Walter Sisulu and Oliver Tambo, decided he had been wrong to reject alliances with other races. They all formed close links with radical Indians in planning the next steps for their movement.

Likewise white communists became increasingly influential in the ANC. The Allied pact with Stalin during the 1939–45 war had led communists for the first time to be respectable in South Africa. Two communist newspapers were for a while published without harassment. In 1947, Lembede's Youth Leaguers tried to have communists excluded from the ANC annual conference, but the older ANC élite had always run the movement as a broad church in which all strands of opinion could find a home, and won the vote to let the communists stay.

In 1950 Malan's government carried the Suppression of Communism Act (for details see page 121), which proved the single most potent boost to communist activity in the ANC. The Communist Party dissolved itself, to forestall the police. Most of its 1,500 members wanted to remain politically active and many of those who had not already diverted their energies into the ANC now did so.

Another significant group for whose support the African nationalists had to thank the post-1948 government was drawn from the coloured community. Formerly the overwhelming majority of the coloureds had been allied to the whites. The Population Registration Act, most of whose victims were coloureds previously accepted as white, and the ban on whites marrying or having sex with coloureds led a substantial proportion of this well-established community of more than a million people to change sides. Most coloureds lived in the Cape and worked in skilled trades. Those of them who joined the nationalist movement brought, as did the Indians, the useful ability to pay dues.

Maintaining the unity of all these groups was not easy. The story of Sophiatown reveals some of the difficulties. Four miles to the west of central Johannesburg, Sophiatown was one of the areas where Africans had succeeded in buying freehold land before Union law forbade it. A nearby municipal dump reduced the area's attraction, enabling many Africans in the early years of the century to afford property there. As segregation was enforced in the 1920s and 1930s, blacks were removed from predominantly white areas and Sophiatown, convenient for industrial jobs, filled up with those who had been displaced. By the 1950s it was a crowded inner-city suburb, with a few rich landlords, both black and Indian, letting out rooms, and many poor householders who went out to work and let space in their homes to top up their incomes. Dr Xuma, the wealthy medical practitioner and until 1949 president of the ANC, lived there. So did wandering vendors of beads and petty services who earned less even than industrial workers and were too poor to afford a cart.

White citizens demanded the removal of this 'black spot' from central Johannesburg. Manufacturers persuaded council and Native Affairs Ministry officials that the consequent loss of their labour supply would be disastrous. For decades no action was taken. After 1948, the government took a more interventionist attitude. It became the policy of the Native Affairs Department to control the number of Africans coming into the towns. Unlike officially-controlled townships, Sophiatown was an informal place where a newly arrived African could earn a little by casual work, prostitution or joining one of the gangs that ran protection rackets, and where he could rent a corner of a room without anyone in authority finding out. More significantly, Sophiatown became a centre of ANC, communist and Indian joint resistance campaigns – against a rise in tram fares, against police attempts to control illegal liquor-brewing (an important source of income for many older black women), against the enforcement of the Pass Laws. Sophiatown acquired the reputation of being a hotbed of resistance. It had to go.

Johannesburg City Council, controlled by the United Party, dragged its feet over the cost of building a new township and over the obligation to offer Sophiatown freehold owners equal title elsewhere. So, in 1951, the Minister of Native Affairs, Dr Verwoerd, announced that the 'black spot' and some adjacent areas with a total population of 58,000 were going to be cleared and a new township built fifteen miles away to house those displaced. Expropriated Africans, he made it clear, would not be granted freeholds.

The ANC saw Sophiatown as a challenge. The government seemed to regard success as crucial to the implementation of apartheid. For the African nationalist alliance too it became a key battle. However, the ANC found some new allies with whom it was unhappy. Its national leaders' commitment to use non-violent methods was overruled by local leaders who enlisted criminal gangs to support the cause. One Sophiatown ANC leader, Robert Resha, had gangsters in mind when, in February 1955, a few days before the removals were due to start, he told the young men of the area 'to stop playing dice, abusing women and going to the bioscope [cinema] for the next twelve days. The police know they are helpless to stop crime here in Sophiatown . . . You must show them that the removals are uppermost in your minds . . . Boycott pleasure.'

The ANC called a stay-at-home throughout Johannesburg on the date set for the first removals, to keep the police busy far from Sophiatown, but the government simply advanced the date and moved in eighty lorries and two thousand police. Officials had skilfully chosen to start with families who did not object to the extra journey to work from the new township and who were attracted by the prospect of possessing a private tap and lavatory. The selected residents moved quietly and, during the five years that the removals continued, the government successfully divided owners from tenants, Indians from Africans, the criminal from the law-abiding, to secure a total victory. Those who had doubted Verwoerd's ability to carry out major removals under the Group Areas Act were routed. The authorities later built a vast housing estate for the white working class on the site of Sophiatown and named it Triomf, triumph.

The ANC too had its successes. In 1952, with its allies, it organised the most sustained and, in terms of the numbers involved, successful resistance in its history, the defiance campaign. ANC, Indians and coloureds agreed on a plan 'for the defiance of unjust laws'. They wrote to Malan, the Prime Minister, asking him to repeal the Pass Laws, the Group Areas Act 1950, the Bantu Authorities Act 1951, and a few other acts and warning that if he refused, defiance would begin. Malan's secretary replied that they had no business writing to the Prime Minister – they should address themselves to the Native Affairs Department – and if they defied the law, the government would 'make full use of the machinery at its disposal to quell any disturbances and deal adequately with those responsible'.

The defiance campaign was planned in the spirit of Gandhi. One of its supporters was to be his son, Manilal, who lived in Natal. The 7,000 ANC members, with their Indian, coloured and communist partners, instructed volunteers how to set about non-violently courting arrest. The objective was to embarrass the government and overcrowd the prisons. Every act of defiance was performed by a group, who first attended a meeting where they were told exactly what to do and usually prayed and pledged themselves to discipline and cleanliness. They were made to swear that, however roughly they were handled on arrest, they would not retaliate with violence. The organizers sent the police notice of their plans, sometimes even including a full list of the names of the volunteers, so they would be sure to come to make the necessary arrests. Then, with the press also invited to watch, the campaigners performed their acts of defiance. One of the songs they sang went, 'Hey, Malan, Open the jail doors, We want to get in . . .'

Nelson Mandela, co-founder of the first black law firm in Johannesburg and a Youth Leaguer, was appointed national volunteer-in-chief. He led a group of fifty-two men who broke the curfew law by simply walking on the streets of central Johannesburg, a white area, after 11 p.m. They were duly arrested. Groups of Africans walked through the 'Europeans Only' entrances of railway stations, went to the whites-only counters in post offices, assembled without their passes, refused to dip cattle (in antiseptic, a compulsory measure to counteract disease). Groups of Indians also walked into 'Natives Only' locations. Enthusiasm for the defiance campaign swept the country, until groups were publicly defying selected laws in the twenty-four main towns. Offered the choice of a fine or imprisonment, campaigners chose to go to prison. Some youngsters, given no choice, were sentenced to be whipped.

The campaign's success and duration led it to degenerate into violence. Police chiefs resented doing exactly what the campaigners wanted. So, when they received notice of a forthcoming act of defiance, they took to ordering their men to prevent it. Clashes followed, and the ever-growing groups of watchers – asked by the organizers not to join in the acts of defiance which were to be carried out only by trained volunteers – turned against the police and sometimes against bystanders. Defiance organizers stopped notifying the police of their proposed acts. Some, returning to work on completing their prison sentences, were refused their former jobs. Spontaneous strikes erupted, in spite of the organizers' decision that strikes were not part of the plan.

At the peak of the campaign, in September 1952, India again moved that the race policies of South Africa be debated by the General Assembly of the United Nations, which resolved to set up a commission on apartheid – for the government a deeply offensive intrusion into their internal affairs. This inspired the campaigners to final, heightened displays of defiance. Then, after five months, the joint planning council of the African and Indian Congresses which had been master-minding the campaign decided that, with the spread of rioting and murder and with magistrates imposing increasingly heavy penalties for mere technical offences, defiance must be called off.

Some eight thousand blacks and Indians had been sent to prison for defiance offences, as well as a few white women and one notable white man, Patrick Duncan, son of a former governor-general of the Union. The ANC claimed that the number of its active branches rose from fourteen at the start of the campaign to eighty-seven at its end and that its paid-up membership rose from 7,000 to 100,000.

The defiance campaign led to the replacement of that group of middle-class, black ANC leaders who had for so long resisted mass action. The new President, elected shortly before the campaign was

called off, was Albert Luthuli, a Christian schoolmaster whom a tiny
Zulu village had chosen as its chief. Luthuli was no hothead. He came
to prominence through the defiance campaign – but initially through
resisting it.

Sent as a member of the Natal delegation to the ANC conference at
the end of 1951, Luthuli had found that plans were advanced for the
defiance campaign in other provinces. But in Natal no preparations
had been made. He told the conference that this was so and argued
for delay. The audience was unsympathetic and one woman shouted,
'Coward! Coward!' Luthuli replied: 'It is better for me to express my
cowardice here than that I should keep silent and then go away and
play the coward outside.'

Natal did not, in the event, play a major part in the defiance
campaign, but Luthuli stuck devotedly to the cause, touring the
province in efforts to organize support. As a result the Native Affairs
Department dismissed him from the office of chief. This was a major
reason for his sudden rise to popularity in the movement and his
consequent election as ANC President. He was to prove a calm,
capable and hard-working leader whose commitment to non-violence,
multi-racialism and tolerance held the ANC and its allies together
through the government's counter-attack.

Already the Malan ministry had equipped itself with a remarkable
battery of repressive laws. Its Suppression of Communism Act had
defined communism as, 'Any doctrine or scheme . . . which aims at
bringing about any political, industrial, social or economic change
within the Union . . . by unlawful acts or omissions or by the threat
of such acts or omissions . . . or under the guidance of any foreign or
international institution.' In December 1952, Nelson Mandela, Walter
Sisulu and eighteen others were tried under the provisions of the Act
for leading the defiance campaign. The judge commented that the
charges had 'nothing to do with communism as it is commonly
known', and added: 'I accept the evidence that you have consistently
advised your followers to follow a peaceful course of action and to
avoid violence in any shape or form.' He sentenced them to nine
months' imprisonment, but suspended the sentences for two years.

That was not good enough for the government, which promptly
introduced the Criminal Law Amendment Act, one clause of which
laid down that 'Any person who in any way whatsoever advises,
encourages, incites, commands, aids or procures any other person
. . . or uses language calculated to cause any other person to commit
an offence by way of protest against a law . . . shall be guilty of an
offence' – punishable by up to three years' imprisonment.

The defiance campaign also led the government to tighten up the
law on separate provisions for blacks. Some demonstrators who had
been arrested for occupying premises reserved for whites had won

their cases in the supreme court by arguing that if separate facilities were provided for different races they should be of equal standard. The government responded with the Separate Amenities Act, making it clear that separate facilities did not have to be equal and spelling out the right of owners of public facilities to exclude people on grounds of race or colour. The United Party, even more uncertain of its line on race after Smuts's retirement than it had been when he was its leader, did not oppose either of these measures.

The government claimed that the majority of blacks were really happy with its policies – which were in the black man's interests as much as the white's – and that such activities as the defiance campaign were the work of agitators and communists. This theory was now put to the test. The government imposed 'banning orders' on the principal ANC leaders, restricting their movements and forbidding them to attend public meetings. This was a clever move. Rather than make martyrs of their opponents by imprisoning them, the government restricted them to their homes or the surrounding areas. Some were even able to continue with their jobs. But they were prevented from touring the country or engaging in political activities. If they did so they would be imprisoned, and they could not claim public sympathy since they would have been guilty of breaching an apparently humane restraining order.

The bannings were imposed under the Suppression of Communism Act. Thus Luthuli, the ANC President, was banned on the grounds that he was a communist, when he was in fact a Christian anti-communist, who insisted that the ANC admitted communists to membership only if as individuals they supported African nationalism. And Mandela, newly elected ANC vice-president, was banned as a communist, when as recently as 1947 he had argued that communists should be excluded from the ANC. The terms of the act gave the Minister of Justice sole discretion over banning orders. No appeal to the courts was possible. In 1953, some hundred ANC, Indian Congress and trade union leaders were banned.

This tactic seriously impeded Congress activity by preventing the leaders from meeting each other or from addressing their followers. But the followers found ways to keep going. A large ANC procession marched past a house in Johannesburg when they learned that Luthuli was briefly staying there, and he stood at the gate waving to them. Messengers travelled between members of the executive. And from time to time the ban on a member would expire and he would have a brief spell of freedom before the large but inefficient bureaucracy imposed a fresh one. Much as the bannings slowed down the African nationalist movement after the defiance campaign, they failed to stop it.

The movement fought back against its attempted repression. In

June 1955 it proved that it had survived by holding a 'Congress of the People', an assembly whose purpose was to study and, if possible, to adopt a 'Freedom Charter'. For too long the demands of the nationalist movement had been negative – begging relief from measures introduced by the government. The Freedom Charter was intended to set out the movement's positive objectives in a way that would be acceptable to all the partners in the semi-clandestine enterprise – blacks, Indians, coloureds and a few white liberals, communists and churchmen.

From all parts of South Africa, 3,000 delegates travelled to Kliptown, a village near Johannesburg. Preparations had been handled by people as yet unknown to the authorities. And they accomplished their purpose, even though the leading figures who might have been expected both to attract attendance and dominate the debates were absent. But the Congress of the People laboured under the disadvantage that the enclosure where it was held was surrounded by large numbers of policemen. They too accomplished their purpose – photographing delegates as they entered the sessions and, on the last day, searching all participants and confiscating all documents, including two that were to be among the most famous exhibits in a subsequent trial: notices from the food-stall reading 'Soup with Meat' and 'Soup without Meat'. The new generation of leaders had made themselves known to the authorities.

The Freedom Charter which they drew up remained the manifesto of the ANC and its principal associated movements for more than thirty years. Its main provisions read:

We, the people of South Africa, declare for all our country and the world to know:
– that South Africa belongs to all who live in it, black and white, and that no government can justly claim authority unless it is based on the will of all the people;
Every man and woman shall have the right to vote for and to stand as a candidate for all bodies which make laws;
There shall be equal status in the bodies of the state, in the courts and in the schools for all national groups and races;
The preaching and practice of national, race or colour discrimination and contempt shall be a punishable crime;
The national wealth of our country, the heritage of all South Africans, shall be restored to the people;
The mineral wealth beneath the soil, the banks and monopoly industry shall be transferred to the ownership of the people as a whole;
Restrictions of land ownership on a racial basis shall be ended, and all the land redivided amongst those who work it, to banish famine and land hunger . . .

The Congress of the People provided the police with eighteen months' work, checking, collating, building up dossiers, collecting more documents. The banning of the leaders for being communists had neither quelled the movement nor impressed world opinion. The government now hoped to achieve both. The evidence they had gathered proved, they believed, that a vast group were engaged in a conspiracy to commit treason. Luthuli said that this was ridiculous. In response to the desperate police search for the ANC's plan, he commented: 'What plan? You've been present at our discussions. We've published our "plan". You're already in on the secret.' He added: 'The only future possibility of secret master plans will come if they drive us underground.'

Eventually, in December 1956, satisfied that they could convince the courts and the world, the police carried out a massive dawn arrest of 156 people – 105 blacks, twenty-three whites, twenty-one Indians and seven coloureds. From all over the country they were brought to prison in Johannesburg. Racial segregation was, of course, enforced, but Luthuli, after bans had for three years prevented him from getting to know the full ANC executive, found he was at last able to confer with most of them. 'It was,' he wrote, 'rather like a joint Executive of the Congresses . . . Distance, other occupations, lack of funds, and police interference had made frequent meetings difficult. The government . . . now insisted on [them]. Delegates from the remotest areas were never more than one cell away.'

The trial – which became internationally famous as the Treason Trial – was to last from 1956 until 1961. It was the longest and largest trial in South Africa's history and laid claim to being the world's longest. For the government it was a fiasco. The charge of treason was levelled against people who during the defiance campaign had established themselves as firmly and skilfully dedicated to non-violence. Newspaper editors across the world sensed a story. Since the Freedom Charter, the African nationalist movement had made little impact. Now it found itself receiving the sympathy of distant strangers – often accompanied by cheques. A large international Defence and Aid Fund was organized, initially in South Africa and later from St Paul's Cathedral in London. For the next thirty years it was to raise substantial sums of money and be a continual annoyance to the South African authorities. The fund immediately hired three of the best lawyers in southern Africa, who persuaded the court to release the accused on bail – an unusual decision in a treason trial.

The accused were charged both with treason and with being communists. The latter, something of an obsession with the National Party, was a mistake. The prosecution relied heavily on Professor Andrew Murray of Cape Town University, an expert witness on Marxism and communism. He pointed out, irrefutably, that ANC documents were full of words like 'proletariat', 'imperialism', 'oppressed colonial masses', 'comrade' and 'capitalism'. The same words appeared comparably frequently in the writings of Lenin, Stalin and their associates. Murray therefore held that his case was proved. One of the defending lawyers asked if Murray could definitely identify an author's politics on the basis of an extract from his work. Murray said he thought he could. An extract was read to him and he said he was sure that the author was a communist. The lawyer then revealed that the extract came from a book Murray had written himself. The prosecution, after several months of such embarrassments, dropped all charges against sixty-five of the accused, and restricted its charges against the remaining ninety-one to treason.

The trial revealed remarkable political qualities in one of the accused, Nelson Mandela. He had been one of the young Africanists who, with Anton Lembede, had founded the Youth League and tried to energize the ANC. The law firm he had set up in Johannesburg with another young ANC leader, Oliver Tambo, had become the first many Africans thought of when they were in trouble, irrespective of whether they could afford fees. So, even during the treason trial, Mandela and Tambo were constantly hurrying to remote police stations at all hours of the day and night to protect clients from abuses of the law. Then, when he took his seat in court for his own trial, Mandela's distinction as a political leader and thinker became manifest.

Mandela was from the royal family of the Xhosa. As a boy he had watched his uncle and guardian, the paramount chief, preside over judicial hearings. He might have succeeded to the largely formal chieftainship, had not his uncle's choice of a bride for him led him to flee to Johannesburg and there earn his own living. Until the treason trial he was one of a small group of prominent radicals in the movement.

The prosecution questioned him as spokesman for the accused, largely on the basis of his own speeches and writings, and the 440 pages of the official record of his evidence reveal the evolution and breadth of his thought.

Prosecution: Do you think that your People's Democracy could be achieved by a process of gradual reform?

Mandela: We demand universal adult franchise and we are prepared to exert economic pressure to attain our demands, and we will launch defiance campaigns and stay-at-homes, either singly or together, until the government should say, 'Gentlemen, we cannot have this state of affairs, laws being defied and this whole situation created by stay-at-homes. Let's talk.' In my own view, I would say, 'Yes, let us talk.' And the government would say, 'We think that the Europeans at present are not ready for a type of government where there might be domination by non-Europeans. We think we should give you sixty seats – the African population to elect sixty Africans to represent them in Parliament. We will leave the matter over for five years and then review it.' In my view that would be a victory, my lords. We would have taken a significant step towards the attainment of universal adult suffrage for Africans, and we would for five years say, 'We will suspend civil disobedience' . . . At the end of the period if the government says, 'We will give you again forty more seats', I might say, 'That is quite sufficient, let's accept it' and still demand that the franchise be extended, but for the agreed period we should suspend civil disobedience . . . In that way we should eventually be able to get everything that we want . . . Whether that is Congress's view, I don't know, but that is my view.

Bench: Can you ever achieve that by the methods you are using?

Mandela: Already since we applied these new methods . . . we have won ground. Political parties have now emerged which themselves put forward the demand of extending the franchise to the non-European people . . . Now it is true that these parties, both the Liberal party and the Progressive party, are thinking in terms of some qualified franchise. But if your lordship bears in mind the fact that when we initiated this policy there were no political parties – none – which thought along these lines, then your lordship will realize the revolution that has taken place in European parties . . . You have an organized body of opinion among whites who put forward the view that some limited form of franchise should be extended to Africans.

Bench: Has Congress considered whether the white supremacy in South Africa would without a show of arms surrender that which if surrendered would mean its end?

Mandela: We will force the whites by using our numbers, our numerical preponderance, to grant us what we demand, even against their will. We considered that and we felt that that was possible . . . We worked on the basis that Europeans themselves, in spite of the wall of prejudice and hostility which we encountered, cannot remain indifferent indefinitely to our demands, because we are hitting them in the stomach with our policy of economic pressure. It is a method which is well organized.

Bench: Isn't your freedom a direct threat to the Europeans?

Mandela: No, it is not a direct threat to the Europeans. We are not anti-white, we are against white supremacy . . . and have the support of some sections of the European population . . . The Congress has consistently preached a policy of race harmony and we have condemned racialism no matter by whom it is professed.

In March 1961, three judges of the supreme court finally delivered their verdict. By then charges had been withdrawn against a further sixty-one of the defendants, leaving only thirty to survive the whole course of the trial. The unanimous view of the three judges was that the ANC and its allies had been working to replace the government 'with a radically and fundamentally different form of state'; that illegal means had been used during the defiance campaign; that some of the defendants had made sporadic speeches inciting violence, but that the state had failed to prove a policy of violence. The senior judge asked the remaining defendants to stand and told them: 'You are found not guilty and discharged. You may go.'

Although the charge against Albert Luthuli had been dropped mid-way through the trial, the government had continued to press the charges against others in the movement he led. Yet Luthuli himself was without doubt a man of peace, a Christian, who saw the ideal future in terms of African 'participation' in government rather than absolute control of it. Luthuli believed in mass demonstrations, suffering and sacrifice by Africans, but not in order to tear South Africa away from the whites. His objective was to induce a change of heart among them. Unlike some of the Youth Leaguers who had voted him into office, he still placed faith in the moral impact of African struggle.

A police force and government that prosecuted Luthuli and Mandela for communism and treason had plainly not bothered to read their speeches or writings with due care. The British in India had repeatedly imprisoned Gandhi before they learned that he was a leader who, in response to reasonable concessions, would put a stop to violence. The South African government never appreciated that in Luthuli they had a man of similar principles. In spite of the views of some young activists, like the local ANC man in Sophiatown who had enlisted the support of gangsters, Luthuli's continued immense standing in the movement proved that his commitment to non-violence and tolerance were backed by the vast majority of ANC members.

CHAPTER THIRTEEN

Bantustans, 1958–66

National Party ministers based their policy of depriving all blacks of South African citizenship and making them residents of 'homelands' on a hope that seemed reasonable. Critics kept complaining that it was unfair to restrict 70 per cent of the population to 13 per cent of the land. Ministers believed that the answer to this challenge would take the form of a great gift to the state.

In 1909, when the British Parliament passed the Act establishing the Union, its preamble envisaged 'the eventual admission into the Union of such parts of South Africa as are not originally included therein' and laid out the procedure to be followed when the time came to hand over three huge territories. Bechuanaland, roughly as big as France and Germany put together, consisted mostly of the Kalahari desert and therefore sustained only half a million people, but its addition to the Union promised significantly to add to the 13 per cent. Basutoland, about the size of Belgium, was mainly mountainous and sustained a population of only a million. It was wholly surrounded by Union territory, and its economy depended on sending men to work in the Transvaal mines; so its eventual incorporation into South Africa seemed inevitable. And Swaziland, about the size of Wales, land-locked between South Africa and Mozambique, equally seemed fated to be absorbed. With all three added to the native homelands, the proportion of an enlarged South Africa available to blacks would be raised from 13 to 47 per cent.

The Tomlinson report, realistically facing up to the failure of successive governments to buy the land needed even to meet the 13 per cent target, had stated that the only hope of accommodating the blacks who were to be expelled from white areas was to acquire Basutoland, Bechuanaland and Swaziland. Successive British governments, anticipating the transfer of these territories to South Africa, had declined to spend taxpayers' money on them and had governed them on the cheap. If South Africa now secured them and invested in them some of the £104 million Tomlinson had proposed be spent on the reserves, the land policy of apartheid would become much easier to defend.

In 1935 Britain had promised the inhabitants of Basutoland, Bechuanaland and Swaziland that they would not be transferred to South Africa 'without consultation'. But Britain did not promise 'no transfer without consent'. When in 1954 Strijdom became Prime Minister, obtaining the territories was high on his list of ambitions. While a member of Malan's government, Strijdom had been contemptuous of those who failed to see as clearly as he did that the link with Britain must be broken, that South Africa must as soon as possible be declared a republic. But when he became Prime Minister he set this objective aside, because he thought it more important to sweet-talk the British into handing over the three vast areas which used the South African currency, which were linked to South Africa in a customs union and which most white South Africans thought should have been theirs since 1910.

The British stalled. Successive South African governments had asked for the transfer, but British ministers, Conservative and Labour alike, had held firm. Even when the territories became a drain on the United Kingdom exchequer and Strijdom, changing tactics, had his representatives hint that he would institute economic sanctions against them if they were not handed over, Britain resisted. The transfer had originally been withheld (see pp. 51–2) until South African race policies conformed to imperial ideals, and that condition had still not been met.

During Strijdom's years in office, the pressures on Britain to refuse South Africa's request grew. It had not yet occurred to the British government that these three nations, ruled by Colonial Office men from London as in the nineteenth century, might achieve sovereign independence. In the 1950s, that was thought to be an appropriate end only for populations and territories that were viable – and none of these three was. But with Ghana, independent in 1957, joining India in an increasingly Afro-Asian Commonwealth, British ministers began to think that they stood to lose more than they could gain if they gave in to Strijdom's ever more pressing demands. The longer Britain stalled, the clearer it became that South African hopes of absorbing the lands of the Basuto, the Tswana and the Swazi were to be disappointed. Strijdom had deferred the fulfilment of his republican dream to no purpose.

In 1958 he died in office. The National Party's choice of his successor was a surprise. Early the previous year, Hendrik Frensch Verwoerd, the Minister of Native Affairs, had offered to resign. His concept of apartheid – in particular his careful building up of a new political structure for Africans – seemed to be leading towards self-government for blacks in the homelands. Many in the National Party feared that embarking on this path might lead to demands for independence. It certainly seemed to conflict with Strijdom's clear assertion that apartheid meant *baaskap*. Party members accused Verwoerd of turning his department into a vast new empire, a state within the state. Some attacked him as a liberal and a friend of the blacks, and pointed to senior officials in his department who wanted both to spend the full Tomlinson £104 million on the native reserves and to give them self-government. The attacks were sufficiently frequent to make Verwoerd wonder whether the burdens of office were too much for him.

In the end, he stayed on, but he was the butt of United Party propaganda in the 1958 election, much as Hofmeyr had ten years earlier been the butt of the nationalists. The UP depicted Verwoerd as a man so crazed by his dream of complete territorial segregation of the races as to want to carve South Africa – the Union they were all so proud of – into small portions. Having previously failed in his attempt to win a seat in Parliament, Verwoerd, for his first eight years as a minister, had remained an appointed member of the Senate. Only as a result of the 1958 election, just four months before Strijdom's death, did he become an elected MP.

In 1958, the voters rewarded the National Party, not only by giving it for the first time a majority of votes but also 103 parliamentary seats to the United Party's 53. After such a victory, the nationalists no longer needed a leader whose primary skill lay in political management. Nevertheless, in a community proud of its parliamentary tradition, Verwoerd hardly had the experience to become Prime Minister.

He was chosen because apartheid, for a decade one of a number of policies about which the governing party was concerned, had slowly become its dominating obsession: if they could only get that right, then everything else would fall into place. The 150 MPs and senators who met to make the choice saw Verwoerd as the one man who could make it happen. In intellect, will-power and administrative efficiency he stood head and shoulders above any other minister. If the immense task of social engineering that they had begun was to be carried through, they needed a man with his qualities to lead them. In his moment of triumph, after the National Party caucus had elected him, Verwoerd, who unlike Malan was not a particularly religious man, told reporters: 'I believe that the will of God was revealed in the ballot.'

The *Cape Times*, an English-language newspaper strongly opposed to the National Party, commented:

With four months as an elected member, Dr Verwoerd is unlikely to have absorbed the traditions, the conventions and tolerance which make a parliamentarian. On the contrary, our system of parliamentary government was to him 'British-Jewish liberalism' . . . As Minister of Native Affairs he has been an autocrat, contemptuous of criticism and public opinion. He is a declared racialist . . .

The Broederbond and the National Party now accorded Verwoerd the title *Volksleier*, people's leader. In 1941, as editor of *Die Transvaler*, he had marked Malan's accession to that title with an editorial saying that it was necessary for the leader to occupy the same position in South Africa as Hitler did in Germany. Now Verwoerd had the title. Just as Hitler, born in Austria, had come to love his adopted country more fiercely than most Germans, had led his adopted nationalist movement with an extremism that made many of his fellow-countrymen blanch, had ground down populations that seemed different or threatening and had defined them by law as racially inferior, had constructed a bureaucratic system to carry out policies of crazed heartlessness and brutality, so now would the Dutchman turned Afrikaner nationalist.

Scholars may argue for years about whether Verwoerd was a Nazi. What is scarcely disputable is that he was not, in the normal sense of the word, a democrat.

One of Verwoerd's first acts as Prime Minister was linguistic. Several English-language newspapers had dropped the term 'Natives' and begun to refer to blacks as Africans. Verwoerd jumped on this. He said he would not answer any questions about Africans, since he did not know of any such race. Nor would he tolerate the continued description of the blacks as 'Natives', a term to which the whites had equal claim, since they had arrived in South Africa, Verwoerd and many other whites continued to maintain, at about the same time as the blacks or in many cases earlier. The proper word for all future use, he decreed, was 'Bantu', the name of the principal group of languages spoken from the Equator to the Cape. The name-plates outside the Ministries of Native Affairs and of Native Education were promptly changed, as were the titles of the ministers. All henceforth were 'Bantu'.

In the past, segregation had been applied unevenly. In the labour compounds built by mining companies and large manufacturers, everybody was black. In European clubs and boardrooms, everybody was white. But until 1948 and the arrival in power of the National

Party, South Africa had, as human societies tend to do, defied such attempts as had been made to impose consistent rules. In newspaper offices, factories, first aid posts and churches, whites met blacks whom they liked and respected. The experience was often awkward. Nelson Mandela described how, in the early 1940s when he was articled to a firm of white lawyers in Johannesburg, one of the typists, a white girl, asked him for extra work. One day when he was dictating to her, a white client came into the office. The girl, to conceal the fact that Mandela was her superior, gave him sixpence and asked him to go out and buy her some shampoo.

Some inconsistencies were more serious. After the Boer War, the British government had rewarded many blacks for their loyalty to the Crown by giving them grants of freehold land. In the Transvaal and Natal this was mostly land in what were subsequently to be designated 'white' areas. Many black families had also bought land in such areas. The rights of these landowners were protected by the law of property. Contrariwise, some whites ran businesses in native or, as everybody now had to learn to say, Bantu reserves, and their rights to occupy premises were also protected by law. While the authorities in the cities and larger towns had built townships for blacks, well away from the white or business areas, many blacks, Indians and coloureds had chosen – and had the right – not to move into them. And in many smaller towns the black and white areas were adjacent or even intermingled.

When Verwoerd became Prime Minister, the master-plan that had slowly been evolving in his mind was at last nearing its completion. His mission was to replace all this confusion by order. Segregationist practices that had been maintained by unwritten codes of behaviour would in future be enforced by law. No bureaucratic inertia would stand in his way, no excuses would be allowed. 'Black spots' in white areas were to be eradicated, even if this meant shifting whole communities that had been settled for decades or passing special Acts of Parliament to override property laws and negate title deeds. Verwoerd's blueprint required that trading and professional services for each race must be provided by its own. So those whites who had traded or farmed in black areas were to be moved out. When he was appointed Minister of Native Affairs, his policies had been supported by only a minority of the electorate, his party had had only a shaky majority in Parliament, and many of his civil servants were not convinced that his schemes were practicable; now all those obstacles were removed.

Verwoerd's first measure as Prime Minister was the 1959 Promotion of Bantu Self Government Bill, which provided for the founding of eight national homelands. These were simply the existing 260 scattered native reserves, except that over them eight Bantu homeland authorities would now be created, with powers to tax their own people (as defined by the government in Pretoria), control public works and allocate licences and trading rights. These homeland authorities were based on Verwoerd's new, improved tribal system, with the Minister of Bantu Affairs retaining the right to approve all appointments of chiefs and headmen and to veto their decisions. The new authorities and the areas they controlled at once became known as 'Bantustans'.

Until he became Prime Minister, Verwoerd had always been cautious about the final status of the homeland authorities. When critics had accused him of planning to give them independence, he and the officials of his old department had denied it. The homeland authorities, they asserted repeatedly, were to have only local government powers. But Verwoerd faced an intellectual problem. As a matter of principle he considered it essential to remove all representatives of the blacks from Parliament; they must not remain where they might become the thin end of a wedge. But a residue of Hertzog's 1936 Act survived. Although the advisory Natives' Representative Council had been abolished, the seven white MPs, able to use their parliamentary votes to defend native interests, remained. In the 1950s, these seven MPs could hardly be removed without giving the blacks, the majority of the population, something by way of compensation. This was the kind of dilemma to which the new Prime Minister loved to turn his extraordinary mind.

Verwoerd convinced himself that he was being fair to the blacks when, in 1959, he announced his solution: black representation in the Assembly would be abolished forthwith, but if the Bantu had the ability their new homeland authorities might, in the distant future, be allowed to attain full independence. Verwoerd continued his speech in Parliament by suggesting that they might eventually form a South African Commonwealth, with white South Africa serving as its core and guardian. A National Party MP, Japie Basson, went the whole way and argued that the proposed disenfranchisement could be justified only by the granting of genuine independence to the Bantu areas. Verwoerd had him expelled from the party.

Sir John Maud, British High Commissioner to South Africa from 1959 to 1963, met Verwoerd regularly and recalled:

When he spoke of the Bantu (as he always called black South Africans) his voice took on a slightly soapy tone, suggesting the avuncular concern of a trustee for these primitive children . . . I recall Harold Macmillan (Britain's Prime Minister) asking in 1960 what would be the position of the Bantu in that 87 per cent of the Union which was reserved for the 3 million whites. A majority of the 11 million Bantu in the Union would presumably go on living in 'white' South Africa, their labour indispensable. Verwoerd's answer was firm and clear: 'Like Italians working as miners outside Italy, they will have no political rights outside the homelands; their position will be that of honoured guests.'

Macmillan wrote of that occasion:

I had long discussions with Dr Verwoerd . . . and it was only during these days that I began to realize to the full extent the degree of obstinacy, amounting really to fanaticism, which he brought to the consideration of his policies . . . Even in small matters he had pressed apartheid to its extreme. In a country where there is at least the advantage of being able to enlist African staff, he refused to have a single African in his house. An old and rather incompetent Dutch butler looked after us.

The Prime Minister, with his quiet voice, would expound his views without any gesture or emotion. At first I almost mistook this calm and measured tone for a willingness to enter into sincere discussion . . . However, I had the unusual experience of soon noticing that nothing one could say would have the smallest effect upon this determined man. Normally in politics there is a certain give and take . . . even in questions which raise deep feelings in the House of Commons or in party controversy, most people try to understand, meet or sometimes partially accept the argument of their opponents. But here it was a blank wall.

Sir John Maud continued his description of the conversation between Macmillan and Verwoerd:

And would there be homelands for the Cape coloureds and the Asiatics in Natal? 'No,' was the answer, 'that has still to be worked out.' But that was the only question to which Verwoerd had no answer. About all forms of sport, for example, he was emphatic that there could be no compromise: the simple principle must be applied that people of different colours should not mix but develop separately, and other countries must recognize South Africa's right to decide that question for herself. It was in the interest of all races that members of each race should keep themselves at all points to themselves.

Given his academic background, Verwoerd naturally placed a high priority on ensuring segregation in the universities. Most of them were segregated already. The Afrikaans-medium universities – Potchefstroom, Pretoria, Orange Free State and (after Afrikaans became an established language) Stellenbosch – had from their foundation restricted admission to whites. Of the English-medium universities, Rhodes was all-white and Fort Hare in practice non-white; the remaining three, while more open, were by no means fully multi-racial. Natal admitted non-whites, but kept its classes racially segregated. Cape Town and Witwatersrand admitted students to courses without regard to race but applied a strict colour-bar in social and sporting events. In 1957, when the government had begun the slow process of forcing the universities to become completely segregated, Natal, Cape Town and Witwatersrand had 1,225 non-white students out of a total enrolment in all residential universities of 25,000.

Verwoerd required university segregation to be total, but he faced a tradition of academic independence, derived as much from the Netherlands as from Britain. In the English-speaking universities, his old fellow-professors maintained that, when assessing an applicant, they should consider only his brains and ability to advance learning. While he had been Minister of Native Affairs, they had mustered former students in high places to help fight him off. But Verwoerd was a skilled campaigner and used support in the party and control of the bureaucracy to wear down his opponents. In 1959, soon after he became Prime Minister, his government introduced the Extension of University Education Act, making it a criminal offence for a non-white student to register at a hitherto open university without the written consent of the Minister of Internal Affairs.

To make up for the exclusion of non-whites from existing universities, the government founded new ones, in the Transvaal and Zululand for blacks and in the western Cape for coloureds. Fort Hare, based on the famous nineteenth-century mission college at Lovedale, had been an English-language university open to all, though recently all its students had been non-white. It now became a university for Xhosas only. A new Afrikaner principal was appointed and many of its former staff, including its vice-principal, one of South Africa's leading black academics, Professor Z. K. Matthews, were dismissed. The university reforms had an unexpected effect. Many white students supported blacks in their protests, something new in South African history. And the universities of Cape Town and Witwatersrand became – even more than they had been already – fact-gatherers, analysts and critics of the government's measures.

When Verwoerd became *Volksleier*, the National Party and the Afrikaner population were united. Malan and Strijdom had consolidated them. At last the Afrikaners were on top and felt if not secure, then less insecure. So Verwoerd turned to the concern that had dominated Smuts's career and also, in his latter years as Prime Minister, Hertzog's: uniting all the whites. For the full attainment of apartheid, white unity was essential. Divisions in the white community were the one challenge Verwoerd thought capable of undermining his plans for the blacks. The bitter disputes of English *v* Afrikaners had by no means been stilled in the Malan-Strijdom years as the National Party and the Broederbond pushed English-speakers out of top jobs wherever they could. Verwoerd decided that the time had come to win over the English-speaking whites.

He appealed to them to join the National Party and stressed the need for whites to stand together in face of the growing threat of African nationalism. Britain had conceded independence to Ghana and Nigeria. France was advancing its African colonies rapidly to independence. The Congo, suddenly in 1960 abandoned by Belgium, was sinking into chaos. At his party's congress in 1961 Verwoerd said: 'I see the National party not as an Afrikaans party, whatever it might have been in the past. I see it as a party which stands for the preservation of the white man, of white government, in South Africa.' To drive the point home, he went on to speak for half an hour in English, which puzzled his Afrikaner audience, since it was neither their first language nor his. Subsequently he appointed two English-speaking members to his Cabinet.

In 1960, as Verwoerd was beginning his campaign to win over English-speakers, the British Prime Minister, Harold Macmillan, visited South Africa. His blessing on apartheid, even his acceptance of it, would have greatly helped the cause. That was why Verwoerd devoted so much time to explaining his policies patiently. But when Macmillan addressed a joint sitting of both houses of Parliament in Cape Town, he publicly repudiated South Africa's racial policies. Macmillan spoke of an irresistible wind of change blowing through Africa.

It has been our aim in the countries for which we have borne responsibility to create a society . . . in which men are given the opportunity to grow to their full stature – and that must in our view include the opportunity to have an increasing share in political power and responsibility [with] individual merit alone as the criterion for a man's advancement whether political or econo-mic . . . Our policy therefore is non-racial. It offers a future in which Africans, Europeans, Asians . . . will all play their full part as citizens and in which feelings of race will be submerged in loyalty to new nations . . .

As fellow-members of the Commonwealth it is our earnest desire to give South Africa our support and encouragement, but I hope you won't mind my saying frankly that there are some aspects of your policies which make it impossible for us to do this without being false to our own deep convictions . . . We ought, as friends, to face together, without seeking to apportion credit or blame, the fact that . . . this difference of outlook lies between us.

LEFT: Chief Albert Luthuli, President of the African National Congress, 1952-67, and Nobel Peace Prize winner, 1961.

BELOW: Mandela is arrested for defying the law, June 1952.

BOTTOM: Nelson Mandela (centre right) with Jusuf Dadoo of the Indian Congress at a meeting during the Defiance Campaign, 1952.

TREASON TRIAL

The ACCUSED

DECEMBER 1956

This picture was cut and pasted – it is a carefully constructed montage of several photographs. The photographer had arranged to pose the accused in a natural arena near the court. But when the park-keeper learned who was to be photographed, he withdrew his consent.

Sharpeville, 21 March 1960.

TOP: Before the shooting.

CENTRE: And after.

LEFT: Crowds return, with police.

TOP: J. G. Strijdom, elected National Party leader, and therefore Prime Minister, 1954.

ABOVE: B. J. Vorster, Prime Minister 1966-78. He had no soft feelings about imprisonment without trial, having suffered it himself.

RIGHT: Dr Hendrik Verwoerd, principal creator of apartheid, Prime Minister 1958-66.

ABOVE: Murdered by the police in 1977, Black Consciousness leader, Steve Biko, is here seen speaking at the council of the South African Students' Organization at Natal University, 1971.

LEFT: Chief Kaiser Matanzima, Prime Minister and later President of the Transkei, which in October 1976 became the first black homeland to be given 'independence'.

BELOW: B. J. Vorster with the leaders of the black 'homelands' in 1973. All were reliable allies of the apartheid state, except Chief Gatsha Buthelezi, near left, Prime Minister of KwaZulu.

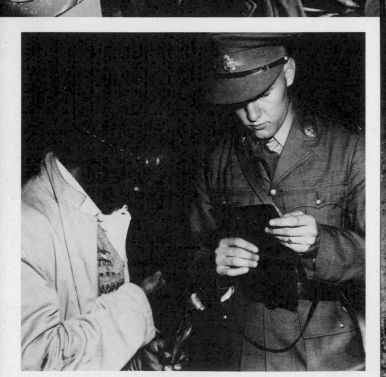

Apartheid in practice.

TOP: A removal, thoroughly supervised. Between 1960 and 1983, more than 3.5 million people were compulsorily moved to 'homelands'.

ABOVE: A pass-book inspection.

RIGHT: 'Bachelors' single-sex dwellings', twenty-five migrant labourers per room. Each shelf is one man's only living space for up to a year.

A repeated form of defiance: a funeral is used as an ANC demonstration. Nelson Mandela's wife, Winnie, helps carry the coffin.

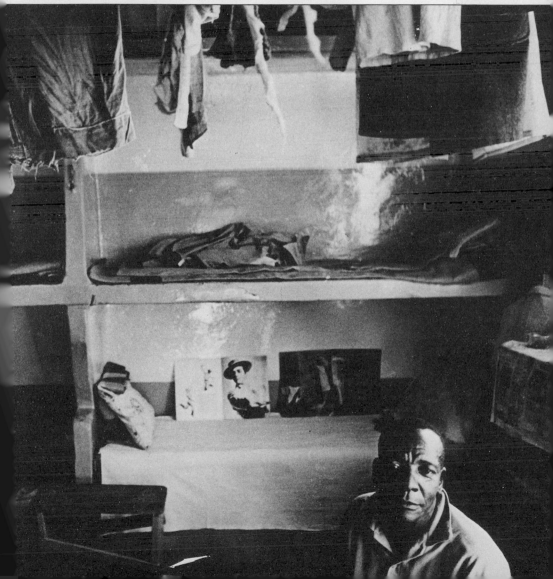

TOP: P.W. Botha, Prime Minister 1978-83, then State President.

ABOVE: Oliver Tambo: since Mandela's imprisonment in 1962 and Luthuli's death in 1967, leader in exile of the African National Congress.

ABOVE RIGHT: Rev. Allan Boesak, a founder of the United Democratic Front.

RIGHT: Bishop Desmond Tutu. In 1983, he became the second black South African to win the Nobel Peace Prize.

The speech was broadcast live. Macmillan had not shown Verwoerd a copy of his text, but Verwoerd was to move the formal vote of thanks. Recognizing that no single speech in South Africa had ever offered such encouragement to the enemies of apartheid – not only blacks, Asians and coloureds, but white journalists, teachers, church leaders and trade unionists – Verwoerd, after a courteous thank you, launched into a half-hour impromptu rebuttal, putting the case for 'justice for the white man', telling Macmillan that by the policies he proposed, 'the very objects you are aiming at may be defeated', and asserting that, if the survival of the white race seemed to warrant it, South Africa would abandon accepted values.

That evening the two prime ministers dined together, unaccompanied, in the official residence, Groote Schuur, which Cecil Rhodes had left to the South African nation. It was an awkward meal. They talked about everything but Macmillan's speech. The extent to which it had shaken Verwoerd was revealed by the way in which, months afterwards, he went on delivering defiant replies.

Macmillan's blow in February 1960 was followed in March by another – this one from Verwoerd's own police. A group of Africanists and anti-communists, followers within the ANC of Anton Lembede and his former Youth League ideas, had broken away to form a new movement called the Pan-Africanist Congress (PAC). They announced that 21 March was to be Anti-Pass Day and called on all Africans to leave their passes at home and surrender themselves to the police. Demonstrations were to be non-violent, no resistance was to be offered, and the police would have no choice but to fill the prisons. The plan was in the tradition of Gandhi, Luthuli and the ANC's defiance campaign of seven years before, except that demonstrators were not trained.

The PAC had a smaller following than the ANC. In many parts of the Union its call was ignored; in others, those who presented themselves pass-less at their local police station were few and the police just took their names and sent them home. Elsewhere the police played the part assigned to them and arrested hundreds without mishap. But in two African townships things went wrong; above all in Sharpeville.

Sharpeville was a model township. It is a satellite of Vereeniging, a steel manufacturing centre fifty miles south of Johannesburg which had expanded rapidly to produce munitions during the Second World War. Vereeniging's old African location had become overcrowded, insanitary and disease-ridden; and, since it was near the centre of the growing town, it was of increasing value as a site for property development. So the local authority built a new township, which was named after the mayor, John Sharpe. Construction began in 1942 and was, by the standard of the times, impressive. The neat rows of houses had running water, sanitation and, in some cases, bathrooms, and the township enjoyed street lighting, a brewery, a clinic and weekly film shows. Removals from the old location to Sharpeville had been gradual, over fifteen years, without compulsion.

For more than twenty years, Vereeniging and Sharpeville had had no political violence. Local officials described the township as 'peace-loving and law-abiding' and said that 'riots and boycotts instigated by the Bantu' were unknown. In 1952, Africans in Sharpeville had attended a meeting about the defiance campaign and had agreed not to support it. The ANC had tried to establish a branch there but had failed. Then in 1959 the seeds of trouble were sown. Seventeen years after building work had begun, Sharpeville was completed and the remaining residents of the old location were told they must leave. Some had been reluctant to move to the model township, because the rents there were too high. Some 5,000 who persisted in their refusal were evicted to the reserves. Thus a large proportion of Vereeniging's settled black population was suddenly expelled.

In 1960, in addition to the 50,000 blacks in Vereeniging district who lived in municipal townships like Sharpeville, 11,000 men lived in employers' compounds. This was another source of trouble. The big factories recruited mostly migrant labourers on short-term contracts whom they transported in from the reserves. Young people brought up in Sharpeville had difficulty finding jobs.

So Sharpeville was a good recruiting ground for the PAC which succeeded on 21 March 1960 in assembling a crowd of some 5,000 outside the police station. Unaccustomed to trouble from the local Africans and surprised to see so many, the police did not know what to do. They could not arrest 5,000 people – they had neither the courage nor the cells – nor could they persuade them to go away. Low-flying Sabre jets frightened crowds outside some nearby police stations and thus dispersed them, but at Sharpeville this tactic was unsuccessful. Some in the crowd were expecting an announcement about the Pass Laws and refused to disperse until they heard it. Some said they would not disperse until told to do so by the PAC leader, Robert Sobukwe. Having assembled by 10 a.m., the crowd was still there at 1.15 p.m., watching as reinforcements brought the number of police in the station compound up to 300.

The police station was surrounded by a wire fence and, at about 1.15 p.m., a scuffle broke out near one of the gates. A police officer was pushed over. The incident excited the interest of the crowd who, wanting to see what had happened, surged forwards. Police witnesses said that at this stage stones were thrown at them. Some young constables, without receiving orders, began firing. The crowd turned and fled, but the firing continued. Sixty-nine people were killed and 180 wounded. Nearly all were shot in the back.

At Langa, a township near Cape Town, a similar disaster occurred, though on a much smaller scale. For people round the world, the word 'Sharpeville' came to mean massacre. The United Nations Security Council, the United States government, the Dutch Parliament, MPs in Britain and many countries throughout the world publicly deplored the police action. The anger and horror that reports about apartheid had for years been building up were released upon South Africa in an avalanche.

In South Africa itself, the funerals of the victims were attended by vast crowds. A stay-at-home was called by Luthuli, the ANC President, to mourn those killed. For the first time, Africans were roused to offer a nationwide response to the brutality of apartheid. For many weeks the authorities were unable to contain it. If, until now, Verwoerd had deceived himself into thinking that his policies enjoyed African consent, as he repeatedly asserted, the events of March 1960 should have opened his eyes. So widespread were African strikes and demonstrations that police and troops in many places were given the task of forcing Africans out of the townships and into the factories. Their failure and the fear of more conflict led to an economic panic. Foreign investment in South Africa halted. A sharp outflow of capital hit the value of the South African currency, the rand. House prices and the share market slumped. The country's gold and foreign exchange reserves fell, over the following year, by more than half.

Verwoerd's response was repression. His government introduced laws to declare the ANC and PAC illegal and, at the end of March 1960, under new emergency regulations, it detained 18,000 people, of whom more than 5,000 were held for several months. Albert Luthuli himself, after he had publicly burned his pass book as an act of sympathy with those killed at Sharpeville and Langa, was sentenced to a year's imprisonment or a £100 fine. The fine was paid by friends.

The government, disoriented by Sharpeville, was shattered when, just a month later, a deranged white farmer shot two bullets from close range into Verwoerd's head. The prospect that the country might need a new Prime Minister aroused strong hopes – at least in the business community and the English-language press – of a change of policy to come to terms with African demands. Even SABRA (the South African Bureau of Racial Affairs), the National Party's think-tank on apartheid, began to have second thoughts. Now that it was clear that the government would not spend the money Tomlinson had shown was essential to make the homelands viable, that the additional territories expected from Britain were not going to be forthcoming, that Africans had risen in a sustained, nationwide protest against apartheid and that the international community was not only condemning the policy but also withdrawing its funds,

SABRA members put forward alternative schemes. Some wanted to bring the coloureds back into the white electoral system, to deprive the Congress of some of its allies. Others argued that apartheid was now plainly revealed as nothing but *baaskap*, certain to provoke an increasingly violent reaction, and that the party must offer a 'new deal' in racial policy.

Verwoerd, recuperating from the attempted assassination, rejected all such advice. A political leader who has just been spared from death acquires, for a while, added authority. He wrote a long statement which was read to Parliament on his behalf in May.

The recent disturbances in certain urban areas and the state of emergency which followed have given cause for general reflection. Certain authorities have submitted ideas and proposals to the government. However good their intentions, those who made proposals often did not have sufficient facts at their disposal . . . One must guard against the tendency among some people . . . to see the disturbances in the wrong perspective, and against the attempts of opponents to try to use the events and the atmosphere to encourage a revision of policy . . . The government sees no reason to depart from the policy of separate development . . . On the contrary, the events have more than ever emphasized that peace and good order and friendly relations between the races can best be achieved through the policy . . . The good things it envisages must now be done in the unfavourable atmosphere of suspicion and incitement created by organizations and persons, some of them white, who are imbued with communistic aims.

Later in the year, he addressed a National Party gathering, where he was treated with the adulation due to one risen from the dead. The completeness of his recovery was amazing. He suffered no long-term effects except a small scar on one cheek and slight impairment of the hearing in one ear. His will-power, if anything, seemed to have been strengthened. He told his party faithful that the government would have to stand 'like walls of granite' on the colour policy because the nation's existence was at stake. When his press adviser, Piet Meirinck, who had been with him as news editor of *Die Transvaler* and through his eight years at the Ministry of Native Affairs, confided that he was finding it increasingly difficult to persuade foreign journalists to listen to pro-apartheid arguments, Verwoerd stopped talking to him – and later dismissed him.

Verwoerd did his best to proceed as though the shootings at Sharpeville had not happened. He, at least, was not disoriented. He had already decided to hold a referendum among the white voters to decide whether the Union should become a republic, and at the end of

1960 he went ahead as planned. The electorate was fairly evenly divided, 850,000 voting for a republic, 776,000 against. But the majority was enough for Verwoerd to claim a popular mandate and at last, after more than 150 years, to send the British Crown packing. In 1961, challenged by intrusive questions from Afro-Asian heads of government, he withdrew the Republic from the Commonwealth, thus breaking the last constitutional link with Britain. For most Afrikaners, as for Verwoerd, this was the fulfilment of a lifetime's dream. The Afrikaner nation cheered itself hoarse in welcoming him back from Britain after the final breach. His authority in Parliament was now absolute.

But to carry out his policy of separate development Verwoerd needed to impose his will on Africans, and that was becoming less easy. In March 1961, after the verdicts of not guilty had been delivered at the end of the treason trial, he decided that the courts, in spite of the promotion of Afrikaner judges by Malan and Strijdom, could not be trusted to give the government the backing it needed. He therefore searched out the toughest man he could find to take charge of internal security and of the government's overseeing of the judiciary. In July 1961 he appointed as Minister of Justice Balthazar Johannes Vorster, the former Ossewa-Brandwag general who had been imprisoned without trial by the Smuts government during the 1939–45 war for being a Nazi and a danger to the state. Vorster later recalled the meeting at which Verwoerd appointed him:

I remember saying to Dr Verwoerd that he should let me deal with the threat of subversion and revolution in my own way. I told him that you could not fight communism with the Queensberry rules, because if you did then you would lose. He agreed with me and said that he would leave me free to do what I had to do – within reason.

At the end of the treason trial, the law firm of Mandela and Tambo went out of business. ANC leaders, including Luthuli, had instructed Tambo to leave the country in order to ensure that, whatever happened in South Africa, an ANC organization survived outside. He opened the first overseas offices in London and Dar es Salaam to build on the international support brought to the cause by the Sharpeville shootings. Mandela, at his own suggestion, was instructed to start something rather different.

While Luthuli and the ANC leadership remained dedicated to non-violence, the government's response to the defiance campaign in 1952, to the Freedom Charter in 1955, and to Macmillan's speech and the Sharpeville shootings in 1960, had caused groups of young blacks throughout the country to demand a change of method. If non-violent protest, external pressure and economic collapse had failed to move the government, they argued, then the only remaining option was violence. Some made it plain that if the ANC did not back them they would themselves launch violent resistance movements locally. As soon as Mandela was released at the end of the treason trial and before the government had had time to re-arrest him, he volunteered to vanish and to adopt a new way of life – that of the homeless, secretive, constantly mobile organizer who would direct and channel the energy of young recruits. The ANC offshoot of which he became leader was named Umkonto we Sizwe, the Spear of the Nation.

'Umkonto,' Mandela subsequently recalled, 'was to perform sabotage; and strict instructions were given to its members right from the start that on no account were they to injure or kill people.' This was not just in deference to Luthuli's principles: to attempt to launch an all-out war against the government would have been to invite certain failure and to provoke an overwhelming response. Sabotage launched against economically important facilities would, Mandela hoped, result in increased pressure on the government to start talks.

In December 1961, Luthuli was awarded the Nobel Peace Prize. His Christian pacifism and the long-suffering of the African people had kept the nationalist movement peaceful far longer than the government had reason to expect. A week after the announcement of Luthuli's prize came the change. Umkonto launched the first of a series of some two hundred fire bombs which exploded over the next eighteen months in government offices, post offices and electrical sub-stations. Most were, as Mandela had laid down, so placed as to avoid injuring people, but twenty-three attacks on policemen, informers or alleged collaborators, some twenty bombs placed in railway buildings and five bombs placed in beer halls were a risk to life. Umkonto, in which communists both white and black played a large role, also sent some three hundred volunteers to Russia, China and sympathetic African countries for training as guerillas.

By 1964, Umkonto was squashed. The police had, from the time of Vorster's appointment, begun fairly frequently to use torture as a means of extracting information from political prisoners. And, following the humiliation of the treason trial, they had built up a network of thousands of black informers – people who preferred cash in hand now to the remote prospect of freedom in the future. So the police were able to catch most of the Umkonto leaders at a farm in Rivonia, just north of Johannesburg, where many of them lived. Papers found there helped police track down the rest. After what became known as the Rivonia trial, many ANC leaders, including Nelson Mandela and Walter Sisulu, were locked away, to stay imprisoned for almost a quarter of a century – well into the 1980s.

The Pan-Africanist Congress, organizers of the Sharpeville

demonstration, also responded to the killings by setting up a military wing. It was called Poqo, Xhosa for 'pure', and was both less organized and more violent than Umkonto. Inspired by a belief in a spontaneous, mass black rising that would overwhelm white South Africa, Poqo produced an evening's violence in Paarl, near Cape Town, where a plan to attack a police station was diverted into the murder of some local whites. It also generated a few score other attacks, terrifying to the whites against whom Poqo youths turned, but never a threat to the state. As with Umkonto, it was all over by 1964, when the police had arrested most of the leaders and many activists and secured convictions in court.

In this way, Verwoerd's government sailed successfully through the rough political waters whipped up by Sharpeville. Vorster, the new Minister of Justice, did as he had promised. He strengthened the already restrictive security laws and gave the police increased freedom to ignore civil liberties. His firm hand in control of state security broke the back of the first violent resistance movement thrown up by African nationalism. Investors who had withdrawn their money in the time of uncertainty were quickly reassured. Import controls and blocks on the export of capital and profits staunched the outflow of reserves. Within five years a revival of political confidence led to an unprecedented spurt of growth and prosperity. English-speaking businessmen began to echo Afrikaner farmers in describing Verwoerd as a great Prime Minister.

He was able to return to his grand design, especially to the most satisfying of all tasks for intellectual bureaucrats: writing the constitutions of new states. The 'self-governing' homelands or Bantustans were, along with Bantu education, Verwoerd's most distinctive invention. In 1963 he set up the first homeland government, with the passing of the Transkei Constitution Act.

A minor local chief named Kaiser Matanzima had realized that the South African government might be able and willing to make him the top man in the Transkei, the area in the eastern Cape that formed by far the largest consolidated native reserve. When in the mid-1950s Verwoerd, as Minister of Native Affairs, had tried to persuade the Transkei Bunga to abolish itself and to make way for local government by chiefs (as laid down in the Native Authorities Act), Matanzima was one of the young chiefs who supported the proposal enthusiastically. He saw the government as the great chief in whose retinue a lesser chief like himself could enjoy rewards, protection and a share of power. Matanzima and the officials of the Native Affairs Department worked well together and his influence increased. In return for his support of official policies, Matanzima's men were allowed a large measure of freedom to settle matters in the Transkei as he thought fit.

In 1961, Verwoerd encouraged the Transkei local government set up under the Native Authorities Act to explore ways of strengthening its own powers. It appointed a committee with Matanzima as chairman, and Verwoerd ensured that he was provided with the necessary guidance to draw up a constitution that would enable the two of them to describe the territory as self-governing. The Prime Minister's close interest in the work of Matanzima's committee enabled him to say publicly what he expected its drafting to produce: 'It will be no multi-racial Transkei as far as its government is concerned. The whites there will be represented in the Republican Parliament, just as the Bantu voters, Xhosas, in the white areas will be represented in the Transkeian parliament.'

A deal was struck. Matanzima and the group of chiefs he now led would secure substantial powers over their fellow-citizens and their tax revenues, in return for backing Verwoerd's scheme for separate development throughout South Africa. Matanzima exacted a price. Verwoerd had to instruct his officials to buy land from neighbouring white farmers to enlarge the Transkei. To avoid political trouble, the displaced whites were generously compensated. The Transkei assembly voted to reward Matanzima and his brothers for their 'faithful service in the development of their country' by grants of farms in the transferred area. One of the brothers, George Matanzima, said frankly: 'Of course, Kaiser who worked so hard to acquire the land will be among the beneficiaries.'

Matanzima was related to Nelson Mandela and was regarded by tribal custom as his nephew. He judged that his brilliant uncle's political activities, in spite of the great popularity they had won him, had led only to defeat and imprisonment. Matanzima knew that, when his committee drew up precisely the constitution for 'self-government' in the Transkei that Verwoerd wanted, he would not become popular, but nor would he find himself in jail counting the years.

The terms of the constitution, which was to be the model for future 'self-governing' homelands, gave the Transkei its own legislative assembly, cabinet, citizenship, flag and national anthem (Matanzima shrewdly chose 'Nkosi Sikelel i-Afrika', the anthem of the ANC). Transkeian ministers were to exercise powers over finance, justice, forestry, education and roads but were to leave defence, internal security, postal services, railways, immigration, banking and, of course, foreign policy to the government of South Africa. The laws passed by the Transkei legislative assembly were subject to the approval of the South African government.

The government-paid chiefs and headmen assented to the scheme – by 1979 the number of employees on the government payroll in the Transkei had reached 170,260 – but most of the Xhosa who were to be the citizens of 'self-governing' Transkei disliked it. Long and bitter revolts broke out against the government and the chiefs, notably in a part of northern Transkei called Pondoland. Several attempts were made on Matanzima's life. Most of the sixty-five chiefs appointed to sit in the Transkei legislature supported him and the policies he recommended, but when the first elections were held, all the forty-five democratically chosen members were against him.

In December 1963, the legislative assembly had to choose the Transkei's first Prime Minister. Chief Victor Poto, who supported a multi-racial South Africa, won forty-nine votes and Matanzima, supporting separate development, succeeded in scraping home with fifty-four thanks only to the overwhelming support of his fellow-chiefs. The total defeat he had suffered in the popular vote compelled Matanzima to cling to power by relying on the South African security forces and on a state of emergency which he maintained for more than twenty years. He and Verwoerd together gambled on power securing acquiescence.

With such a disputed and unsafe political base, was there any way of making the 'independent' homelands economically viable? Verwoerd firmly rejected suggestions from white businessmen that, given suitable inducements, they might invest there. To allow that, he argued, would be to subject the Bantu to the renewal in their own areas of the white domination from which the homelands policy was rescuing them. Verwoerd had told the House of Assembly in 1956:

The Bantu must start on a small scale. Psychologically he is not adapted to industrial life and certainly not to private enterprise . . . on a big scale. Nor would he be in a position in ten or twenty years' time to take over big industries which have been developed there if his relationship towards industry has been simply that of the recipient and the outsider . . . It is only when he mainly spends his own money with moderate assistance . . . that he has an opportunity of adapting himself psychologically to the demands of industrial life; but he will not have that opportunity if the spoon-feeding which has been so disastrous in the past in the rural sphere is applied in this sphere.

Instead, Verwoerd encouraged white businessmen to open factories on 'white' land close to the borders of the homelands. This, he held, would bring jobs to the homelands without diminishing the Bantus' autonomy inside them. Untroubled by the danger of spoon-feeding white industrialists, he made government subsidies available to them to start 'border industries'. Most of the beneficiaries were Afrikaners. Among the advantages of the arrangement, from the point of view of the industrialists, was the absolute lack of rights enjoyed by blacks in these areas. They were not permitted to take any legal action to protect their rights at work, because within white South Africa they were merely temporary visitors – aliens.

A few textile and other factories were founded on the borders of the Transkei and other homelands. But relative to the desperate hunger and unemployment in the rapidly growing populations there (see page 154), the few hundred jobs provided by border industries were of little significance. Like many of Verwoerd's ideas, they were trumpeted to the world as a great scheme designed entirely for the benefit of blacks, while in reality such benefit as came from them went almost entirely to whites.

The reserves, according to the government's own study, the Tomlinson report, had no hope of becoming viable without massive government investment. On this issue Verwoerd minimally relented. In 1959, he set up the Bantu Investment Corporation to take the initiative in establishing black industries in the homelands. Its launching capital of £500,000 was less than a half of one per cent of the £104 million Tomlinson's careful study had said was urgent and essential.

When Dr Verwoerd had taken up apartheid, it had been merely a political slogan, a clear term concealing a muddled prejudice. In an unusually segregationist society, it had indicated a vague will to go further down the racialist road. He turned it into a rigid system of social engineering, controlled from Pretoria by an enormous bureaucracy of Afrikaners. And, to make white South Africa safe, he created the basis for 'independent' states, each with its own Matanzima, each ready to claim dominion over its allotted 'tribal' blacks, wherever they might have been born or be living, and each small and weak enough to have no hope of ever challenging the whites. In justification of his creation of potentially 'independent' Bantustans, he used to say that he preferred a small white South Africa to a large black South Africa. But what he constructed, with his repeated assertion that his policy was in the best interest of the blacks, was a state and a group of satellites so absolutely in the interests of the whites that they could not last. Some who knew him said that, during the last months of his life, he began to wonder if he had overplayed his hand.

On 6 September 1966, Verwoerd was sitting in Parliament, waiting to make his first speech of the new session. While the bells summoning members to the chamber were still ringing and MPs were hurrying to their places, a uniformed parliamentary messenger came up to him. The messenger's name was Demetrio Tsafendas. He had a Greek father and a Portuguese-African mother and had been born in Mozambique. He had worked in many countries and had been in no fewer than eight mental institutions in the United States, Germany, Portugal and Mozambique. He had come to South Africa only the previous year and had been taken on to the temporary staff in Parliament five weeks before the start of the session. His fellow-messengers said he spent most of his spare time reading a Greek Bible. He said later that he was driven to what he now did by a diabolical tape-worm that was eating his insides.

Tsafendas leaned down towards the Prime Minister, as though to give him a message, pulled out a dagger and stabbed him three times in the throat and chest. MPs seized him. Others rushed to help Verwoerd. But the principal maker of the apartheid state was dead.

CHAPTER FOURTEEN

Police State, 1966–77

During Verwoerd's final years, a growing proportion of his time was taken up with, of all things, sport. He had thought it was one of those matters that, once logically thought through, was settled for ever: the survival of the white race in South Africa required the avoidance of racial mixing; sport was a potential danger-point because blacks were undeniably good at some sports and the companionship and enthusiasm of the field could lead to unthinkable risks; so the total segregation of sport had to be enforced. This merely required, as in so many fields, that South Africa's normal practice be codified in law and enforced by the police. In 1962, Verwoerd's Minister of the Interior, Jan de Klerk, spelled out their policy:

The mixing of races in teams taking part in sports meetings in the Republic and abroad must be prevented. The government cannot allow teams from the Republic to be composed of whites and non-whites. Conversely, foreign teams which are so composed cannot be permitted to enter the Republic.

On such issues, a new form of power – world opinion – proved able to intervene in South Africa's internal affairs. Between 1946 and 1965, the number of Afro-Asian members of the United Nations rose from fifteen out of fifty (less than a third) to seventy-three out of 125 (well over half). In 1963, in the aftermath of Sharpeville and the consequent United Nations votes, the International Olympics Committee decided that South Africa must eliminate racial discrimination from its teams if it was to be invited to the next Olympic Games. Verwoerd refused to consider the suggestion; international do-gooders and multi-racialists were not among those to whom he was prepared to listen. The invitation to South Africa to take part in the Olympics, hitherto regularly renewed every four years, was withdrawn.

In 1965, a South African rugby team toured New Zealand. Some of the best players were Maoris, and the New Zealand Rugby Union made it plain that, in the changed international climate, they could not continue to exclude Maoris from teams they sent to tour South Africa. This drew from Verwoerd a typical magisterial pronouncement.

At present we are engaged in an argument in a sphere which I should prefer not to discuss, namely our rugby team in New Zealand. But . . . much is being openly written in opposition newspapers which has compelled me to state my own and the government's attitude very clearly and unequivocally . . . We have not changed our attitude. As we behave in other countries, so we expect them to behave here – in accordance with our customs; and everyone knows what they are.

The New Zealand Prime Minister, Keith Holyoake, said this amounted to South Africa telling the New Zealand selectors which players to include in their teams, which was unacceptable. The New Zealanders, when next invited to send a team to South Africa, declined.

This seemingly minor problem was inherited by Verwoerd's successor, the Minister of Justice whose ruthless campaign against black political organizations had been so successful. Balthazar Johannes Vorster was no thinker. His colleagues raised him from being one of the most junior members of the cabinet to the prime ministership because they thought he was tough. His distinctive contribution to his country's history was to secure for the police the power to hold suspects without charging them or bringing them before a court for twelve days (1962), ninety days (1963), 180 days (1965), for an unlimited period if authorized by a judge (1966) and without such authorization (1976). He claimed to understand political detention better than most ministers of justice, having himself suffered twenty months' imprisonment without trial during the Second World War. Vorster later said:

I had no real hard feelings about my own internment. I had come out in opposition to the government of the day, that government identified me as a threat to established order and so neutralized me. It did what it felt was necessary at the time. I adopted the same approach.

When he became Prime Minister, journalists and politicians expected him to continue as the policeman of Verwoerd's policies. He surprised them by his flexibility, his first display of this talent being devoted to sport.

White sports enthusiasts eager to welcome foreign teams had petitioned and pleaded with Verwoerd. He had resisted, not conceding an inch, until his murder in September 1966. A mere seven months later, in April 1967, Vorster changed direction, announcing that he would not tell visiting sports organizers which athletes to select. Later that year, South Africa undertook to send a multi-racial team to the next Olympic Games, and the International Olympics Committee recommended that the Republic should be readmitted. Newly independent African countries pointed out that within South Africa sport would continue to be segregated. They therefore threatened to boycott the games and thus prevented the committee's recommendation from being implemented. Some National Party supporters complained not just that Vorster's deviation from the Verwoerd line had been unsuccessful, but that it had been skittishly radical.

In diplomacy, Vorster carried through a similar adjustment. South Africa happened to be on the African continent, but most whites tried to pretend the country was an island. In 1963, when the Organization of African Unity (OAU) was founded, its members, the newly independent black governments, had begun a campaign to isolate and weaken the apartheid state. Most of them had refused to recognize it. Verwoerd had dismissed the comments of black presidents and the OAU as ignorant and mischievous. But the Foreign Ministry advised that such displays of unwavering disdain could be damaging. Some black governments deprived South African Airways of landing rights at profitable stopovers on its routes to Europe, others closed their markets to South African exports. Their votes had led to South Africa's removal from the Commonwealth and later from such useful forums as the specialized agencies of the United Nations. And the vocal antagonism of African states nourished the Africanist spirit among young blacks in South Africa itself, threatening to provoke trouble.

While Verwoerd lived, his government accepted the costs and cold-shouldered black Africa. In 1962, Sir Abubakar Tafawa Balewa, Prime Minister of Nigeria, had asked to be allowed to visit South Africa and, in 1964, Dr Kamuzu Banda, President of Malawi, had offered to establish diplomatic relations. Verwoerd had refused them both. Soon after his death, however, officials in the Foreign Ministry persuaded his successor to reverse the policy. Vorster launched a 'peace offensive'. As the richest and most 'advanced' state on the continent, South Africa began to offer technical and financial aid, particularly in mining and medicine, to those black states whose governments were willing to talk.

One early target of the South African government's wooing was Malawi, an impoverished former British protectorate. Its President, Kamuzu Banda, had in his youth, like thousands of his country's citizens, walked 1,500 miles to work as a migrant labourer in the Rand gold-fields. When, three years after his offer of diplomatic relations had been turned down by Verwoerd, Banda received an approach from Vorster, he raised his price. He made South Africa pay for the construction at Lilongwe of a new capital city for Malawi. In 1967, he appointed a white ambassador to Pretoria.

In 1971, President Banda paid a state visit. A former mine clerk in Johannesburg, he enjoyed mixing as an equal with the whites. And he now challenged apartheid openly. He insisted on appointing a black ambassador. This was a shock to those white South Africans who had come to regard Verwoerd's concept of total apartheid as permanent and unchangeable. A visiting black head of state, though displeasing, was tolerable because, amid all the pomp of such occasions, he was cut off from everyday life. But an ambassador would remain among them, would live, Banda insisted, in a white suburb, not an African township or a homeland, and would be allowed, Banda again insisted, to enter whatever hotels and restaurants he pleased even though the law reserved them for whites only.

Vorster gave in, as Verwoerd would sooner or later have had to do. The South African government needed neighbouring black states to co-operate with its plans for the future security and economic development of the region. But Vorster's speedy shift from the line to which Verwoerd had adhered brought him trouble. The admission of a few black sportsmen for brief tours and the forging of diplomatic links with black states aroused within a section of the National Party the cry 'Back to Verwoerd'. Dr Albert Hertzog, son of the former Prime Minister J. B. M. Hertzog, resigned from the Cabinet and in 1969 said of the inclusion of Maoris in a visiting New Zealand rugby team: 'It will lead to social integration, since they will dance with our Afrikaner girls at social functions.' It was not a casual remark but the voicing of an anxiety so deep-rooted that Vorster thought it necessary to expel him and a number of others who shared his views from the party. Collectively they were known as the *verkramptes*, the narrow ones.

To widespread surprise, Vorster himself became the leader within the National Party of the *verligtes*, the enlightened ones. Their enlightenment did not go deep. They persisted with all the main elements of Verwoerd's policies, in particular the extension of the Bantustans, the eviction of blacks from towns and 'white' areas, the completion of the apartheid structure. The *verligtes* merely wanted to place a few black ambassadors and athletes in South Africa's shop window to impress the world. But the intensity of the *verkrampte* backlash gave Vorster pause. Hertzog and his colleagues were summoning up the *swart gevaar*. It threatened to revive all the Afrikaner bitterness and xenophobia that Hertzog's father and Malan had, in previous decades, harnessed at election times to defeat Smuts.

Vorster was no Smuts. In the art of arousing Afrikaner nationalist fervour and racial prejudice he was unsurpassed, and he quickly reasserted his and his party's role as the sole voice of the volk. He rededicated the administration to the ideals of Verwoerd – in particular, to the implementation of the keystone of his policy of separate development, the revolution in the homelands.

This comprised two parts. One was choosing millions of Africans who were living in white areas, loading them and all their possessions on to lorries and removing them to those homeland areas in which the government thought they belonged. The other was finding black leaders willing to take the 'homelands' down the constitutional path towards 'independence', thus providing the public justification for depriving blacks of any claim to rights in 'white' South Africa. The white electorate had come to accept Verwoerd's idea of 'independence' for black homelands once they had grasped that the word, when used by the government in this context, was always in invisible inverted commas.

The territories Vorster set about packing with displaced people and advancing to 'self-government' – with 'independence' as their eventual goal – were the 260 jigsaw pieces that the Tomlinson commission had said needed to be consolidated and urgently developed. In the years since the Tomlinson report was published, the infertility of much of their land, the poverty of most of their people and the desperate need for investment to enable them to provide for their new inhabitants had not changed. Their condition remained as described in 1953 in an Oxford thesis by Piet Koornhof, a young Rhodes Scholar, who was later to become the National Party minister in charge of them:

An inquiry into the living conditions of the reserves reveals strikingly that the inhabitants find it impossible to supply even the bare necessities for living on a subsistence level . . . Opportunities for gainful employment are almost non-existent. [The reason is that] the easier the living in the reserves, the less the labour is available for outside employment. The temptation for European employer-legislators not to improve the living has, therefore, always been strong and it has been the economic force, represented by the demand for labour, which has usually decided the issue.

Improving the reserves was consequently never a serious priority for the government, which did not even complete the purchase of additional land to bring their proportion of the total area up to the 13 per cent promised in Hertzog's 1936 Native Trust and Land Act. The Bantu Affairs Department revealed that by 1962, more than twenty-five years after the Act was passed, of the quota of 7.25

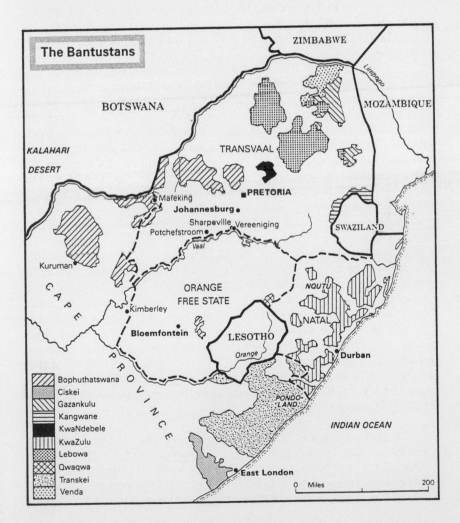

million morgen (16 million acres) prescribed for purchase, almost a third had still to be acquired. The reserves remained as the Tomlinson report had found them, populated by more people than they could feed and so over-farmed that the fertility of their land was declining. Economic historians disagree over the precise date at which the 'collapse' of agriculture in the reserves took place. Over-population was becoming a problem from the 1920s onwards. All who have studied the subject agree, however, that by the 1960s the 'collapse' had reached desperate proportions, with starvation widespread.

Into these impoverished areas, Vorster's government sent millions of displaced blacks. The exact numbers will never be known, but the closest study, by the Surplus People's Project, a group formed to monitor and relieve the hardship caused, puts the total of blacks moved by the state to homelands between 1960 and 1983 at 3.5 million. They came from 'black spots' – from shanty-towns, from 'white' farmland and from established townships that whites now found inconveniently located.

A vast project of social engineering develops its momentum slowly. Verwoerd had proved that he could evict blacks, coloureds and Indians even from a freehold township like Sophiatown, and that he could find black allies to be his agents even in a territory accustomed to a partly representative local administration like the Transkei. He had bequeathed to Vorster a vast army of civil servants who had proved that they could impose apartheid in a succession of difficult test cases and had worked out the procedures needed to complete its nationwide, routine enforcement. Flexible though Vorster might be over peripheral matters like sport and black diplomats from abroad, in dealing with the core of apartheid he was as tough as Verwoerd. He took the policy from its development stage to implementation on a mass scale.

Soon after Vorster became Prime Minister, the Secretary for Bantu Administration and Development wrote to all the officials in his department who were to carry out the policy, explaining what they must do. His General Circular no. 25 of 1967 states in part:

It is accepted government policy that the Bantu are only temporarily resident in the European areas of the Republic for as long as they offer their labour there. As soon as they become, for one reason or another, no longer fit to work or superfluous in the labour market, they are expected to return to their country of origin or the territory of the national unit where they fit ethnically . . . No stone is to be left unturned to achieve the settlement in the homelands of non-productive Bantu at present residing in European areas.

The Bantu who . . . have to be resettled in the homelands are:

(i) The aged, the unfit, widows, women with dependent children and families who do not qualify for accommodation in European urban areas;

(ii) Bantu on European farms who become superfluous' as a result of age [or] disability . . . or Bantu squatters from mission stations and black spots which are being cleared up;

(iii) Doctors, attorneys, agents, traders, industrialists, etc. [who] are not regarded as essential for the European labour market.

The Secretary went on to explain that those Bantu who 'are financially in a position to bear the cost of staying there' should be moved into homeland townships with 'full services'. These were for 'Bantu employed in industries founded in the border areas' – to enable their inhabitants to travel daily to work in white South Africa. Most communities of evicted blacks, however, required less elaborate facilities: 'Normally only a rudimentary lay-out on the basis of agricultural residential areas is undertaken and the delimitation need not be carried out by a surveyor.' Lorry-loads of Africans, in short, were to be dumped on open ground.

A priest, Cosmas Desmond, reported of one group, deported to Limehill in northern Natal in 1968: 'We found the first arrivals sitting in the bare veld surrounded by their belongings looking bewildered and utterly lost. A little distance away was a water tank and a pile of folded tents, which the people did not know how to erect – nothing else.'

Circular no. 25 of 1967 went on:

In the case of squatters from European farms, they usually possess some cattle . . . As a result of a shortage of adequate land, it is not possible to settle all these people together with their cattle in the homelands. Consequently it is imperative that they must first sell their cattle, sheep and goats. District officers must give all possible help by arranging cattle sales in good time in order that they may obtain the best possible prices for their livestock.

The government knew that it was sending displaced blacks to land that could not accommodate another cow or sheep, but ministers repeatedly insisted that all blacks who moved to the homelands did so voluntarily. M. C. Botha, Minister of Bantu Administration and Development, said in 1969: 'The Bantu people like being moved . . . They like the places where they are being resettled.' As in Nazi Germany, most whites did not know what their government was doing. The convoys of lorries carrying deportees avoided passing through white cities. Vorster, when he was Minister of Justice, had shown his competence at one kind of police operation. Now as Prime Minister he had proved he was equally good at another.

A documentary film, 'The Dumping Grounds', made in 1970 by Granada Television, showed what 'removals' involved. The township of Schmidtsdrift, near Kimberley, housed 7,000 Africans in territory that had been legally protected for African occupation. But it was in the middle of European land, so in 1968 officials and police had loaded most of the Africans into lorries and driven them away. Soon afterwards, two British doctors, Donald and Rachel Mackenzie, running a mission hospital in an African reserve in Kuruman on the edge of the Kalahari desert, were surprised to see convoys of lorries bringing new residents into their arid region. The passengers from Schmidtsdrift were simply left in a place where the soil, according to an independent British analyst, was 'totally unsuitable for crops or grazing in conditions of low annual rainfall'.

The deported Africans complained that they could grow nothing to mix with the mealies (a kind of ground maize) of which they had brought huge bags. The Mackenzies reported that the deportees, who were fairly fit when they arrived, quickly began to suffer from diseases caused by starvation, and that several hundred died. Two years later, the starvation was unabated. The Mackenzies' successor as medical superintendent of the mission hospital wrote: 'The incidence of malnutrition here is shocking, even to someone accustomed to African conditions.'

No work was to be found in the desert, so those of the deportees who had formerly worked in Kimberley went back in search of their jobs. Living 150 miles from Kimberley as they now did, their home visits were reduced to one a year. But at least some of them were able to send their families small remittances.

The Granada film next moved 750 miles to the east, to the district of Nqutu in Zululand, where Dr Anthony Barker, for twenty-five years medical superintendent of the Charles Johnson Memorial Hospital, reported regular deaths from the under-nutrition diseases, kwashiorkor and pellagra, and others from straight starvation. Soil erosion was getting worse because of the extra people the government was introducing. The need for the men to stay in far distant towns to earn a living led, Dr Barker said, to 80 per cent of first babies in this area being illegitimate.

To save the bother of drawing up a separate constitution for each homeland, Vorster's government created a general framework in a single law, the Bantu Homelands Constitution Act of 1971, which empowered it to give, by proclamation, successive Bantustans the formal appurtenances of 'self-government' (and later of 'independence'). The pattern was an exact copy of Verwoerd's constitution for the Transkei. In 1972, Bophuthatswana (made up of nineteen fragments, some of them hundreds of miles apart) and Ciskei became partially self-governing; in 1973 Gazankulu and Venda; in 1974 Qwaqwa. The next in line, KwaZulu (made up of twenty-nine major and forty-one minor fragments), came to 'self-government' soon after. In every case, these new sub-states were created in the manner Machiavelli taught his prince: by a firm display of power, by binding chiefs and headmen to the state apparatus with land grants, subsidies and licences, and by suppressing all opposition.

One of Vorster's first acts on becoming Prime Minister had been to create a Bureau of State Security (BOSS), reporting directly to him, with a fellow former Ossewa-Brandwag member and wartime detainee, Hendrik van den Bergh, as its chief. This secret police force helped all the chiefs who were to head the Bantustan governments to deal with their opponents. In every Bantustan, the legislature, as in the Transkei, contained only a minority of elected members. Bantu Affairs Department officials advised the majority of the legislators, the appointed chiefs:

Be your own police in your own interest, find out those men who respect authority and tribal institutions and band them together as the chief's and headmen's *impi* [attacking force] which will turn out when called to help keep your tribes and locations clean and well behaved . . . Use moderate violence . . . just like a good chief should do.

Vorster's police state seemed to be working. After Sharpeville and the brief eruptions of Umkonto we Sizwe and Poqo, the police had tracked down and imprisoned an entire generation of black political and trade-union leaders. As a result of the policy of driving blacks into the homelands, some African townships suffered a decline in population, further breaking down radical political networks. The apparent restoration of stability in the country attracted a fresh inflow of foreign capital, financing a further enlargement of manufacturing industry. To the government and its supporters, apartheid seemed to be firmly on course.

However, one of Dr Verwoerd's policies had a consequence he had not predicted. Sending black students to all-black universities – the Africans called them 'tribal colleges' – created a hothouse for a new growth: a movement called Black Consciousness. This was partly a development from Anton Lembede's Africanism, partly an adaptation of American Black Power, partly a response to the fact that, now that they were all in separate universities, black students no longer found that the liberal National Union of South African Students adequately voiced their concerns. Black Consciousness was not an organization, but a set of ideas that helped create a mood. Its fury was reflected in poetry:

When did the revolution-war begin?
It began the day the white put his foot on the land.
It began when your forefathers were brought in chains to work the fields.
They killed Shaka – it began.
They incarcerated Sobukwe, Mandela, Sisulu – it began.
Now it is on – the revolution
       – because they killed my brother
       – because they muted our leaders.

The leading writer and thinker of the Black Consciousness movement was a medical student at Natal University's non-white medical school, Steve Biko.

Black Consciousness [he wrote] seeks to channel the pent-up forces of the angry black masses to meaningful and directional opposition . . . But the type of black man we have today has lost his manhood. Reduced to an obliging shell, he looks with awe at the white power structure and accepts what he regards as the 'inevitable position' . . . The black man has become a shadow, completely defeated, drowning in his own misery, a slave and ox bearing the yoke of oppression with sheepish timidity.

Black Consciousness, with its contempt for the compromises of previous generations, spread from universities to schools. In 1975, the Minister of Bantu Education issued an instruction that arithmetic and social studies in all Bantu secondary schools must be taught in Afrikaans. Parents, pupils and teachers united in protest. Nearly all the black teachers spoke English; many knew no Afrikaans. Parents and pupils protested that English was the main language of industry and commerce, and therefore of jobs, and was the lingua franca of Africans in the towns. Afrikaans they considered the language of police, pass office and prison.

They sent their protest to the appropriate department, the office of the Deputy Minister of Bantu Education, Dr Andries Treurnicht, a *verkrampte* whom Vorster had kept in the party and recently appointed a junior minister. Treurnicht was not the man to show sympathy for black concerns, particularly for their objections to his own language. He stood firm on the policy.

In May 1976, a black leader Desmond Tutu, the Anglican Bishop of Johannesburg, sensing the bitter mood of Black Consciousness in the air, wrote a letter to the Prime Minister: 'I am writing to you, Sir, because I have a growing nightmarish fear that unless something drastic is done very soon then bloodshed and violence are going to happen in South Africa . . . A people can only take so much and no more . . . A people made desperate by despair and injustice will use desperate means.' Vorster, like Treurnicht, ignored the warning.

In June 1976, in Soweto, the south-west townships ten miles from central Johannesburg, a group of secondary school students called a demonstration. Some 15,000 pupils converged on Orlando West Junior Secondary School. The moment of explosion of Black Consciousness in the schools – and, via them, throughout South Africa – had arrived.

Soweto, where it happened, had been designed in the 1930s as barracks for migrant blacks, nearly all mine-workers. It therefore had few modern amenities: no mains electricity, no shopping centres, no entertainments. In the 1950s and 1960s came rapid expansion. Wide roads were laid down, though mostly unmetalled, semi-detached concrete houses were built, with water supplies and drainage. Considering that the government was setting out to provide only 'temporary sojourn' for migrant labourers, its standards were not horrifying – more like a dusty sprawl of sub-standard English council estates than a third world slum. The seemingly endless rows of houses were supposed by 1976 to accommodate 600,000 people. But the job market had for several years raced ahead of official house-building and most experts agreed that Soweto housed well over a million. The lack of electricity led to a pervasive smokiness from the coal stoves, especially when evening meals were being cooked. The lack of shops led Soweto Africans to bus, drive or share taxis for shopping in white-owned central Johannesburg. Most Sowetans had passes, some education and jobs – since those without were constantly being expelled to Bantustans. Economically, the people of this strange, planned sub-city were the élite of black Africa.

The violence that was to startle the world began with the half-friendly first ritual of confrontation. Among the slogans the pupils carried, mostly painted on cardboard, were, 'Afrikaans stinks', 'Afrikaans is an oppressors' language' and 'If we must do Afrikaans, Vorster must do Zulu'. A hastily summoned police detachment tried to disperse the crowd of schoolchildren and their supporters with tear gas and, when that failed, opened fire, killing two and injuring many.

The young people scattered. Soon thousands of them were surging through Soweto, taking revenge. They threw stones at passing cars, put barricades of rubble across streets, set fire to shops, beer-halls and government buildings. They killed two white officials.

Within days, youths were rampaging through several other towns. The minister closed the schools. The pupils closed shops and offices, prevented buses from running, set fire to petrol pumps, threw bricks.

Even though it had no national leaders or organization, the schools protest had become a national confrontation with the government. Police patrols and government buildings were the favoured targets. The police retaliated with batons, *sjamboks* (rhinoceros-hide whips) and bullets, often taking the initiative against black youths whom they suspected, rightly or wrongly, of being rioters. The death toll rose. Black schools in most of South Africa were deserted.

A month after the start of the troubles, in an effort to reopen the schools, the government dropped its order to teach in Afrikaans. But those schools that reopened soon found themselves suffering police raids, as the authorities tried, often brutally, to identify the ringleaders of the revolts and drag them away. The children quit their schools again. Between August and November 1976, they four times forced Johannesburg to a standstill by calling general strikes, which they enforced by preventing workers from leaving their townships. The only part of the Republic in which the towns were relatively unaffected was Natal. Throughout the following twelve months, schools continued to be disrupted. Official figures – almost certainly underestimates – put the total number killed in the course of the uprising that began in Soweto at 575 and the wounded at 2,389.

Vorster's period in office may be remembered for his flexibility over sport and black diplomats, for the millions he deported to the homelands, for his strengthening of police powers or for the Soweto troubles. But probably it will be most remembered for a single mistake. On 12 September 1977, in police custody in Pretoria, a detainee died. Since 1961, when Vorster was put in charge of the Ministry of Justice, forty-five detainees had died in police care. Most of them, the police claimed, had committed suicide, usually by hanging, had slipped on bars of soap severely injuring their heads or had fallen out of windows. No member of the security police had been officially held responsible for any of their deaths.

Death number forty-six was different. The dead man was Steve Biko. Only thirty years old, Biko had already established an extraordinary standing as a leader of Black Consciousness and as an intellectual. He was known and respected among white liberals and had met United States senators and embassy officials. Donald Woods, a South African newspaper editor, wrote of Biko: 'In the three years that I grew to know him my conviction never wavered that this was the most important political leader in the entire country, and quite simply the greatest man it had ever been my privilege to know.'

Vorster's regime, accustomed to imprisoning black people without trial and to brazening it out if they unaccountably died in police hands, knew at once that Biko's death would cause problems. Journalists and lawyers from all over the world flew to South Africa to ask questions. Evidence given at his inquest by police, warders and doctors revealed that, from the day after his arrest on 18 August 1977, he had been kept naked and manacled for twenty days, during which time he was not allowed out of his cell even for air or exercise. On 2 September, a magistrate had visited him and Biko asked for soap to wash himself. 'Is it compulsory that I have to be naked?' Biko asked, 'I have been naked since I came here.' The magistrate did not reply. On 7 September, Biko was told to dress and was taken to an interrogation room, where he received various blows. Some to his head caused brain damage. Several doctors examined him. Five days later he died.

Two days after Biko's death, the Minister of Justice, Jimmy Kruger, told a National Party congress:

> I am not glad and I am not sorry about Mr Biko. It leaves me cold. I can say nothing to you. Any person who dies . . . I shall also be sorry if I die. [Laughter]. . . Incidentally, I can just tell congress, the day before yesterday one of my own lieutenants in the prison service also committed suicide and we have not yet accused a single prisoner. [Laughter]

The police had regarded Biko as exceptionally dangerous. They had detained him under a clause of the Terrorism Act, on the basis of a recent court ruling that for a member of the Black Consciousness movement to be found guilty of terrorism, no act of terror or of violence or of any plans for terror or violence had to be proved. Biko and his Black Consciousness colleagues had not wanted to be banned, like the leaders of the ANC and PAC, so they had been careful to obey the law, limiting their activities to philosophical and political speeches and social work. Biko himself had put much effort into raising funds for self-help clinics in black areas. Nevertheless, in 1974, the authorities had banned him, restricting him to King William's Town, in the east of Cape Province, and forbidding any political activity. Consequently he had kept comparatively quiet and could not be accused of any offence when, in January 1975, nine Black Consciousness supporters were put on trial for terrorism.

No act of terror nor of recruitment for military training was alleged by the state. The issue on trial was whether publishing the Black Consciousness philosophy itself constituted terrorism. The evidence consisted only of speeches and pamphlets. Compared to the speeches and pamphlets produced by the Afrikaner nationalist movement in the early 1940s, when Malan led the party and many Afrikaners supported the Ossewa-Brandwag and other Nazi groups, the patter of the Black Consciousness philosophers was not specially inflammatory.

At the end of the trial the judge concluded: 'While freedom of speech and of assembly must be regarded as fundamental in our democratic society, it does not mean that everyone with opinions or beliefs to express may address a group at any public place and at any time.' He accepted that the Black Consciousness activists did not manage any revolutionary group. But their concepts, he concluded, did encourage feelings of hostility between blacks and whites and their depiction of the system of white power as one of murder, oppression, exploitation, fascism, robbery and plunder amounted to 'an act of terrorism'. Accordingly he convicted them as 'terrorists'.

Thus the policy of apartheid had at last provoked among young blacks a total, angry rejection that allowed no compromise. And it had led the state, whose supporters liked to think of themselves as heirs to the traditions of the seventeenth-century Dutch republic and the British Parliament, to destroy significant parts of what they claimed to stand for.

Steve Biko's death may have been no worse than several dozen others. It was merely the one that attracted world attention and can therefore be described in most detail. Biko was never found guilty of any crime, never arrested for inciting violence, never accused of it.

During the ten years following the death of Dr Verwoerd, the idea of apartheid had ridden high in white South Africa. The government that implemented his policies had been confident and self-righteous. Its morale had been high. Afrikaner political leaders had persuaded most of their supporters, and some may even have persuaded themselves, that they were not merely defending their own interests but, as Verwoerd had repeatedly asserted, doing what was best for the blacks. They had maintained that they were the defenders of democracy and justice, indeed of western civilization itself.

The Soweto rising and the death of Steve Biko marked a turning-point. Afrikaners began to think again, the professors in their universities and the reflective columnists in their newspapers to use words like 'crisis', 'decisive hour', 'fear' and 'confusion'. The Federated Chambers of Commerce sent a memorandum to the Prime Minister stating that only by having urban middle-class blacks 'on our side' could white South Africa contain 'the irresponsible economic and political ambitions of those blacks who are influenced against their real interests from within and without our borders'. The events of 1976–7 brought home to leading Afrikaners a simple message: to continue to follow the pattern laid down by Verwoerd was impossible.

CHAPTER FIFTEEN

The Beginning of the End, 1977–87

The Soweto troubles brought South Africa all the economic and financial backwash that had followed the 1960 Sharpeville shootings, only more so. Capital again flowed out of the country. Businesses and the housing market collapsed. Instead of the normal yearly influx of a few thousand whites, 1977 and 1978 saw more than 3,000 net departures. Gloom descended on a white community that could not see the way ahead.

Vorster at first said nothing. Verwoerd had responded to Sharpeville by promptly telling all who argued for change that they were wrong, but for three months after the Soweto outbreak Vorster made no public comment. The reason was that his ministers and civil servants were abuzz with radical ideas and he did not know which way to turn. Gradually the reformers secured the ascendancy. Verwoerd's strict recipe for apartheid was abandoned. The years 1977–83 in South Africa came to resemble 1905–17 in Tsarist Russia. Reforms came late and, given the survival in power of the old regime, surprisingly fast. But they fell far short of the demands of the regime's critics. To the outside world the National Party began to seem like an ageing lion trying to persuade captive lambs that it was no longer a carnivore.

The National Party did not embark on what it considered a daringly radical process just because it was shaken by the post-Soweto disturbances or made guilty by its treatment of Steve Biko and others; these were merely the events that stirred the reformist impulse to flower. Its roots lay in economic and social changes.

Vorster, the policeman of apartheid, stressed that the reasons for opening the doors to change were economic – above all the need to enlarge the pool of skilled black workers. For the first two decades of National Party rule, job-apartheid had been successful: white workers had been available to fill most skilled jobs and hundreds of thousands of blacks had been removed from the towns. In the years before and after Verwoerd's murder in 1966, a shift occurred. The growth in the manufacturing sector of the economy overtook the capacity of the white population to deliver skilled workers.

The vigorous Afrikaner-first policies of Malan, Strijdom and Verwoerd had lifted a large proportion of the Afrikaner workforce out of the blue-collar job market. In 1948, when the National Party came to power, 9.6 per cent of private businesses (excluding farms), one per cent of the mines and 16 per cent of all posts in the professions were in the hands of Afrikaners. By 1975 these figures were up to 20.8 per cent, 18 per cent and 38 per cent respectively. Sanlam, the Afrikaner insurance group, was challenging the Anglo-American mining corporation for the title of the most powerful company in South Africa and, along with Anton Rupert's Rembrandt group (owners of the Rothmans/Stuyvesant tobacco company) and the Volkskas bank, provided training and leadership to Afrikaner businessmen. Sanlam had even bought the General Mining Company from Anglo-American, thus at last securing Afrikaner control of a major corporation in the country's biggest foreign-exchange earner, gold. And the civil service, before 1948 almost totally dominated by English-speakers, by the end of the 1970s was 90 per cent Afrikaans.

Consequently, in the 1960s and 1970s, factory managers who filled the newspapers with job ads could not find the white recruits the colour-bar said they must employ. To deal with this problem they evaded the law. One technique they developed became known as 'diluting' the colour-bar. When workers were needed for a skilled job which the law defined as 'white', managers promoted whites who had formerly been doing the job, calling them supervisors, and recruited blacks at lower wages to fill the gap. To conceal from the authorities the fact that black men were doing white men's work, job titles were changed.

To build a house in Johannesburg meant either waiting for months for a white, expensive, legal building gang, or finding a black gang, perhaps with a white nominally in charge in case an official came inquiring. Most customers opted for the quicker, cheaper service.

When white trade unions complained at such flouting of apartheid, the police brought the offending black workers to court, and magistrates sent them – valuable and newly trained though many of them were – away to a 'homeland'. The magistrates also fined or imprisoned them. Many employers paid the fines, but it was not they who were guilty of an offence. The law blamed not the company which offered the unauthorised black worker a job, but the black who accepted it.

Through the 1960s and early 1970s informal deals to resolve these problems became increasingly common. Some white trade unions, satisfied that no whites were available to fill the jobs, tolerated 'dilution'. Black workers and their employers bribed the police. The law stated that an African could acquire the right to remain in a prescribed area for more than seventy-two hours – 'Section 10 rights' – only if he or she had lived there since birth or worked there for one employer for ten years or was the child under eighteen of a person with such rights. The industrial managers who won promotion in the 1970s were those who proved themselves most adept at persuading Bantu Affairs Department officials to re-designate black recruits to the workforce as 'Section 10s'. Large parts of industry were able to function only by means of such conspiracies to evade the law.

These were not the only developments that were making apartheid appear ridiculous. In 1971, African townships, previously run by local authorities, were transferred to centrally appointed Bantu administration boards. Instead of being responsive primarily to local needs and pressures, the new boards took their cue from Pretoria, where the official line dictated that the flow of blacks into white towns should be reduced. At a time when industry was drawing Africans into the towns in their thousands, the Bantu administration boards cut back the pace of black house-building. So more and more newly-arrived blacks settled in shanty-towns or crowded into township houses three or four times the numbers they were built for – illegal acts which were punished by eviction to the homelands, again depleting the industrial workforce.

Vorster recognized that such battles between businessmen and apartheid could not go on. In 1977 he appointed two commissions. The first, conducted by P. J. Riekert, studied influx control and recommended that blacks with skilled jobs and proper housing be accepted as permanent residents in the towns. To enable the government to protect these privileged blacks – in effect an enlarged population of 'Section 10s' – influx control must continue to be actively enforced against all others.

The second commission, chaired by Professor Nic Wiehahn, studied industrial relations – and broke new ground by including one black member. Black trade unions were unrecognized and black strikes a criminal offence. Yet when black workers formed trade unions, many industrial managers chose to avoid trouble by talking to them. The newspapers were constantly carrying reports of black unions successfully calling illegal strikes. A major series of strikes in 1973 in Durban and the widespread strikes following the Soweto riots showed that, illegal or not, black trade unions were a growing force.

Further, their members were doing well. The market was driving up black wages faster than white. Between 1970 and 1976, real white earnings rose by 3.8 per cent, black by 51.3 per cent. In the mines, where black wages had always been exceptionally low, the rise was even more dramatic. Between 1970 and 1978, a period of heavy capital investment and the build-up of a skilled labour force to man it, white earnings rose by 79 per cent, black by 390 per cent.

After the Soweto riots, students, church groups and small investors in America and Britain put pressure on international companies not to operate in South Africa. Some companies countered this pressure by announcing that they were paying black workers at the same rate as whites. In New York or London such statements sounded satisfactorily high-principled, clearly flouting the colour-bar. In some industries in Johannesburg and Durban – thanks to the success of Bantu education in depriving blacks of advanced knowledge – this was becoming the only way to recruit skilled black workers, though a convergence in wage rates for skilled industrial workers still left huge differences between the earnings of most whites, which were above these levels, and those of most blacks, which were far below.

The commission on industrial relations advised that job reservation must be abolished and black unions recognized, giving them equal status with white unions, bringing them into South Africa's statutory industrial relations system, with its court, conciliation procedures and right to strike after an official thirty-day notification period. Thus, the African worker who was a 'permanent part of the economy' would be absorbed in 'the protective and stabilizing elements of the system'.

From these two reports the government concluded that white South Africa must make the best of the inevitable and turn the skilled black workforce into collaborators in maintaining the system. Within the white economy, apartheid would be largely dismantled. To those blacks who were economically essential, a share of the fruits of the nation's wealth would be conceded. They must become a stable aristocracy of labour – white society's buffer against the mass of less well-endowed blacks, who must remain outside the system. But they would have no share in political power, and they would have to continue to prove their right to be in the privileged sector. If they became involved in an illegal strike or a riotous assembly or were dismissed from work, they would lose their residence rights. The schemes were calculated to ensure that blacks would become junior partners in white South Africa, but only so long as they were well-behaved.

Ministers had a brilliant idea for presenting these proposals to the outside world. The reforms would be described as marking the end of apartheid. The Cabinet could scarcely contain its excitement at the thought of the victory it was about to enjoy over its international critics. At last South Africa could win the propaganda war in which it had so often suffered defeats. Schemes to train blacks for skilled industrial work were financed by the government and by industry with 100 per cent tax rebates. Houses in black townships, which thirty years of accumulating apartheid legislation had just about removed from the protection of all property laws, so that blacks could neither own them freehold nor on long leases, were made legally purchasable once again on ninety-nine year leases. Business groups advertised mortgages for high quality housing in black townships. In Soweto, a new suburb called Selection Park was developed, with 'élite houses' beside a golf course, many with swimming pools. Black millionaires and professionals bought them, and foreign journalists were brought in their hundreds to see the new face of South Africa. 'That house you see there,' said the guide to a group of foreign journalists in 1980, 'belongs to an employee of Anglo-American. He's a very important black official at Anglo, and he came with his own plan for that house, and since he could afford it he was able to get a double stand to build that very large house.'

Perhaps the most striking reform was an early one. In 1975, the military disciplinary code was amended to give blacks in the defence forces the same status as whites of equal rank; henceforward whites would have to take orders from and salute senior black officers. It all amounted to a good story to tell the world.

For some years Vorster had been preparing the information department for such a task. Concerned about South Africa's poor image, he had decided to launch a secret information invasion of two key targets, Washington DC and London. He had pumped money from the Prime Minister's discretionary fund into the information department and, when that proved insufficient, had turned to the safest source of secret funding, the defence department. Between 1974 and 1978, Vorster put some £30 million into information special projects. The department set out to buy the daily *Washington Star*, using an American citizen as its front-man. When this purchase fell through, the South African government became instead the anonymous owner, on the rebound, of the somewhat less influential *Sacramento Union*.

The department's plan secretly to buy a British publishing company, Morgan Grampian, was unsuccessful, but it managed nevertheless to spend vast sums on persuading western journalists and broadcasters of the reforming and just spirit of Vorster's policies. The scale of the information department's plans would never have come to light but for the survival in South Africa of strong elements both of Calvinist morality and press freedom. The misappropriation of defence funds, investigated first by the official auditor-general and then by press, MPs, judges and committees of inquiry, compelled Vorster to retire from

the prime ministership to the comparative tranquillity and, he hoped,
inviolability of the office of president. Even there he was pursued,
however, and in June 1979, a mere eight months after being elected head
of state, he was forced finally to quit public life.

Vorster had done his best to clothe the policies of economic
convenience that had been forced on him in the rhetoric of morality.
'One does not have the right to belittle and ridicule the human dignity
of others,' he said; blacks must be treated not 'as labour units but as
human beings with souls'.

His successor as Prime Minister, P. W. Botha, had, until entering
Parliament, worked only as a National Party organizer. J. B. M.
Hertzog, Strijdom and Vorster had come to the National Party from
the law, Malan from the clergy and Verwoerd from professorships
and journalism. P. W. Botha had no experience except politics. In
1936 he had left university without completing his degree to work as
a junior fixer for Malan's new Purified National Party when it had
seemed the hopeless cause of a minority of Afrikaner zealots. In 1946,
had been promoted to information officer, co-ordinating the party's
smear campaign against Hofmeyr and helping by press management to
orchestrate the *swart gevaar*. After 1948, as a young MP, he was one of
those who had demanded Verwoerd's appointment to the Native Affairs
Ministry. Later, when himself Minister of Defence, he had direct
responsibility for the information department's secret funding, though
he had skilfully kept his name clear. He was the complete party
apparatchik. Few expected him to arrive in office with a burst of new
ideas.

He surprised the sceptics. In successive speeches up and down the
country he announced:

> We are moving in a changing world, we must adapt otherwise we
> shall die . . . The moment you start oppressing people . . . they
> fight back . . . We must acknowledge people's rights and . . . make
> ourselves free by giving to others in a spirit of justice what we
> demand for ourselves . . . A white monopoly of power is untenable
> in the Africa of today . . . A meaningful division of power is needed
> between all race groups . . . Apartheid is a recipe for permanent
> conflict.

As if all that was not sufficiently startling for his party activists, he
went on to question the need for the Mixed Marriages and
Immorality Acts by saying that people of different colours could
'really love each other and want to get married'.

What did all this mean? South African spokesmen overseas said
that it meant the end of apartheid and the fulfilment of those
democratic principles that had always lain near the Afrikaner heart.
Piet Koornhof, the Oxford scholar of the 1950s whom Botha

appointed to his Cabinet as Minister of Co-operation and Development (the same department that had once been called Native and
later Bantu Affairs), told the National Press Club in Washington that
apartheid was dying: the National Party had seen the light and was
firmly changing direction. Some who had for years been fierce critics
of the South African government were convinced that the conversion
was genuine.

Botha appointed the former head of the army, General Magnus
Malan, with whom he had worked closely, to succeed him as Minister
of Defence. Together they had studied the guerilla wars of the
previous twenty years – including the Rhodesian war immediately to
their north – and they had concluded, in Malan's words, that survival
could not be secured by military strength alone but depended on 'the
continued advancement of the well-being of all South Africans'. The
Defence Department considered that its job was to defend South
Africa against external threats. If failures of internal policy led to the
army being used against the country's own population, its capacity to
repel invaders would be undermined. Malan therefore took an active
role in shaping policy in areas unconnected with defence. He stressed
the need to win the 'trust and faith' of the blacks, and pressed
strongly for large public works in the black townships and
homelands. He argued that major social improvements in black
communities were essential for his 'total strategy'.

Botha agreed with General Malan's view, but he was enlarging the
circle of those who influenced policy-making, and he came
increasingly under the influence of a rival group of reformers. These
were advisers from the business community. Until 1948, business
leaders had enjoyed regular access to ministers, and the English-
speaking community had therefore generally felt that its vital
interests were well looked after under Smuts and even, by and large,
under Hertzog. But the National Party governments of D. F. Malan,
Strijdom and Verwoerd placed a high priority on knocking
English-speaking business leaders off their perches. The key group
influencing decisions under these prime ministers had been the
National Party caucus, dominated by Afrikaner trade unionists and
farmers. They had favoured such policies as driving skilled black
workers out of the towns despite industry's need for them. Botha was
determined not to repeat this mistake.

The businessmen among his new group of technocratic advisers
persuaded him that what South Africa needed above all was a revival
of economic growth, which would both restore white confidence and
provide the means to buy black support. And the surest path to
growth was to give businessmen the freedom to get on with the job.
This meant removing unnecessary controls – 60 per cent of
supermarket prices were subject to controls, as were housing,

transport, utilities and building materials – and reducing the government's share in spending the nation's wealth. Rather than build the major investments in black areas that General Malan wanted, Botha decided to let the money be invested by businessmen to get the economy moving. A sympathetic newspaper, the Johannesburg *Sunday Times*, summarized the new policy in a headline: 'Go for growth and apartheid falls away.'

P. W. Botha's plans for the future of South Africa were not yet fully worked out when the 1981 election led him to put the brakes on. Albert Hertzog's breakaway *verkramptes* took roughly a third of the Afrikaner vote. The National Party was still comfortably re-elected, but Botha's belief that he could lead Afrikanerdom away from Verwoerd's policies with the confidence Verwoerd had shown when introducing them was scotched. The Progressive Federal Party (PFP), part-successor to the United Party and similarly based on English-speaking votes, won twenty-nine seats and hoped to back Botha against his own right wing in bringing blacks, coloureds and Indians into the government and legislature. Distressed at his post-election backsliding, its spokesmen challenged Botha to admit that 'white domination' was now his policy. He replied, 'For the present, yes.'

He did, however, persist with schemes to change the constitution. Afrikaners had long been troubled by the position of coloureds and Indians. In 1960, Verwoerd had admitted to Harold Macmillan, 'That has still to be worked out', and more than twenty years later it still had. Vorster and P. W. Botha had claimed that every black had a homeland in which he could exercise his rights. But the coloureds and Indians had no homeland and no political rights. Even if the Afrikaner voters were not ready to bring the urban black élite into the political structure to collaborate in defending the whites' position, surely they would not resist a gesture towards the coloureds and Indians? In 1976 Vorster had set up a constitutional commission with P. W. Botha as chairman. It had produced a proposal for the whites, coloureds and Indians each to have a House in a three-chamber Parliament and a cabinet dealing with its 'own affairs', though blacks, as foreigners, would have no representation. In 1977, on its publication, the scheme was derided. It was then forgotten.

But not by P. W. Botha. He came from the Cape, where most coloureds lived, and he described coloureds and whites as 'relatively one nation'. In 1983, after every possible alternative scheme had been canvassed and reported on, with the sole exception of one-person one-vote (which nobody in the ruling élite thought worth considering), he announced the introduction of a new constitution along the lines he had first thought of. Whites, coloureds and Indians would each have a separate House – of Assembly, of Representatives and of

Delegates – with the number of members in each roughly proportionate to the numbers of the population, in the ratio 4:2:1, representing the Republic's 4.5 million whites, 2.5 million coloureds and 0.8 million Indians. Thus the whites could be sure of dominating. Whites alone took part in the referendum on the new constitution.

Alexis de Tocqueville, the French nineteenth-century political theorist, wrote:

> Experience teaches us that the most perilous moment for a bad government is when it seeks to mend its ways. Only consummate statecraft can enable a king to save his throne when, after a long spell of oppressive rule, he sets out to improve the lot of his subjects. Patiently endured so long as it seemed beyond redress, a grievance comes to appear intolerable once the possibility of removing it crosses men's minds.

In addition to chambers in Parliament for coloureds and Indians, the government introduced a scheme for blacks to elect local authorities in the townships. These innovations meant that it could hardly ban political campaigning. It had created the legal space for its opponents to manoeuvre.

The Indian Congress called upon all Indians to boycott the first elections to the new all-Indian House of Delegates. In January 1983, it invited Rev. Allan Boesak, a coloured and President of the World Alliance of Reformed Churches, to address a meeting in Johannesburg. Boesak said:

> Working within the system for whatever reason contaminates you. It wears down your defences. It whets your appetite for power . . . And what you call 'compromise' for the sake of politics is in fact selling out your principles, your ideals and the future of your children . . . Churches, civic organizations, trade unions, student organizations and sports bodies should unite on this issue, pool our resources, inform the people of the fraud that is about to be perpetrated in their name, and expose those plans for what they are.

Boesak's suggestion matched the public mood. When, in August 1983, a co-ordinating committee announced the inaugural rally of the federal campaigning body he had called for, more than 400 organizations sent members. Prominent among them were the trade unions, which the government had legalized because it could not enforce the law that required their suppression. It had meant them to function only in industrial relations. But they had promptly become channels for political demands, seized by their members as the only such channels available – and highly effective, by means of strikes and boycotts, at getting their way. The unions, like the other founder-bodies in the new organization, were giving expression to a ferment of political hope and determination. They hired the civic centre at Mitchell's Plain, the coloured township near Cape Town. The building is huge, but applications for tickets were too numerous for it. Since outdoor political meetings were banned, the organizers hired, in addition to the hall, a large marquee to cover the overspill. An estimated 10,000 people of all races attended. They called the new body they launched the United Democratic Front (UDF). Boesak spoke again:

> We are here to say that the government's constitutional proposals are inadequate, that they do not express the will of the vast majority of South Africa's people . . . The time has come for white people in this country to realize that their destiny is inextricably bound with ours . . . They will never be free as long as they have to lie awake at night worrying whether a black government will one day do to them as they are doing to us . . . To be sure, the new proposals will make apartheid less blatant in some ways. It will be modernized and streamlined, and in its multi-coloured cloak it will be less conspicuous and less offensive to some. Nevertheless it will still be there.

The UDF was to prove powerful partly because of its elusiveness. All its member organizations had committees, many had premises. The UDF had neither. It had a long list of patrons, but no property or formal leaders for the police to seize. And when Boesak and other UDF patrons were put in prison, the UDF continued, at times more of an idea than an organization, until member-groups next decided to activate it. The only policy it adopted was a watered-down version of the Freedom Charter (see page 123), so bland in its praise of democracy, freedom and other noble ideals that none of the nurses' guilds or sports clubs that were affiliated could object – nor could the police. In a careful piece of drafting, the UDF declared that it did not 'purport to be a substitute movement to accredited peoples' liberation movements'. This meant that it did not seek to replace the ANC, or to oppose it.

In the referendum campaign, the *verkramptes* opposed P. W. Botha's new constitution on the grounds that it opened the gates for the black flood. The UDF and the PFP opposed it for failing to bring in the blacks and therefore totally missing the point. The PFP pointed out that the new constitution strengthened apartheid: to partition the legislature itself on racial lines was to move apartheid even further into the heart of public life. But the white electorate gave the new constitution a substantial majority. In the ensuing election, only 20 to 30 per cent of the coloureds and Indians who were registered actually voted – a small turnout, perhaps even derisory, but not quite farcical. The government claimed it was a start down a road to which there was no alternative.

In September 1984, the new three-chamber legislature met. For the first time, Indian and coloured representatives joined the whites in the Cape Town Parliament House. To those in the National Party who hankered after the memory of Verwoerd, this racial mixing in the legislature was a shock, almost a desecration. It signalled de Tocqueville's moment of peril.

That same month, on the very day that the new constitution took effect, a familiar name hit the news headlines worldwide: Sharpeville. For a second time the former model township – along with a second township called Sebokeng that also housed blacks who worked in Vereeniging – was the starting-point for a wave of violence that was to shake South Africa and leave it permanently changed. This time the killing was not started by the police.

The UDF had helped lead a successful boycott of the council elections in black townships. In many seats officials had been unable to persuade any candidates to stand. Only 2–3 per cent of those registered had bothered – or dared – to vote. The new councillors elected were mostly middle-class blacks who hoped they could help build a bridge between the government and the black majority. Some were attracted by political office and the opportunities they hoped it might offer. They, like the government, failed to appreciate that the anger which had led to the massive support for the UDF and the election boycotts had not worked itself out.

On 3 September 1984, the newly elected deputy-mayor of Sharpeville was hacked to death on his front doorstep. The same day in Sharpeville, two blacks were burned to death trapped in their cars, four people were strangled behind a plundered garage, a man burned to death in a liquor store, many buildings and cars were set on fire. The official tally for Sharpeville, September 1984, was twenty-six dead. With comparable killings in nearby Sebokeng, it marked a new phase in South Africa's history: the moment when blacks turned their anger against those fellow-blacks they regarded as collaborators with the white government.

Nobody knew where the violence might erupt next. In townships all over South Africa the volatile mood of unsatisfied grievances with no channel of expression exploded in bursts of a day, a week, in some places even a month of violence. Between September 1984 and February 1985 the government reported:

5 black councillors killed
4 black policemen killed
109 black councillors attacked
56 black police officers injured
143 black school buildings destroyed
6 black churches destroyed
9 clinics for blacks destroyed
516 private vehicles belongings to blacks badly burned or damaged
1,080 buses in service for blacks badly burned or damaged
147 black councillors 'forced to resign'

Everywhere the violence was 'black on black'. The outside world, which had shown some sympathy for P. W. Botha's attempted reforms, could make no sense of it. Then, on 21 March 1985, the anniversary of the 1960 Sharpeville killings, a crowd set out from the black township of Langa, in the eastern Cape, towards the nearby white town of Uitenhage. Police tried to stop them and, failing, opened fire, killing twenty. Almost at once, such credit as the government's reform efforts had earned was dissipated.

By 1984, the South African uniformed police force was half black and even included sixty black officers, of whom two were colonels. The police were of course the agents of state policy, but to represent them merely as an instrument of repression was misleading. In a famous incident in 1962, when Nelson Mandela was a wanted man, a black policeman had spotted him and given him an ANC salute. Some blacks who joined the police between 1980 and 1984, believing P. W. Botha's promises of reform, found themselves in 1985 facing death at the hands of their own people. At Langa in 1985, as at Sharpeville in 1960, the policemen who opened fire did more damage to their government – and to their own service – than all their enemies. The outside world was eager to see a familiar and simple pattern in South Africa: it was Sharpeville 1960 all over again: white policemen killing black protesters.

The black cause too was damaged by its own excesses. In July 1985, at a funeral in Duduza to the east of Johannesburg, a young girl suspected of being a police informer was stoned, stabbed and beaten, then covered in sticks and grass which were set on fire. Desmond Tutu, Anglican Bishop of Johannesburg and recently awarded the Nobel Peace Prize, said that the television pictures of the young girl's death, beamed around the world, had supported the white claim that the blacks were not ready to govern themselves.

Such violence was to spread, making many townships no-go areas for the police – a principal objective of the young blacks who led local campaigns. At first called 'the children', later more commonly 'the comrades', they saw all allies of the authorities, whether councillors or police, as the enemy. When they caught a suspected enemy and the mood was upon them, they poured petrol into a rubber tyre, placed it round his neck, and set it alight. During 1986, this became the most popular way of killing 'enemies'. The method became internationally known by the name the comrades invented for it, 'the necklace'.

In townships from which police and councillors were excluded by fear, young blacks for the first time in modern South Africa tasted power. Many blacks, working in a white town by day, returned to a black, 'comrade'-ruled township by night. The rule of the comrades was erratic. Some set up people's courts that administered a fair approximation to justice; others administered the blazing necklace and whippings. Many created 'people's parks' (flowers in a derelict site, a gaily painted abandoned car, a few slogans, some tyres), and tried to raise the taxes to maintain schools and local services. Some degenerated into local tyrannies of young criminals, with older blacks waiting hopefully for the return of the police and the army in a military campaign of reconquest. Most of the comrades were less than twenty-five years old. In the words of an elder: 'You have to be a child to be so ready to die.' One twelve-year-old in a township wrote in a school essay: 'The population of the world is surely decreasing. Every hour, minute and second there is someone dying.' Nobody controlled the children, or comrades. In each township they went their own way. Some were supporters of the UDF and responsive to the influence of local UDF affiliates. Often they regarded the UDF and the ANC as the permitted and the banned branches of the same movement and supported both.

Others derived their inspiration from the Black Consciousness movement, several of whose leaders, imprisoned before the death of Steve Biko, had been released at the end of their sentences, during P. W. Botha's reform phase. The released leaders quickly started a new organization in the Africanist-Black Consciousness tradition. They called it AZAPO, the Azanian People's Organization – 'Azania', their name for South Africa, being derived from the Ancient Greeks' term for the mysterious land south of Egypt. Where the UDF was non-racial and ideologically liberal, welcoming white members and supporters and favouring a transfer of power to the majority by negotiation if possible, AZAPO restricted its membership to blacks, coloureds and Indians, called for a total revolution, overthrowing not only white rule but also capitalism, and dismissed talk of negotiation as the babbling of Uncle Toms.

AZAPO and UDF factions battled for control in many townships. Each accused the other of murdering its local leaders. AZAPO was not as widely supported or as strong as the UDF, but it attracted intellectuals and used a revolutionary language that many journalists and teachers found suited the times. The principal weapons in the AZAPO–UDF war were petrol bombs, with which they destroyed each others' homes and killed each others' members. Government agents did what they could to encourage them.

Many of the young leaders of both UDF and AZAPO professed a high regard for Nelson Mandela, who by 1987 had been in prison for twenty-five years – since before most of them were born. Mandela's position was peculiar. After eighteen years imprisoned with fellow-ANC leaders on Robben Island, where they spent much of their time working in a lime quarry, they had been moved in April 1982 to more comfortable quarters in Pollsmoor prison, Cape Town, and Mandela there became a focus of world attention – the one person who might be able to negotiate with P. W. Botha's government on behalf of South Africa's blacks.

Demands for his release had been made from many quarters and had been repeatedly turned down. In June 1981, P. W. Botha had summarized the official position: 'The government is not in favour of the release of Mr Mandela. He has been found guilty, an independent judiciary decided that he shall serve a life term in prison, and I have nothing to add to that.'

In January 1985, Botha changed his mind. He announced that the government would release Mandela in return for a promise not to take action that would lead to his re-arrest. Mandela's reply was read out at a UDF rally in February by his daughter Zindzi.

I am a member of the African National Congress. I have always been a member of the African National Congress and I will remain a member of the African National Congress until I die . . . I am surprised at the conditions the government wants to impose on me. I am not a violent man. My colleagues and I wrote in 1952 to Malan asking for a round table conference to find a solution to the problems of our country, but that was ignored. When Strijdom was in power we made the same offer. Again it was ignored. When Verwoerd was in power we asked for a national convention for all the people in South Africa to decide on their future. This, too, was in vain. It was only when all other forms of resistance were no longer open to us that we turned to armed struggle.

I am not less life-loving than you are. But I cannot sell my birthright, nor am I prepared to sell the birthright of the people, to be free. I am in prison as the representative of the people and of your organization, the African National Congress which was banned. What freedom am I being offered whilst the organization of the people remains banned? What freedom am I being offered when I may be arrested on a pass offence? What freedom am I being offered when I must ask for permission to live in an urban area? What freedom am I being offered when my very South African citizenship is not respected?

Only free men can negotiate. Prisoners cannot enter into contracts . . . I cannot and will not give any undertaking at a time when I and you, the people, are not free. Your freedom and mine cannot be separated. I will return.

The Botha government allowed Mandela a small number of selected visitors, including several foreign politicians who were amazed by his self-confidence and poise (one said Mandela behaved as though the prison officers were his staff), by his grasp of affairs (he received a regular supply of newspapers) and by his moderation. Mrs Helen Suzman, a PFP Member of Parliament who visited him in May 1986, when he was sixty-seven years old, said afterwards:

It is crazy for the government not to take advantage of his position of authority among blacks, authority which I believe he would use to the benefit of all in South Africa . . . I believe Mr Mandela's talents should be used before it is too late and far more radical elements take control of the ANC.

The ANC in Mandela's absence was the subject of much speculation. The government maintained that it was a body of communists and terrorists, determined to use violence to set up a Marxist state and destroy the prosperity and lifestyle of the whites. This was mere propaganda. The ANC had communists as members, including one, Joe Slovo, who was a key figure in its exiled military command, but the government had no more chance of proving the principal leaders to be communists than it had when it had brought the charge against Luthuli and Mandela in the 1950s, only to have it dismissed by South African judges.

The ANC's president since the death of Luthuli in 1967 was Oliver Tambo, Mandela's former law partner who had left South Africa in 1961 to set up the movement's headquarters in exile and had been out of the country ever since. A quiet, reflective, scholarly man, Tambo's manner was that of the committee secretary rather than the leader of a revolutionary insurrection. Like Mandela he was without anti-white prejudice and had been driven to violence only by the government's years of inflexibility. He led the ANC from Lusaka, the capital of Zambia, where it functioned like a government in exile, financed by independent African countries through the Organization of African Unity, equipped with Russian arms, which it was increasingly successful at smuggling into South Africa, and planning and controlling small guerilla campaigns from neighbouring states. The most successful raids were into the Transvaal and Natal.

The 1976 Soweto violence and the subsequent repression had led some thousands of young blacks to leave the country to train for guerilla warfare abroad. Most of them were inspired to this action by the Black Consciousness movement, but, in spite of police suspicion of Steve Biko and his friends, Black Consciousness had no capacity to organize a guerilla army. So the young recruits joined the one liberation movement that had – the ANC.

Until the 1970s, Tambo's guerillas had lacked easy access to their country. White South Africa had enjoyed the protection of friendly buffer states: Mozambique to the north-east, ruled until 1974 by Portugal, and Rhodesia (later renamed Zimbabwe) to the north, ruled until 1980 by a white settler regime. The transfer of power in both territories to independent black governments exposed the Republic's borders, apparently making the guerillas' task easy.

This was a delusion. South Africa possessed the most powerful army and airforce on the continent and used them, in response to any reports of ANC guerilla operations from nearby black states, to launch prompt and devastating raids. The black states, including Zimbabwe, Zambia, Botswana, Lesotho and Swaziland, quickly agreed to stop the use of their territories for ANC guerilla activity. The most militant and Marxist of South Africa's black neighbours, Mozambique, under its charismatic President, Samora Machel, was not so ready to agree. So South Africa hit Mozambique repeatedly and hard, and eventually P. W. Botha secured his reward. In March 1984, at Nkomati on the South Africa–Mozambique border, President Machel, in full military regalia, shook Botha's hand and promised to prevent his territory from being used as an ANC base. Consequently military incursions from abroad failed to make a fraction of the impact of the black activists in the townships.

Despite this limit to its effectiveness, the ANC was generally regarded as the likely winner, were blacks allowed to vote in an election. Its former activities had established centres of support in most parts of the country, the continued imprisonment of its leaders, particularly Mandela, gave it a kind of legitimacy, and many foreign governments accepted its claim to speak for the blacks. In September 1985, a group of white Johannesburg businessmen, led by Gavin Relly of Anglo-American, the huge gold and diamond corporation, flew to Lusaka to meet Oliver Tambo and other ANC leaders and discuss their ideas about the future of the country. This meeting of a group whom the South African government called 'terrorist murderers' with another whom the followers of Black Consciousness called 'capitalist-racist exploiters' was relaxed and friendly. The chairman, President Kenneth Kaunda of Zambia, and the location, under a tree in one of his game parks with hippopotamuses splashing nearby, helped to avert tension.

The British Conservative Prime Minister, Margaret Thatcher, who had for years dismissed the ANC leaders as men of violence with whom she would never deal, in June 1986 had a Foreign Office minister meet Tambo in London. Even the US President, Ronald Reagan, came round to recognizing that the ANC was a major force on the South African scene with which his government would have to do business.

Within South Africa the ANC's principal black opponents were the governments of the homelands or Bantustans. Between 1976 and 1981, four of these, Transkei, Bophuthatswana, Ciskei and Venda, had been formally granted 'independence'. They did not control their own foreign policy or defence, and were therefore not independent by the standards of international law; further, they were plainly a device to sustain apartheid. So their 'independence' was not recognized by any country except South Africa. But the acceptance of nominal independence by the Bantustan governments enabled ministers in Pretoria to declare that their subjects, owing loyalty to a foreign country, had lost their South African citizenship.

All the remaining homelands – Lebowa, KwaNdebele, Qwaqwa, Gazankulu, KwaZulu and KaNgwane – had by 1986 reached the stage of 'self-government', but Verwoerd and his successors had always insisted that they took the next step – to 'independence' – only when their own governments said they were ready. And in the uncertain political climate of the mid-1980s some of them were not at all sure they were ready.

The most notable of these was KwaZulu, the fragmented homeland of the five million Zulu, scattered across Natal. Its Chief Minister, Gatsha Buthelezi, a member of the Zulu royal family, had as a young man at Fort Hare University joined the ANC and the Youth League and remained for many years an ally of the ANC. He was a consistent public opponent of apartheid. Like all the homeland leaders, he ruled with a rod of iron, controlling gangs of supporters and putting down critics more ferociously than the South African government itself. Having become Chief Minister of the largest population group in South Africa, Buthelezi was not P. W. Botha's puppet. He demanded the consolidation and enlargement of KwaZulu, arousing angry resistance from English-speaking, white Natal farmers. His refusal of independence meant that within South Africa, as defined by the government, Zulu continued to outnumber whites.

Buthelezi was preparing for the power-struggle that would follow the end of white rule. His stance was that he and his Inkatha movement – for which he claimed a million paid-up members – could keep order, ensure that business flourished, and thus enable black and white to live prosperously together. He pressed for the creation

of a joint KwaZulu–Natal government and legislature, confident that
the overwhelming Zulu majority there would ensure that he won any
election. Many whites in Natal considered that a Zulu–white coalition
under Buthelezi was preferable to the likely alternative of growing
conflict leading to war.

Most ANC supporters maintained that Buthelezi was selling-out,
that his scheme for a separate settlement in Natal meant giving in to
the original Verwoerd plan: fragmenting South Africa into small,
black states, none of them viable, leaving the bulk of the country,
including the richest farmlands and all the mineral wealth, in the
hands of the whites. To gain Natal for the Zulus and lose the whole of
South Africa for its black majority was, to his black critics, the worst
kind of opportunism. So the ANC's young supporters and Buthelezi's
Zulu gangs regularly clashed in the townships. Until Verwoerd's
time, urban blacks from different parts of South Africa had, while
living in townships, mixed fairly freely. But the architect of apartheid
had required that the authorities separate the 'tribes', compelling the
Zulu to live apart from the Xhosa, the Tswana from the Sotho. Thus,
in large townships, rival urban ghettoes had been created. In the
violence that started in 1984, the fruit of this policy ripened:
gang-warfare between 'tribes' erupted, with 'impis' of urban Zulu
often blamed for the first attacks.

Mandela and Buthelezi continued to speak well of each other –
Mandela the revered leader of almost all the blacks, including many
Zulu, Buthelezi the boss of the largest single black nation and a
formidable political operator. In 1986, Buthelezi refused to take part
in constitutional talks proposed by P. W. Botha's government until
Mandela was released and invited to participate. In the same year,
Mandela said that no talks about the constitutional future could be
held without Buthelezi. None the less, the energies of ANC and
Inkatha were as solidly devoted to opposing each other as to action
against the government.

The gap between the Sharpeville shootings of 1960 and the
outbreaks sparked by the Soweto schoolchildren in 1976–7 was
sixteen years. The next eruption, at the time of the launching of
P. W. Botha's constitution in 1984, came after only seven years. Not
only were the risings becoming more frequent, but also more
widespread and longer-lasting. Sharpeville 1960 and its aftermath
were over in a year. The internal violence and economic disorder
following the Soweto outbreak in 1976 took two years to suppress and
forced a rethink by the whites which was still in progress a decade
later. The 1984 risings were of a different order of magnitude. Two
years after they started, they showed no sign of abating. No sooner
did army and police invade a township, restoring a kind of control,
than comrades or children took over another.

In the anarchy of the townships some orderly structures survived. Here a protection gang 'taxed' a region and organized modest services, there a landlord of shanty-properties employed minders to keep his patch in order. Vigilante alliances of such groups, sometimes actively supported by the police and the army, tried to take control and intermittently succeeded. Bricks, iron bars and knives were the most common weapons in 1985–6, but the ANC managed to bring a few Russian AK47 automatic rifles to its township allies. Teenagers, even twelve-year-olds, were learning to use them with the insouciance of Beirut militiamen. Civil war was spreading.

Most of the violence was 'black on black', but a few bombs were also set off in white areas, killing whoever happened to be nearby. That, however, was not the main threat faced by the government. In their ability to offer whites physical protection, the police and army were scarcely challenged. The government's most difficult problem was the economy.

Not only did the economy have to maintain the high standard of living of the whites; more important, if the government was to secure political stability, it needed to provide jobs for a growing army of young blacks. The estimate of economists was that South Africa needed to maintain a growth rate of 5 per cent each year merely to keep the unemployment rate from growing. The only way was to borrow money overseas and invest at home. South Africa happened in 1985 to have reached a stage of economic growth at which it was particularly vulnerable to a cut-off of its supply of foreign capital. Since 1960, anti-apartheid movements worldwide had been demanding that big companies and banks stop investing in South Africa. The demand had little effect. In 1985, however, the big international banks changed sides. For decades they had insisted that they looked only at balance sheets, that if they worried about the human rights or social policies of governments they would have to withdraw from half the world. But in 1985 the large New York bank, Chase Manhattan, influenced by students, churches and charities that had withdrawn deposits rather than have them invested in South Africa, refused to renew a major South African loan. Other banks quickly followed suit. Suddenly respectable bankers, long committed to avoiding meddling in politics, decided that here things were different. Together they informed the South African Finance Minister and the Governor of the Central Bank that future loans would be forthcoming only if South Africa settled its internal political problems. They made it plain that the reforms P. W. Botha and his ministers were planning were insufficient to produce political calm, the essential precondition for safe investment.

Botha and his Cabinet responded with promises. They would abolish the Pass Laws and amend the constitution to provide a share of power for the blacks. For a few months the loans on which they depended were rolled over. But South Africa's future loans were cut off pending the implementation of satisfactory reforms. And other international pressures were growing. In 1985, the fifty states in the Commonwealth demanded the imposition of economic sanctions. These could hardly be more devastating in their effect than the banks' cutting off their loans, but for many governments economic sanctions had become a politically necessary gesture and some believed they would further increase the pressure on Pretoria.

Before imposing sanctions, the Commonwealth heads of government decided to send a mission to South Africa to try to bring the government and black representatives to the negotiating table. Led by an ex-Prime Minister of Australia, Malcolm Fraser, and a former head of the military government of Nigeria, General Olusegun Obasanjo, the mission met Mandela and P. W. Botha and believed it had devised a formula on the basis of which they could begin talks. What Mandela was prepared to offer, and believed he could deliver, was the suspension of violence during talks, so long as the government undertook in return to suspend violence by the state. But, to the Commonwealth group's surprise, the South African government, after showing some interest in its proposals, suddenly turned unco-operative.

The reason was that talks with Mandela and the freeing of the ANC to campaign in the country would almost certainly have taken power out of white hands. Once talks began, with the withholding of the banks' loans and the introduction of economic sanctions hanging over them, the South African government would have been forced not just to share power with the blacks, which by 1986 it recognized it would have to do, but to cede control. No solution that denied blacks control of the government of South Africa by means of one-person one-vote elections would have been possible. And that was the concession the South African government was not prepared to make.

So, in June 1986, P. W. Botha's government imposed a state of emergency and reverted to the manner of rule familiar from B. J. Vorster's time as Minister of Justice: a harsh repression. The theory behind this policy was that reform had run out of control and could proceed only when the government was once again firmly in charge. Once the townships were restored to order, the next step towards the sharing of power with skilled, urban blacks could be undertaken; not before. 'Reform' was presented to the world as meaning the abolition of apartheid. But Botha's government believed that major elements of apartheid must be preserved. In the homelands or Bantustans it planned to persist with Verwoerd's blueprint. Indeed during 1986, while seeking to impress the international banks with its commitment to reform, it continued to press ahead with its plan to grant 'independence' to

KwaNdebele, thus depriving the seven hundred thousand Ndebele of their claim to South African citizenship. It justified its policy by stating that, whatever might be decided for educated urban blacks, the attempt to impose democracy on rural blacks had failed throughout Africa and had merely led to dictatorships. It preferred, therefore, to go slowly by means of the part-democracy of the Bantustan: allowing the blacks their own controlled equivalent of Tudor monarchs or Romanoff tsars. Whether its arguments were justified or not, it did not seem likely that it would have the time to put them to the test.

BOOK LIST

Benson, Mary, *The Struggle for a Birthright*, International Defence and Aid Fund, 1985. A useful short history of the African National Congress, 1912–65.

Benson, Mary, *Nelson Mandela*, Penguin, 1986. A hagiography, but as yet all there is.

Bernstein, Hilda, *No 46 – Steve Biko*, International Defence and Aid Fund, 1978. Extracts from the transcript of the inquest with some useful additional data.

Bunting, Brian, *The Rise of the South African Reich*, Penguin, 1964. Whether or not one agrees with Bunting's view that after 1948 the National government created a fascist state in the Nazi mould, he marshals his evidence in a way that is always thought-provoking.

Clarke, Stephen and Leslie Woodhead, *The Dumping Grounds*, Granada Television, 1970. Transcript of a brilliant television programme: a short, irrefutable proof that the South African government's principal claims about its homelands policies were lies.

Davenport, T. R. H., *South Africa, a Modern History*, Macmillan, 1984. Useful and occasionally incisive.

Desmond, Cosmas, *The Discarded People*, Christian Institute of South Africa, 1979. A report on the 'removal' of a number of black groups to 'homelands' where they suffered starvation and destitution. The author, a Catholic priest, revealed with this book the aspect of apartheid that, above all others, the South African government wanted kept secret.

D'Oliveira, John, *Vorster – the Man*, Stanton, 1977. A campaign biography.

Elphick, Richard and Hermann Giliomee (eds), *The Shaping of South African Society, 1652–1820*, Longman, 1979. A splendid set of essays summarizing research on the first 170 years of white occupation.

Fisher, John, *The Afrikaners*, Cassell, 1969. An attempt to introduce the Afrikaners to the outside world.

Frederikse, Julie, *A Different Kind of War*, Ravan, 1986. An assembly of cuttings, photographs and interviews, put together by an American radio journalist; more a scrapbook than a book, but useful.

Gerhart, Gail M., *Black Power in South Africa*, California, 1978. A splendid work of scholarship, describing one intellectual current in black politics.

Giliomee, Hermann, *The Parting of the Ways, South African Politics, 1976–82*, Philip, 1982. Selections from a brilliant newspaper column that this Afrikaner historian writes for several South African papers.

Hancock, W. K., *Smuts, The Sanguine Years, 1870–1919*, Cambridge, 1962, and *Smuts, The Fields of Force, 1919–1950*, Cambridge, 1968. Biography on the grand scale. Hancock sympathizes with his subject, and so helps us to understand Smuts in his own terms.

Harrison, David, *The White Tribe of Africa*, BBC, 1985. The producer of the excellent television series of the same name not only offers helpful warnings to those who try to follow in his footsteps, but casts some sharp beams of light into the Afrikaner mind.

Heard, Kenneth A., *General Elections in South Africa, 1943–70*, Oxford, 1974. Useful. Clear. Excellent tables.

Hepple, Alex, *Verwoerd*, Penguin, 1967. Although the author was once leader of the Labour Party in South Africa, he writes about the principal ideologue and builder of apartheid with fairness.

Hirson, Baruch, *Year of Fire, Year of Ash*, Zed, 1979. A study of the Soweto rising of 1976–7. Lovely Marxist invective against the naiveté of Black Consciousness. Hirson, a former physicist at the University of Witwatersrand, is a committed revolutionary and spent ten years in South African prisons as a result.

Ingham, Kenneth, *Jan Christian Smuts*, Weidenfeld and Nicolson, 1986. More critical than Hancock, particularly on Smuts's approach to blacks, Ingham nevertheless belongs to the same liberal tradition.

Jenkins, Simon, 'The Great Evasion', *The Economist*, 1980. First of a series of surveys, by the political editor of *The Economist* who has repeatedly visited South Africa and missed little that matters.

Johnson, R. W., *How Long Will South Africa Survive?*, Macmillan, 1977. The 1976 Soweto riots and Portugal's withdrawal from Angola and Mozambique provoked this brilliant work of scholarship-journalism.

Kiewiet, C. W. de, *A History of South Africa, Social and Economic*, Oxford, 1941. Written with such style and so world-encompassing an understanding that it is still rewarding, although somewhat dated.

Klerk, W. A. de, *The Puritans in Africa*, Collings, 1975. An Afrikaner tries to explain his people by telling their history, with most of its myths.

Kruger, D. W., *South African Parties and Policies 1910–1960*, Bowes and Bowes, 1960. A collection of speeches, policy-statements, etc.

Lacour-Gayet, Robert, *South Africa*, Cassell, 1977. A Frenchman's history designed to show that apartheid was not merely necessary but desirable.

Leach, Graham, *South Africa*, Routledge and Kegan Paul, 1986. The BBC's southern Africa radio correspondent provides a handy update.

Leipoldt, C. Louis, *Jan van Riebeeck*, Longmans Green, 1936. An elegant, literate biography, full of insights into the Dutch East India Company.

Lelyveld, Joseph, *Move Your Shadow*, Michael Joseph, 1986. The *New York Times* correspondent produces descriptive writing about life under apartheid that no novelist could better.

Lipton, Merle, *Capitalism and Apartheid*, Gower, 1985. A formidable school of Marxist historians maintains that capitalism and apartheid buttress each other and may therefore be treated as two sides of the same coin. The author's careful presentation of the data and clarity of argument reveal their view to be over-simple.

Lodge, Tom, *Black Politics in South Africa since 1945*, Ravan, 1983. An English scholar who has settled in South Africa, Lodge has become the world's leading pundit on the ANC and black politics generally and this book is something of a standard text.

Luthuli, Albert, *Let My People Go*, Collins, 1962. Part autobiography, part tract. Luthuli's dignity, modesty and eloquence provide some amazing insights.

Macmillan, Harold, *Pointing the Way, 1959–61*, Macmillan, 1972. Valuable for his account of his 'Wind of Change' trip and his meetings with Verwoerd.

Macmillan, W. M., *Bantu, Boer and Briton*, Oxford, 1963. A unique work: not only eloquent, but also the only means of access to the papers of the London Missionary Society's Dr John Philip, destroyed in a fire at the University of Witwatersrand in 1930, soon after Macmillan finished studying them.

Mandela, Nelson, *The Struggle is My Life*, International Defence and Aid Fund, 1978. A collection of speeches and documents.

Marks, Shula, 'Southern Africa 1867–1886', and 'South and Central Africa 1886–1910', in *The Cambridge History of Africa*, volume 6, Cambridge, 1985. Essays that for the first time put all the pieces into context. Africans, Afrikaners and British are presented in a way that shows understanding of all and of the economic motives that drove them.

Marks, Shula, *The Ambiguities of Dependence in South Africa*, Ravan, 1986. The perfect antidote for those who think South Africa a clear issue of right and wrong.

Marks, Shula and Anthony Atmore (eds), *Economy and Society in Pre-industrial South Africa*, Longmans, 1980. Scholarly essays of high quality, which form the starting-point for a major revision in thinking about South African history.

Meintjes, Johannes, *President Paul Kruger*, Cassell, 1974. Few people have been so brutally libelled by the journalists and historians of the British Empire as Paul Kruger. Meintjes paints a more sympathetic portrait – convincingly.

Moodie, T. Dunbar, *The Rise of Afrikanerdom*, California, 1975. The religious content of Afrikaner nationalism is Moodie's principal interest. Perhaps he makes too much of it, but he presents an intriguing story.

Muller, C. F. J., *500 Years*, Academica, 1981. The authorized, Afrikaner version of the history of the country. I received my copy from Koos Venter, Minister (Information) at the South African embassy in London, whom I should like to thank, both for the book and for much other help.

Neame, L. E., *Some South African Politicians*, Maskew Miller, 1929. Sketches by a lobby correspondent in the Westminster tradition.

Neame, L. E., *General Hertzog*, Hurst and Blackett, 1930. A mid-career biography by the then political correspondent of the *Johannesburg Star*.

Neame, L. E., *The History of Apartheid*, Pall Mall Press, 1962. The author, now ex-editor of the *Rand Daily Mail*, had lost his earlier skill at digesting and analysis.

Pakenham, Thomas, *The Boer War*, Weidenfeld and Nicolson, 1979. One of those rare books that, through the quality of its writing and the detail of its research, adds noise and smell, anxiety and anger, to make history as gripping as the best of novels.

Paton, Alan, *Hofmeyr*, Oxford, 1964. A great biography, brilliantly written, passionately involved, at times rough on Hofmeyr, but only because Paton fully appreciated his virtues.

Patterson, Sheila, *The Last Trek*, Routledge and Kegan Paul, 1957. A readable attempt to explain the Afrikaners.

Pirow, Oswald, *James Barry Munnik Hertzog*, Allen and Unwin, 1958. The author was a barrister, Minister of Justice under Hertzog, and during the 1939–45 war a Nazi who campaigned against the parliamentary system. His biography is a reminder that some deft brains (including, in his final years, Hertzog himself) can thus go astray.

Redcliffe-Maud, John, *Experiences of an Optimist*, Hamish Hamilton, 1981. Britain's last High Commissioner and first Ambassador to South Africa offers some insight on Dr Verwoerd, 1959–63.

Riebeeck, Jan van, *Journals*, Balkema for the van Riebeeck Society, 1952–58. Gulliver's Travels stories, only these are real: landing, storms, building the fort, punishing dissidents, exploring islands and the interior, planting and waiting to see what grows, dealing with the natives. All described with the amazing detail that the Council in Amsterdam demanded of all its agents.

Roberts, Michael and A. E. G. Trollip, *The South African Opposition, 1939–45*, Longmans, 1947. Contemporary history of the key period when Afrikaners turned towards apartheid.

Robins, Eric, *This Man Malan*, SA Scientific Publishing, 1953. Instant journalism, with a few good anecdotes.

Roux, Edward, *Time Longer than Rope*, Wisconsin, 1978. An extraordinary book, part history, part memoir. Its author, a professor of botany, was a white South African caught up in the struggle for black rights and in the Communist Party of South Africa.

Smuts, J. C., *Jan Christian Smuts*, Cassell, 1952. A son's loyal biography of his father.

Stultz, Newell M., *Afrikaner Politics in South Africa, 1934–1948*, University of California Press, 1974. A competent academic study.

Thompson, Leonard, *The Unification of South Africa, 1902–1910*, Oxford, 1960. The making of the constitution of South Africa is here made almost as exciting as that of the American union just over 100 years before. Thompson is one of those blessed scholars who write superbly.

Thompson, Leonard, *The Political Mythology of Apartheid*, Yale, 1985. This is a clever book by one who, as Professor in Cape Town and later in America, has devoted a lifetime to South African history.

Van den Heever, C. M., *General J. B. M. Hertzog*, Afrikaanse Pers Bookstore, 1946. The authorized biography.

Walshe, Peter, *The Rise of African Nationalism in South Africa*, Hurst, 1970. By a South African, educated at Oxford and teaching in America, this is, for the time being, the standard work, up till 1952.

Wheatcroft, Geoffrey, *The Randlords*, Weidenfeld and Nicolson, 1985. A large number of millionaires compete for attention in a single volume. The expectation of a mere swollen gossip column proves wrong. This is serious history, unconventionally handled.

Willan, Brian, *Sol Plaatje*, Heinemann, 1984. An exquisite biography which is making this early African nationalist deservedly well known.

Wilson, Monica and Leonard Thompson (eds), *The Oxford History of South Africa, volume 1, to 1870, volume 2, 1870–1966*, Oxford, 1971. The English edition states, 'Not for circulation in the Republic of South Africa', because the chapter on 'African

Nationalism, 1910–1964' contained references to banned people and papers. Some scholars treated these volumes as the last outpourings of an extinct species, the liberal historians. I found them generally clear and helpful.

INDEX